The Ultimate Visual Guide

Ancient and Medieval World

WINDMILL
BOOKS

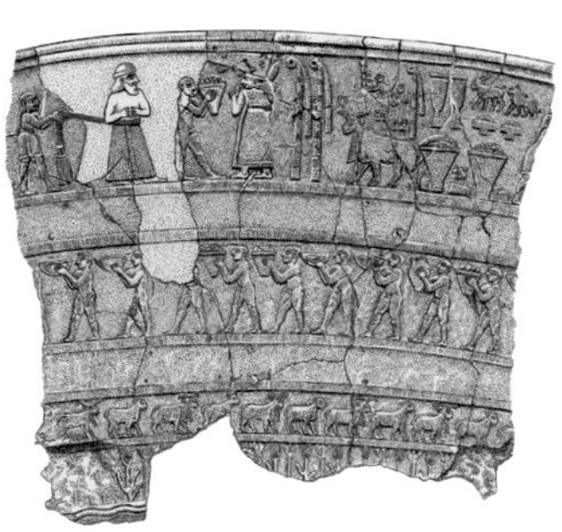

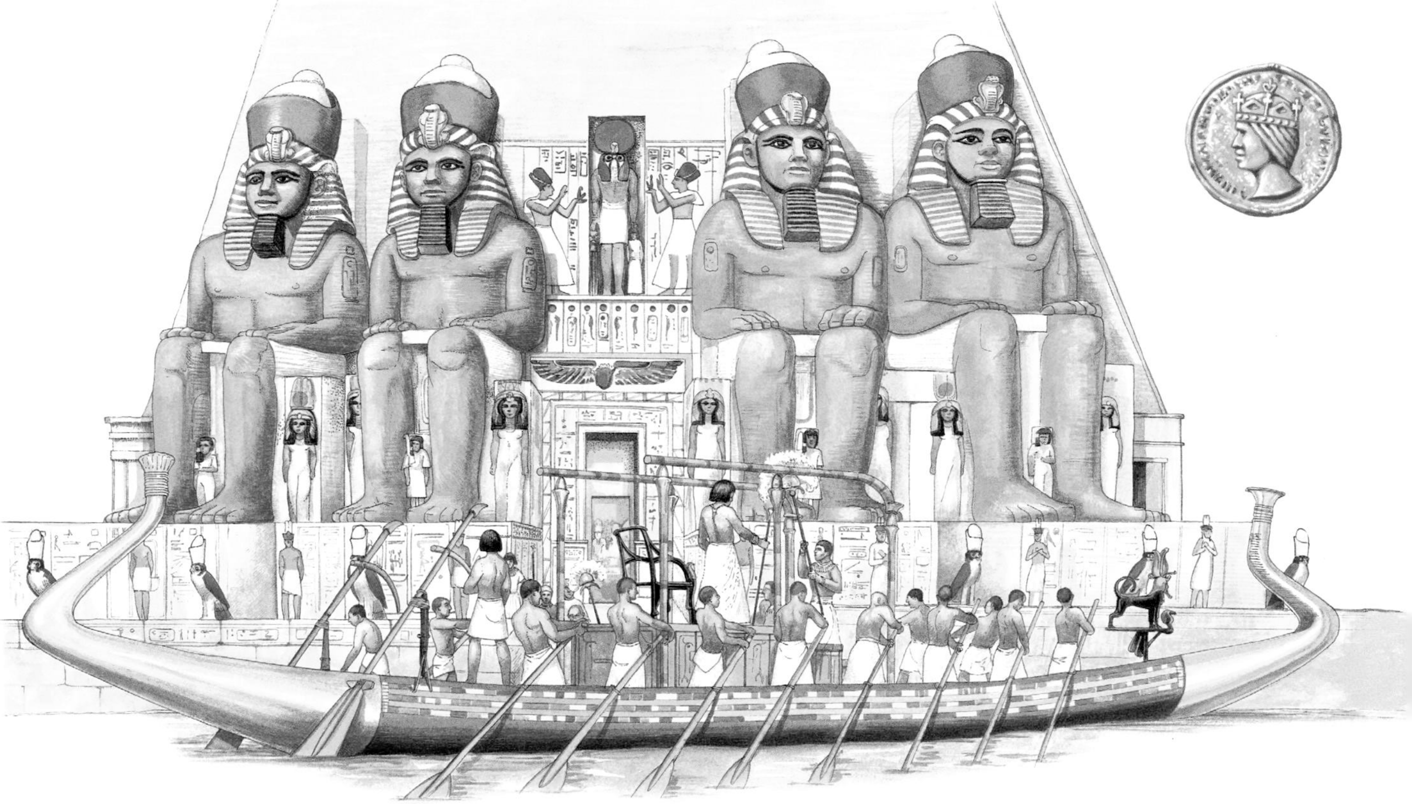

The Ancient and Medieval World

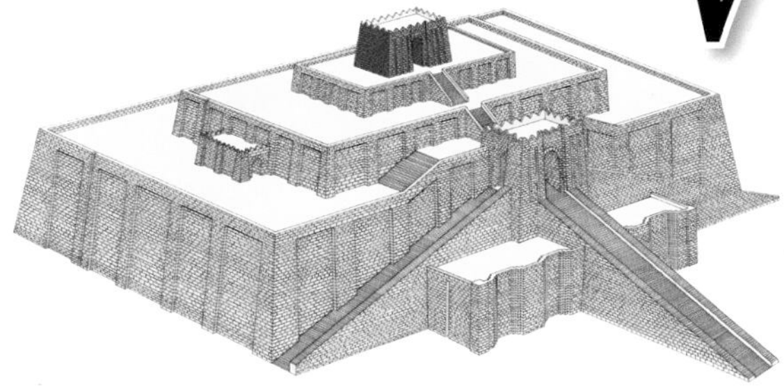

CONTENTS

INTRODUCTION

The story of human history is an enthralling and often inspirational journey. This book is an illustrated guide to all aspects of daily life from the key civilizations of the ancient and medieval worlds—such as the Egyptians, Greeks, and Romans around the Mediterranean Basin, as well as the cultures of ancient China, India, the Americas, and Africa. In Europe, human society was thrown backward into the "dark ages" after the collapse of the Western Roman Empire, and a section of this book shows what life was like in Europe in the Middle Ages, as emerging technologies began to push civilization forward again.

The book is divided into sections, organized chronologically, with an opening map spread setting the scene

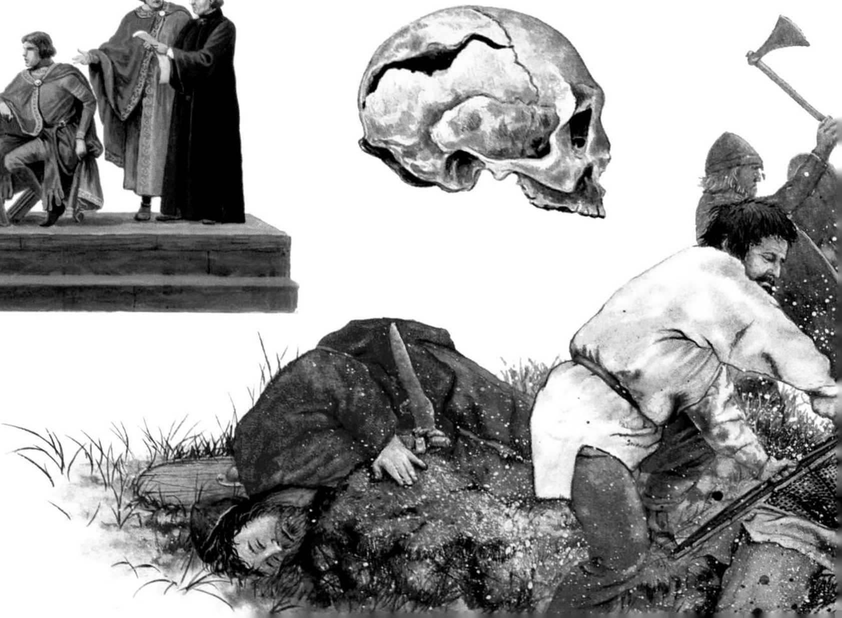

geographically. Each of the theme-based spreads that follow look at key features, such as pyramid building in ancient Egypt, the hoplite armies of ancient Greece, the bathing culture of the Roman Empire, and the pyramids of the Maya and Aztecs.

Each page is packed with lively artworks illustrating themes such as the homes people built, the weapons they fought with, and the gods they worshiped. Major contributions to the world of art, architecture, fashion, and music are highlighted. Informative captions and annotation highlight key features of building design, weaponry and military strategy, technological innovation, and religious ritual to give a flavor of life as it was in the ancient and medieval world.

TIMELINE

4.5 million years ago The earliest bipedal ancestors of humans (*Australopithecus*, the australopithecines) begin to appear in the fossil record.
2.6 million years ago The ancestors of modern humans begin to make simple stone tools. This develops into the Oldowan toolmaking culture, which marks the beginning of the Stone Age.
2.3 million years ago *Homo habilis*, the earliest member of the genus *Homo*, emerges.
1.9 million years ago Hunting and meat-eating are practised by early humans.
500,000 years ago Early hominids begin to use fire for cooking their food.
200,000–150,000 years ago Anatomically modern humans—*Homo sapiens sapiens*—evolve in Africa.
75,000 years ago The earliest examples of human decorative art appear.
12,500 years ago In the Levant, the earliest-known permanent settlements are established.
11–10,000 years ago Sheep, goats, pigs, and cattle are domesticated in the Middle East.
10,000 years ago Humans begin the cultivation of wheat and other crops. The earliest mud-brick towns begin to emerge, and defensive walls are soon added.

PREHISTORY

The earliest known examples of anatomically modern humans date from around 195,000 years ago. Early humans were hunter-gatherers who lived a nomadic lifestyle. They gradually—over tens of thousands of years—spread out from their African homeland to establish themselves all over the world.

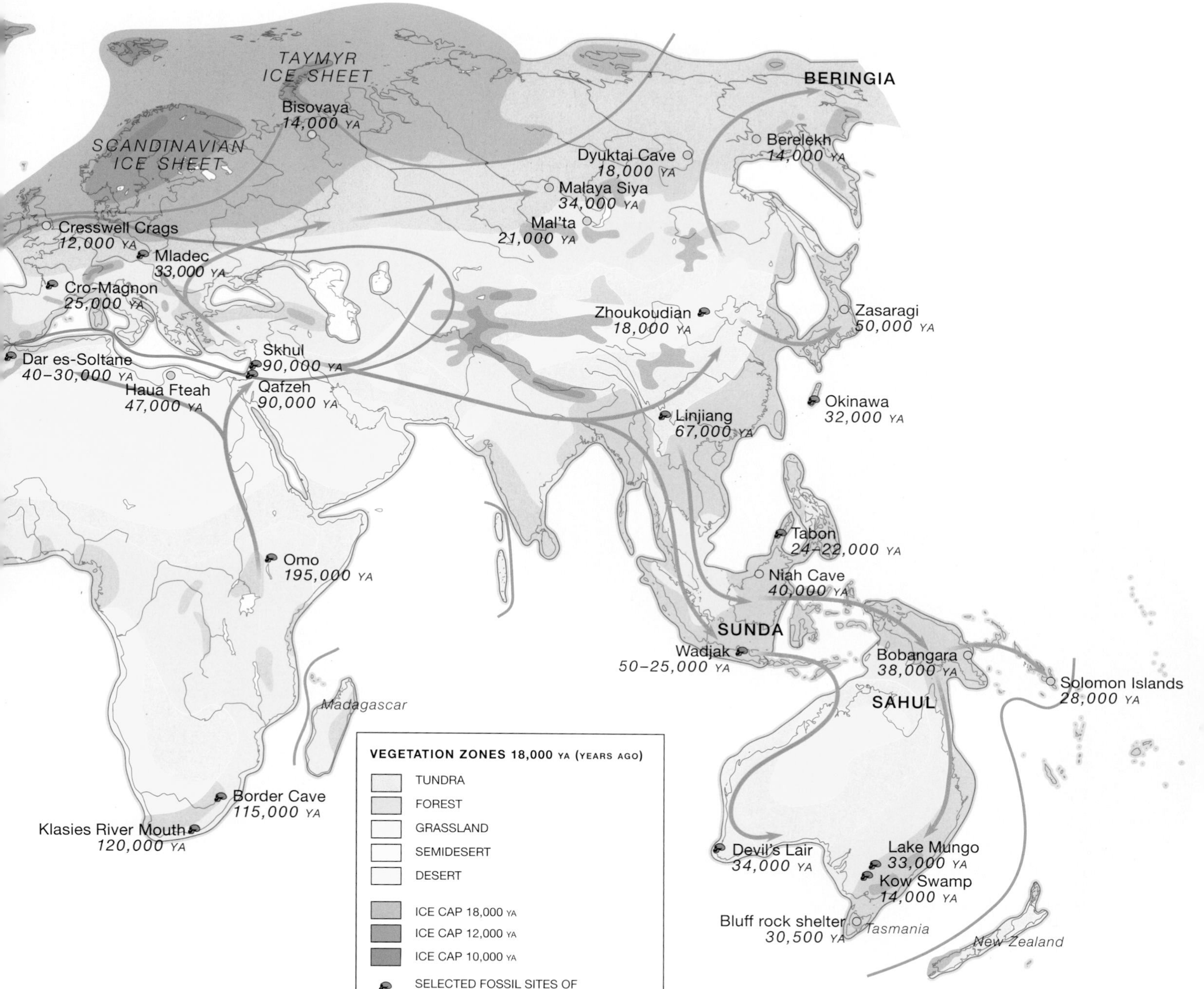

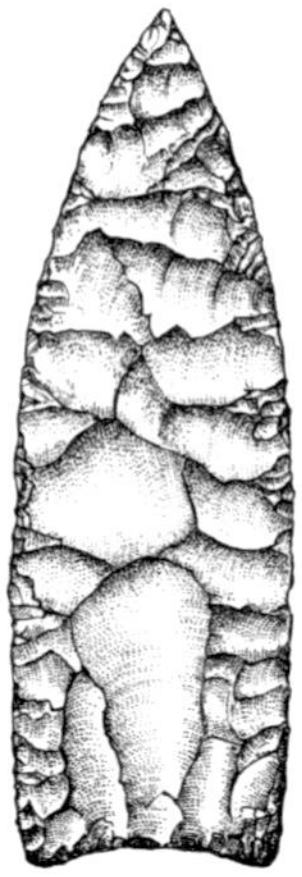

Flint spearhead
By carefully chipping flakes off a piece of flint, it is possible to make very sharp and quite strong blades and points. This discovery allowed humans to hunt and butcher animals.

HUMAN ORIGINS

Human evolution began as Earth's climate cooled toward the end of the Miocene epoch, about 25 million years ago. The forests that had been home to humanity's ape-like ancestors began to shrink, forcing them out into the open savannah. The ancestors of modern humans like the australopithicenes and *Homo habilis* had to adapt to this new environment, walking on two legs for speed and becoming progressively more intelligent. Anatomically modern humans evolved in Africa 200,000–150,000 years ago, long before the most recent ice age.

Males were much larger than females

Australopithicenes
The earliest human ancestors adapted to walking upright, australopithicenes stood 4–5 feet (1.2–1.5 m) tall. They lived in the grasslands of southeast Africa.

Homo habilis
Homo habilis was the first species in the genus *Homo*, of which we are the most recent development. *Habilis'* toolmaking ability enabled it to live in environments too hostile for australopithicenes.

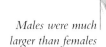

Habilis *looked more like apes than humans*

Fruits and berries were an important part of Habilis' *diet*

Ice Age nomadic hunters
The last Ice Age reached its peak some time between 26,000 and 20,000 years ago. The extreme conditions of this period were a harsh test of human ingenuity.

Stone spearhead
During the late Stone Age (10,000–5,000 BCE) stone tools became increasingly complex and finely made.

Extended family group
Very little is known of early human society. People are thought to have lived in extended family groups, moving their temporary camps as the seasons changed.

THE FIRST FARMERS

About 12,000 years ago, toward the end of the last Ice Age, people in the Near East discovered a new way of obtaining food. It involved the cultivation and domestication of the plants and animals they formerly had to travel to find. The advent of farming dramatically changed human society. Surplus food allowed people to become more specialized, developing important new technologies and teaching others their skills.

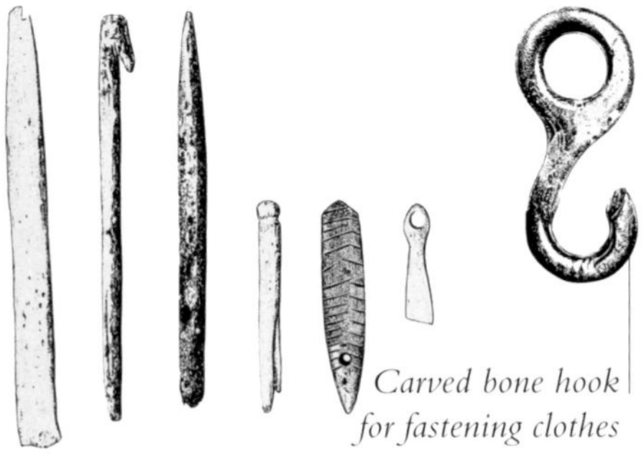

Small tools and fixings
Archeologists excavating ancient houses often find bone needles that were used to make clothes.

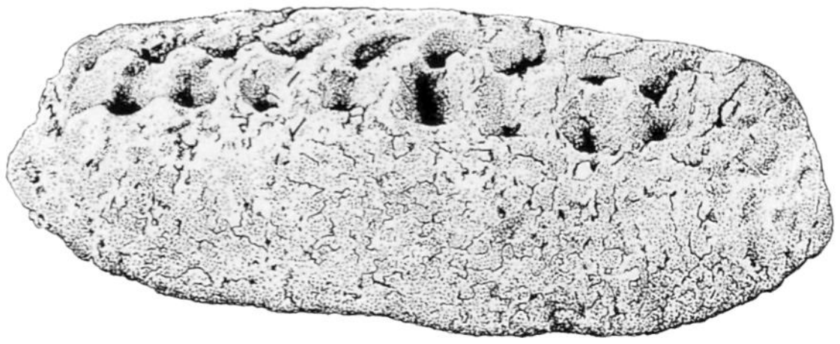

Mud brick
Mud bricks are a strong and versatile building material, still used throughout the world. They are made by mixing mud and straw in a mold then leaving it to harden in the summer sun.

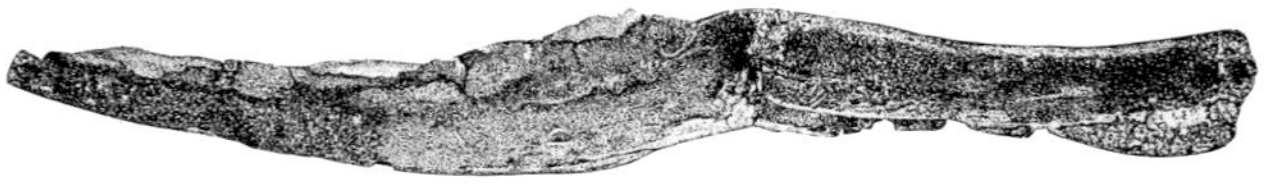

Stone sickle
Stone tools could be quite complex and difficult to make. This sickle has a stone blade attached to a wooden handle using bitumen as glue.

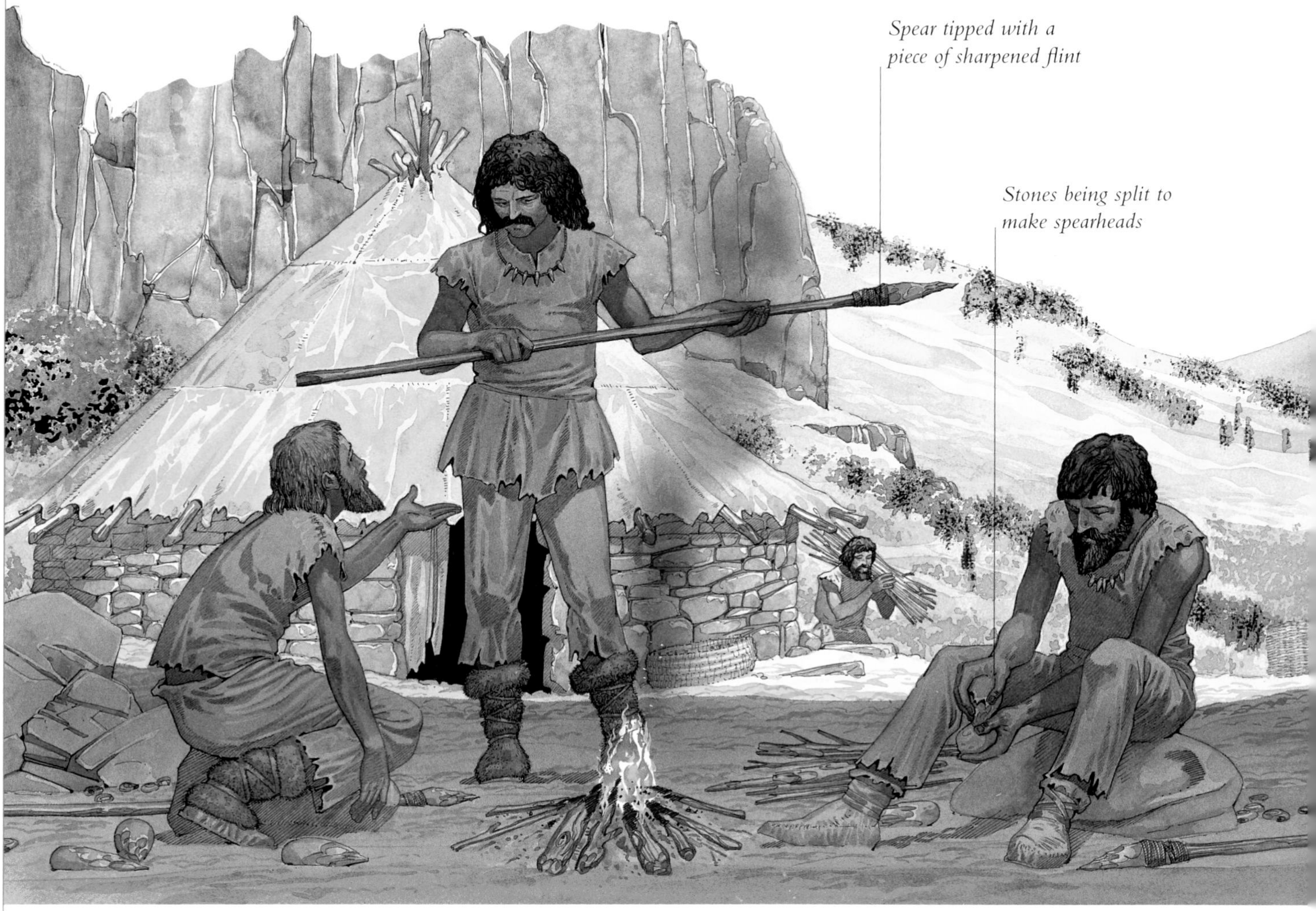

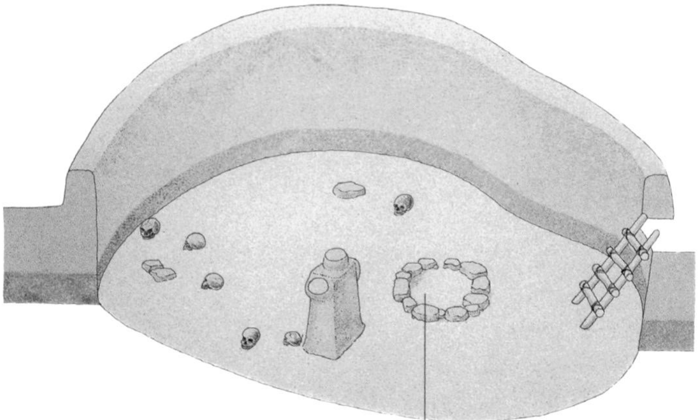

Round huts
The earliest houses were round mud-brick huts sunk into the ground.

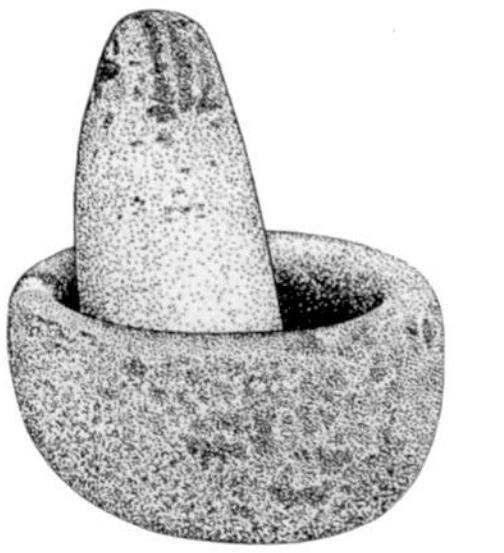

Mortar and pestle
This stone bowl and grinding stone was used to grind seeds and grain into flour.

White ware
Before the techniques for making pottery were understood, vessels were made from a kind of plaster known as white ware.

The earliest settlements
The first settled communities in Mesopotamia were established around 10,000 BCE. The people still hunted, but were able to supplement this often unreliable source of food by herding animals and growing some simple crops.

THE FIRST TOWNS

Farming communities emerged independently in many parts of the world between 10,000 and 5,000 BCE. Farming enabled far more food to be obtained from the land than hunting and gathering, making it possible for large numbers of people to settle in a small area. This led to the construction of the first towns and the creation of the complex social systems required to manage the distribution of land, labor, and other resources.

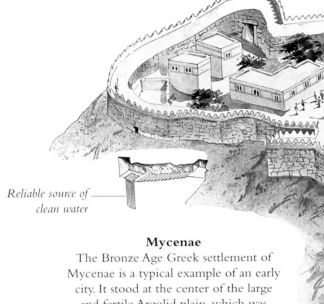

Mycenae
The Bronze Age Greek settlement of Mycenae is a typical example of an early city. It stood at the center of the large and fertile Argolid plain, which was intensively farmed.

Iron Age hill fort
The need to protect a community's wealth from raiders was one of the driving forces behind the creation of towns. Hill forts like this one were built throughout Europe by semi-nomadic herders and farmers.

Ancient Egypt
In Egypt, the fertile Nile Valley enabled the growth of a large and complex society as long as 5,000 years ago.

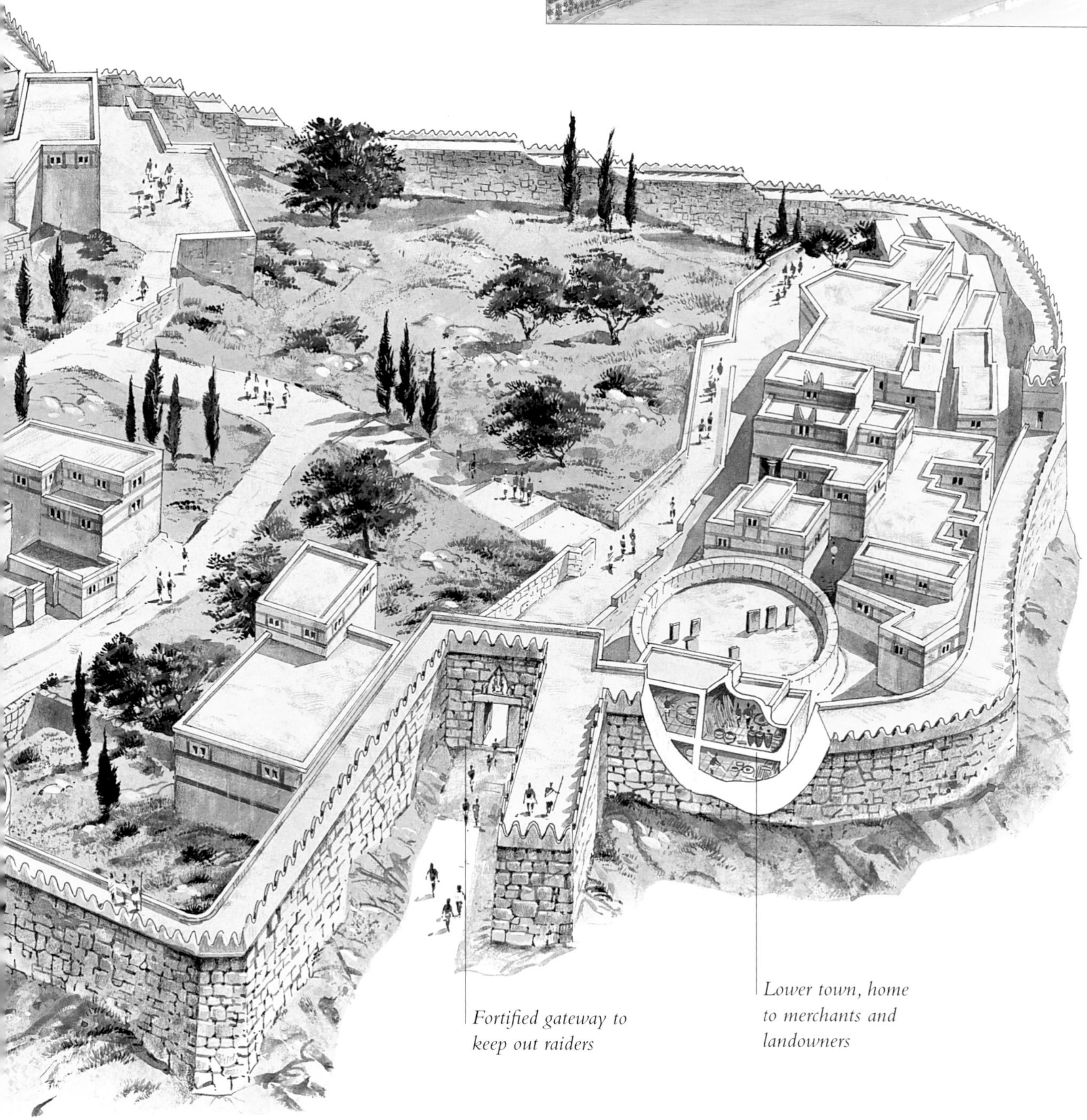

Fortified gateway to keep out raiders

Lower town, home to merchants and landowners

ANCIENT EGYPT

Over 5,000 years ago, the world's first major civilization was born on the banks of the Nile River. Mesopotamia had civilized city-states, but Egypt was a whole country ruled by one king and governed by one set of laws. Its civilization lasted for about 3,000 years.

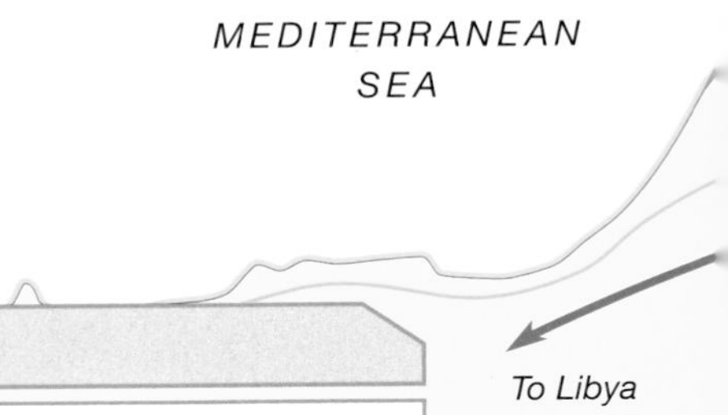

TIMELINE

4500 BCE The first permanent settlements appear along the Nile River.

4000 BCE Naqada culture, named for its principal city, emerges in the upper Nile Valley.

3400 BCE The earliest Egyptian examples of written language appear. Wall paintings and painted pottery also begin to appear.

3400 BCE Earliest evidence of deliberate ritual mummification.

3100 BCE The foundation of the Egyptian state.

2920 BCE The beginning of the Early Dynastic Period.

2650 BCE The earliest known pyramid is built in Saqqara for the pharaoh Djoser.

2575 BCE Start of the period of the Old Kingdom, during which the power and wealth of the Egyptian state grows.

2600–2500 BCE The massive stone pyramids of the Giza Necropolis are built.

2040 BCE The territories of Upper and Lower Egypt are united under a single ruler. This marks the foundation of the Middle Kingdom.

1550 BCE Foundation of the New Kingdom. This period witnesses a significant expansion of Egypt's influence.

1504–1492 BCE The Egyptian empire is at its fullest extent under the pharaoh Tuthmosis I.

1333–1324 BCE The brief reign of the pharaoh Tutenkhamun.

1279–1213 BCE Period of rule of Rameses II the Great.

1186–1155 BCE Reign of the pharaoh Rameses III.

723 BCE Beginning of the Late Kingdom period. This period sees the decline of Egypt as a major power as it is eclipsed by other civilizations.

343 BCE Egypt is conquered by the Achaemenid Persians.

332 BCE The Persians are driven out by Alexander the Great. The Greek Ptolemaic dynasty rules Egypt until the arrival of the Romans in 30 BCE.

Music and entertainment
Musicians played many kinds of instruments, including harps and reed pipes. Dancers performed at feasts.

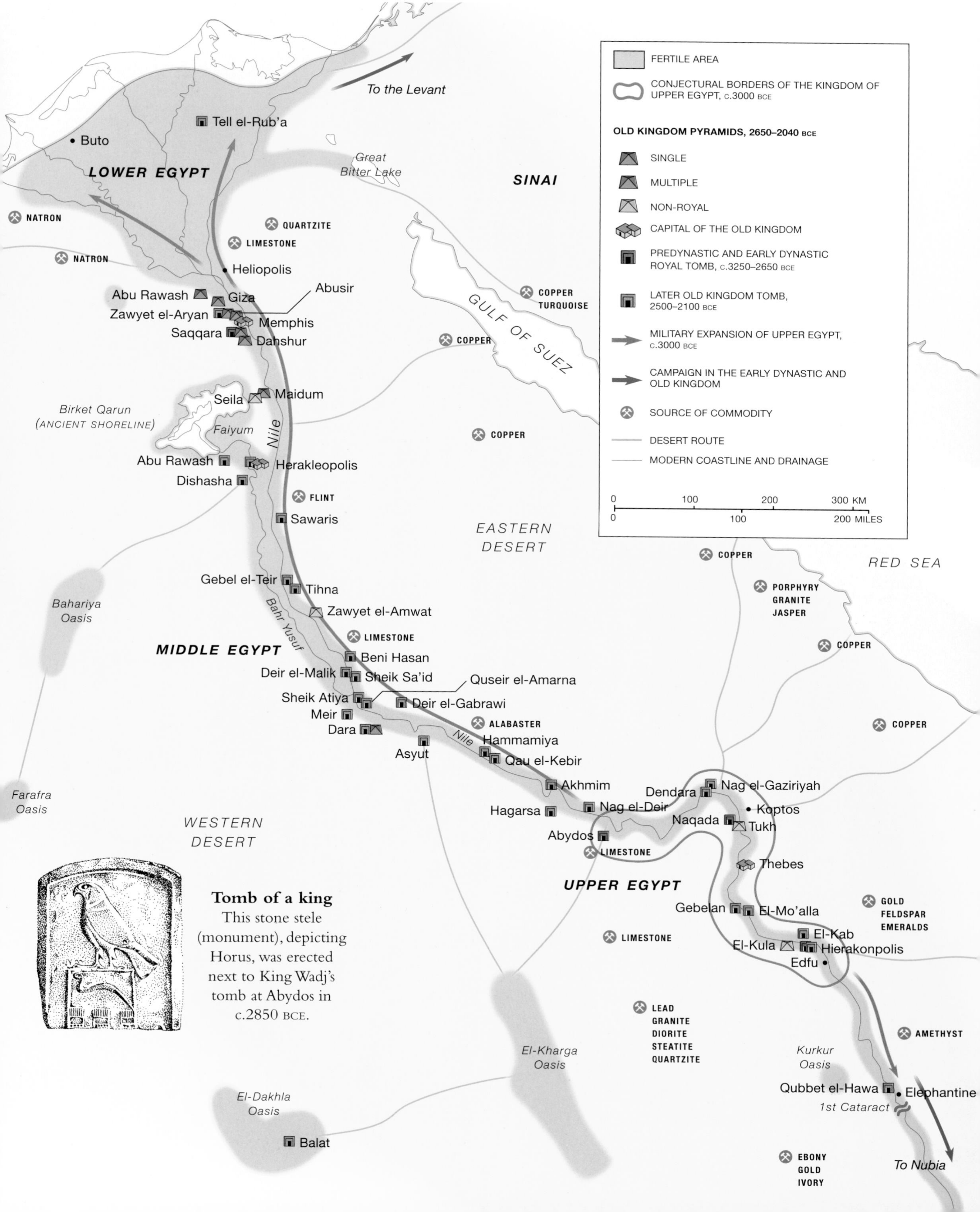
FERTILE AREA
CONJECTURAL BORDERS OF THE KINGDOM OF UPPER EGYPT, c.3000 BCE
OLD KINGDOM PYRAMIDS, 2650–2040 BCE
SINGLE
MULTIPLE
NON-ROYAL
CAPITAL OF THE OLD KINGDOM
PREDYNASTIC AND EARLY DYNASTIC ROYAL TOMB, c.3250–2650 BCE
LATER OLD KINGDOM TOMB, 2500–2100 BCE
MILITARY EXPANSION OF UPPER EGYPT, c.3000 BCE
CAMPAIGN IN THE EARLY DYNASTIC AND OLD KINGDOM
SOURCE OF COMMODITY
DESERT ROUTE
MODERN COASTLINE AND DRAINAGE
0
100
200
300 KM
0
100
200 MILES
To the Levant
Tell el-Rub'a
Buto
LOWER EGYPT
Great Bitter Lake
SINAI
NATRON
NATRON
QUARTZITE
LIMESTONE
Heliopolis
Abu Rawash
Giza
Abusir
Zawyet el-Aryan
Memphis
Saqqara
Dahshur
COPPER TURQUOISE
GULF OF SUEZ
COPPER
Seila
Maidum
Birket Qarun (ANCIENT SHORELINE)
Faiyum
Nile
COPPER
Abu Rawash
Herakleopolis
Dishasha
FLINT
Sawaris
EASTERN DESERT
COPPER
RED SEA
Gebel el-Teir
Tihna
PORPHYRY GRANITE JASPER
Bahariya Oasis
Zawyet el-Amwat
Bahr Yusuf
LIMESTONE
COPPER
MIDDLE EGYPT
Beni Hasan
Deir el-Malik
Sheik Sa'id
Quseir el-Amarna
Sheik Atiya
Deir el-Gabrawi
Meir
ALABASTER
Dara
Nile
Hammamiya
COPPER
Asyut
Qau el-Kebir
Akhmim
Nag el-Gaziriyah
Dendara
Farafra Oasis
Hagarsa
Nag el-Deir
Koptos
Naqada
Tukh
WESTERN DESERT
Abydos
LIMESTONE
Thebes
UPPER EGYPT
GOLD FELDSPAR EMERALDS
Gebelan
El-Mo'alla
LIMESTONE
El-Kab
El-Kula
Hierakonpolis
Edfu
LEAD GRANITE DIORITE STEATITE QUARTZITE
AMETHYST
El-Kharga Oasis
Kurkur Oasis
El-Dakhla Oasis
Qubbet el-Hawa
Elephantine
1st Cataract
Balat
EBONY GOLD IVORY
To Nubia

Tomb of a king
This stone stele (monument), depicting Horus, was erected next to King Wadj's tomb at Abydos in c.2850 BCE.

GODS

The Egyptians considered all their gods and goddesses to be forms of the creator of the world, but with identities of their own. They could be shown in full human or animal-headed human form, are often shown wearing distinctive headdresses, and carry sacred symbols. Some had several forms. Hathor, for example, may be shown as a beautiful woman, the head of a woman with cow's ears, a cow, or a cow-headed woman.

Magic eye
The magic eye, or Eye of Horus, was a good-luck sign and was thought to protect against evil spells.

Ankh
This symbol represented life. It was carried only by gods and kings, because they alone had power over life and death.

Wadjit
The goddess of the delta is here shown with a lioness's head with a cobra (the symbol of Lower Egypt) on top.

Gods and goddesses
Well over 1,000 deities are mentioned in Egyptian texts. Represented below are human and semihuman forms of some of the chief Egyptian gods and goddesses.

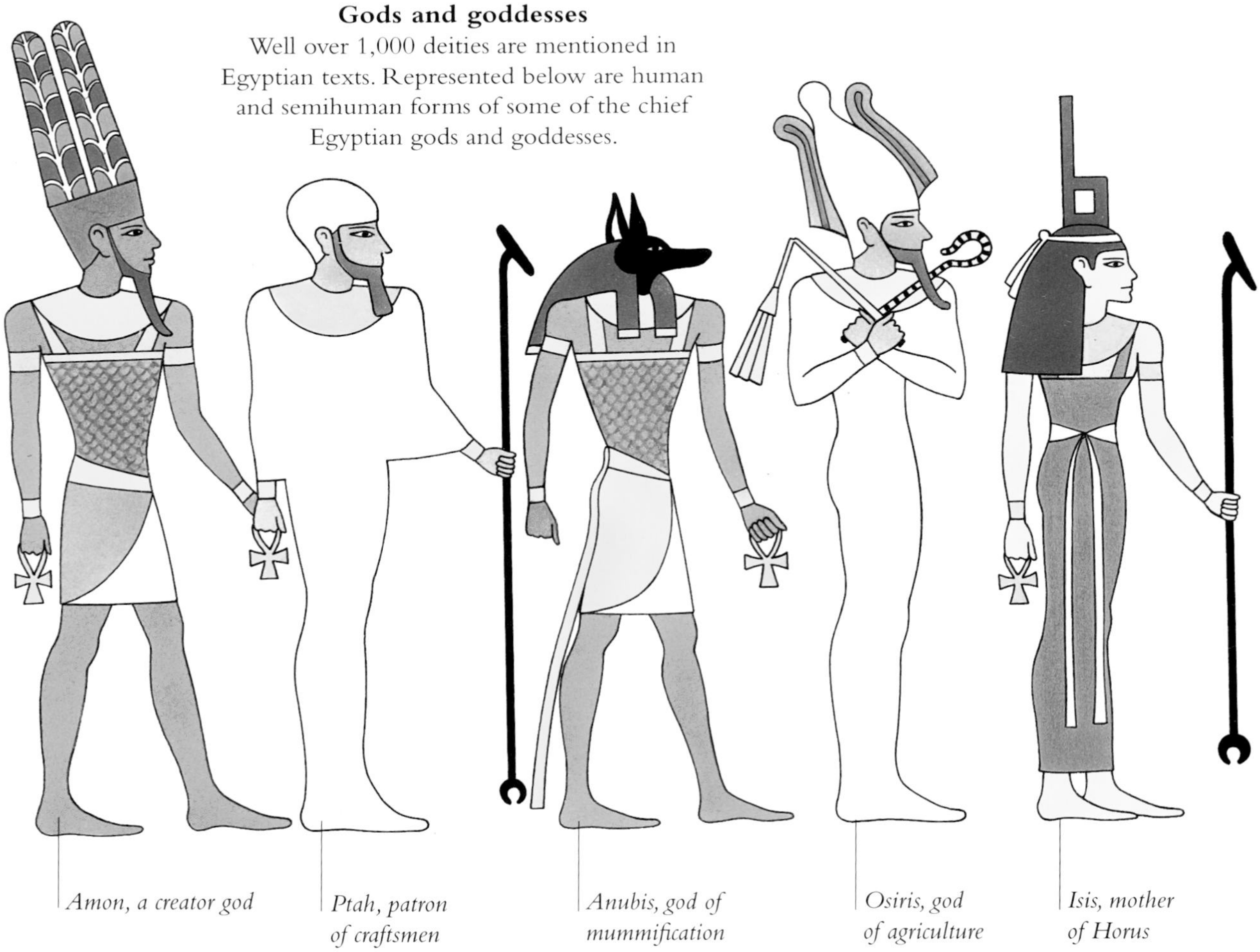

Amon, a creator god

Ptah, patron of craftsmen

Anubis, god of mummification

Osiris, god of agriculture

Isis, mother of Horus

King raises figurine

Daily temple ritual
A pharaoh makes offerings to a statue of the god Amon, standing in a gilded shrine. The chief offering is a figurine of the goddess who represents Maat, the goddess of truth, justice, and order. This act symbolized the king's duty to uphold these qualities.

Priestess raises sacred rattle, or sistrum

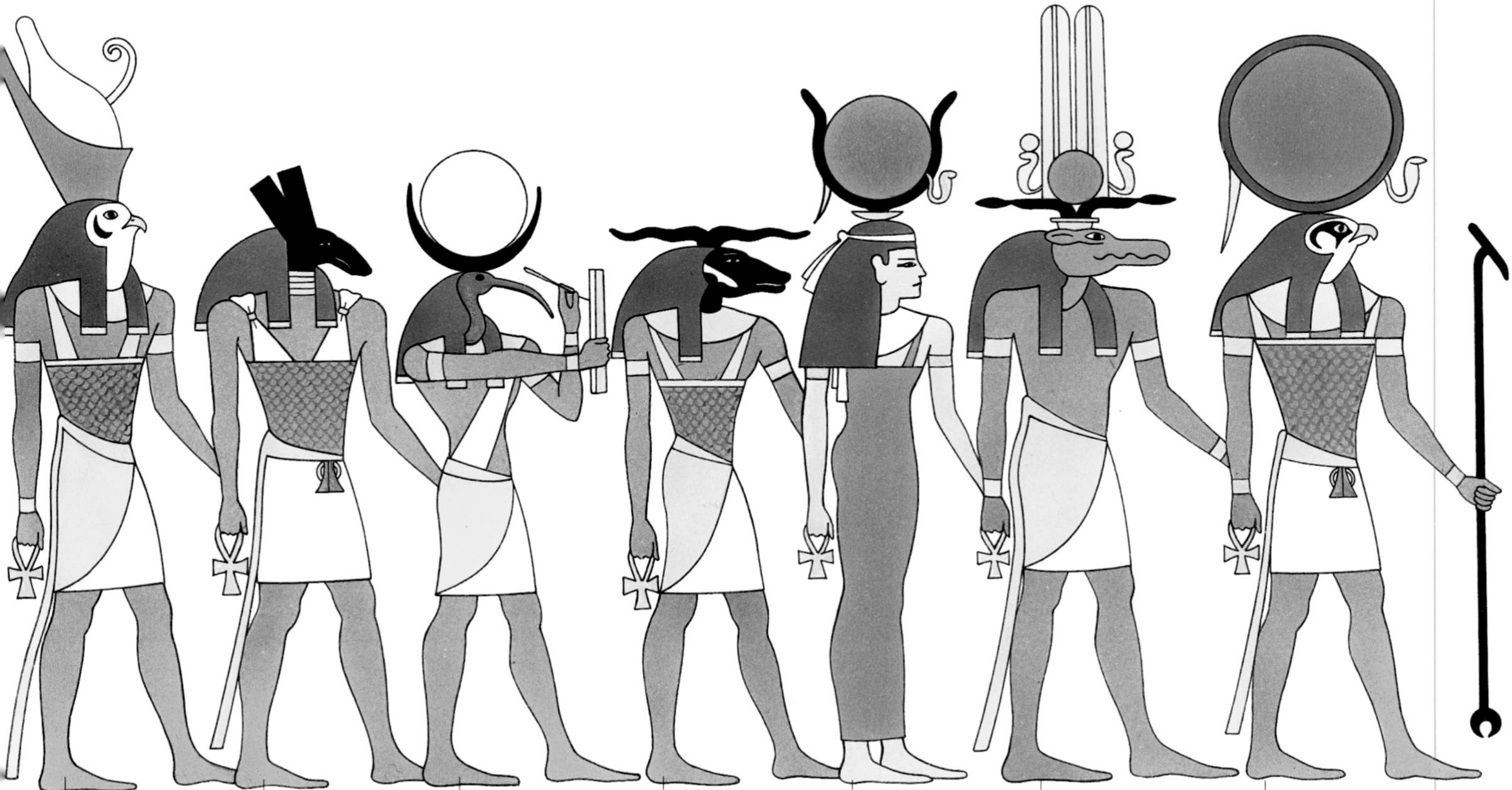

Horus, a sky god linked with kings

Seth, enemy of Horus and Osiris

Thoth, god of wisdom

Khnum, a ram god

Hathor, goddess of love

Sobek, the crocodile god

Ra, the Sun god

WRITING

Writing first appeared in Egyptian society around 3000 BCE. It made it easier to organize society and pass on information. The first Egyptian writing used hieroglyphs based on pictures. Later, the hieratic and demotic scripts were developed for daily use. One of the greatest technological advances of the Egyptians was the invention of paper, which was made from papyrus plants. Inks of different colors were produced, using a variety of minerals mixed with water, gelatin, gum, and beeswax.

Hieroglyphs
Hieroglyphs are little pictures. Some stood for objects and others represented letters of the alphabet (vowels were omitted).

Pens
Pens were made from reeds. The end was squashed to make a pointed nib. Black was the most common color of ink for official documents.

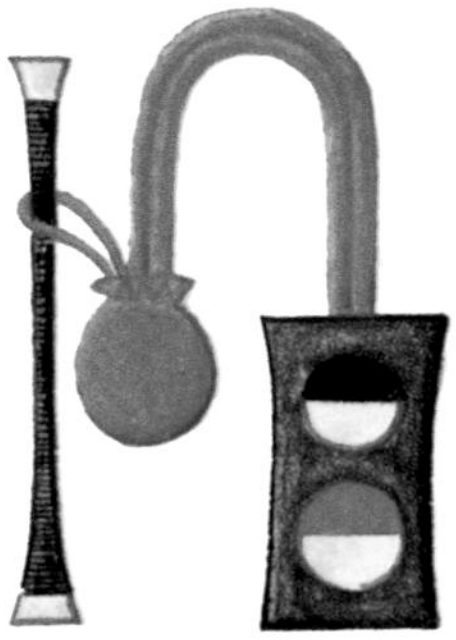

A scribe's equipment
This hieroglyph shows a palette with red and black inks, a water pot, and a papyrus smoother.

HIEROGLYPHS

The hieroglyphic script has about 750 signs, most of which are pictures of people, animals, plants, or objects. There are two main types of sign: sound-signs and sense-signs. Sound-signs can represent from one to four consonants. The vowels were not written out. A sense-sign can be used to write a word or be placed after a word to show the area of meaning. Verbs of motion, for example, have a pair of legs attached. A sentence (from the battle *Annals of Thutmose III*)—"His majesty set out on a chariot of gold"—is set out below. Also shown below is a selection of commonly used sense-signs.

ONE CONSONANT

Y W F M N R T

TWO CONSONANT

ḤR WR WN GM ḤM NB D3

THREE CONSONANT

ḪPR D'M NTR NH HNT W3D WSR

wd̲3	ḥmf	ḥr	wrryt
set out	*majesty his*	*on*	*(a) chariot*

nt	d̲'m
of	gold

SENSE SIGNS

Nose/ joy	Precious metal	Wood	Motion	Woman/ female

Cutting papyrus
Tall stems of the marsh plant papyrus were cut and carried off in bundles.

Stripping the rind
Each stem was stripped of its rind and cut into short pieces. These were cut into long strips.

Preparing the pith
Strips were placed at right angles on top of each other. It was essential to keep the pith (soft plant fibers) moist.

Making scrolls
Two layers of strips were put on a hard surface and beaten until fused. The papyrus sheets were polished and then glued together to make scrolls.

BURIALS AND MUMMIES

The ancient Egyptians took many precautions to make sure that the spirits of the dead could enjoy a life after death. They believed this was only possible if the bodies were preserved. In early times, burial in dry sand preserved bodies naturally. Later, when coffins came into use, some artificial way of preventing decay was needed—mummification. The exact treatment depended on what a family could afford.

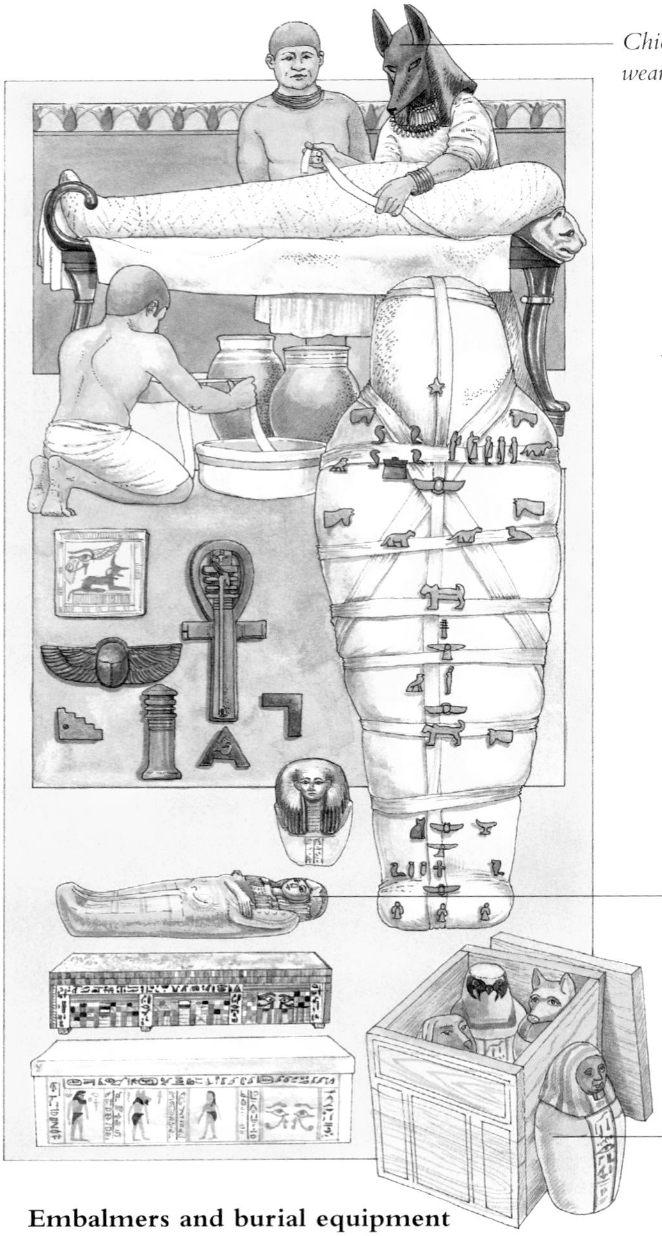

Embalmers and burial equipment
The chief embalmer wears a jackal mask to impersonate Anubis, protector of the dead. Spells were recited as each part of the mummy was wrapped in long strips of linen.

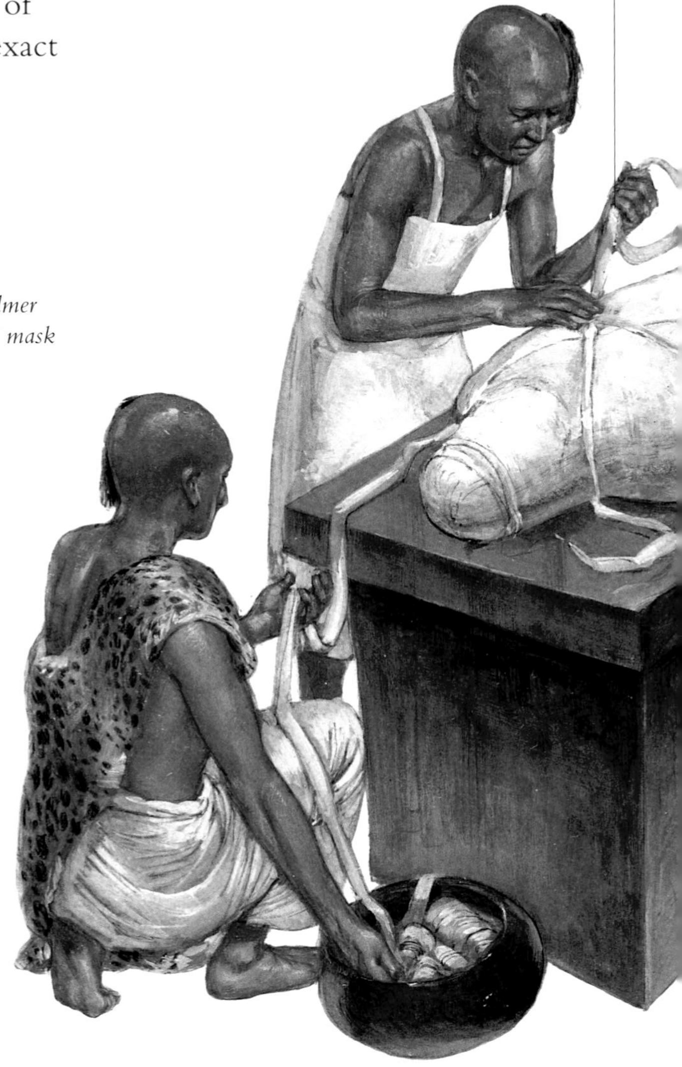

Preparing a mummy
The most elaborate type of mummification took about 70 days. Embalmers took the brain out through the nose and removed the vital organs. When the body was completely dried out, the mummy was treated with perfumed oils and resin before being wrapped for burial.

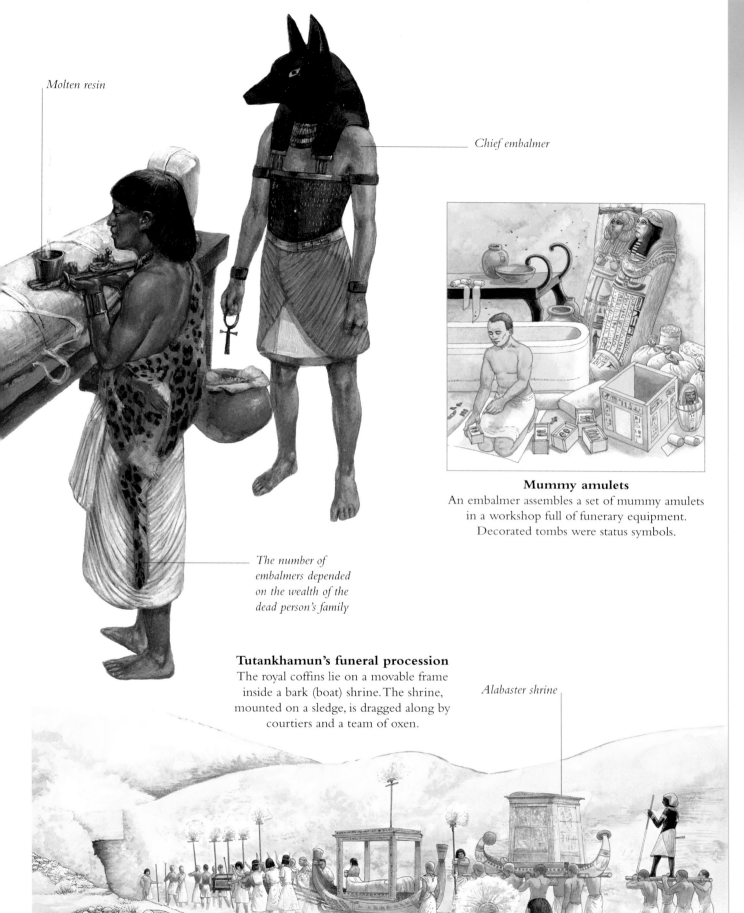

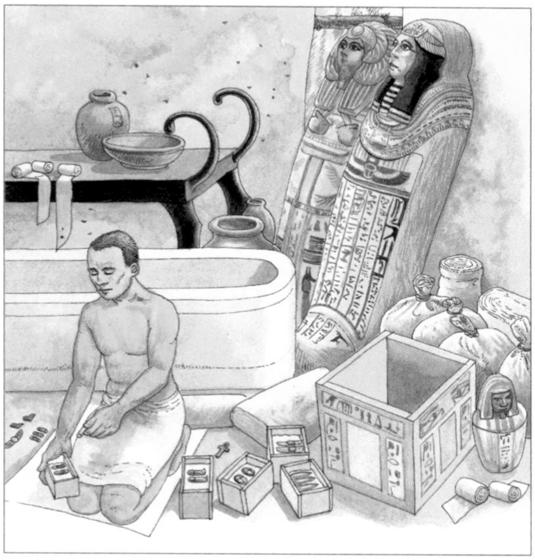

Mummy amulets

An embalmer assembles a set of mummy amulets in a workshop full of funerary equipment. Decorated tombs were status symbols.

Tutankhamun's funeral procession

The royal coffins lie on a movable frame inside a bark (boat) shrine. The shrine, mounted on a sledge, is dragged along by courtiers and a team of oxen.

PYRAMIDS

According to tradition, an official called Imhotep designed Egypt's first pyramid, the Step Pyramid at Saqqara, during the reign of King Djoser around 2630 BCE. Like the later pyramids, it was both a royal tomb and a temple where the spirit of the dead king could be worshiped. Pyramid building accelerated and became more sophisticated in the period 2600–2500 BCE, when the giant pyramids of Giza were constructed.

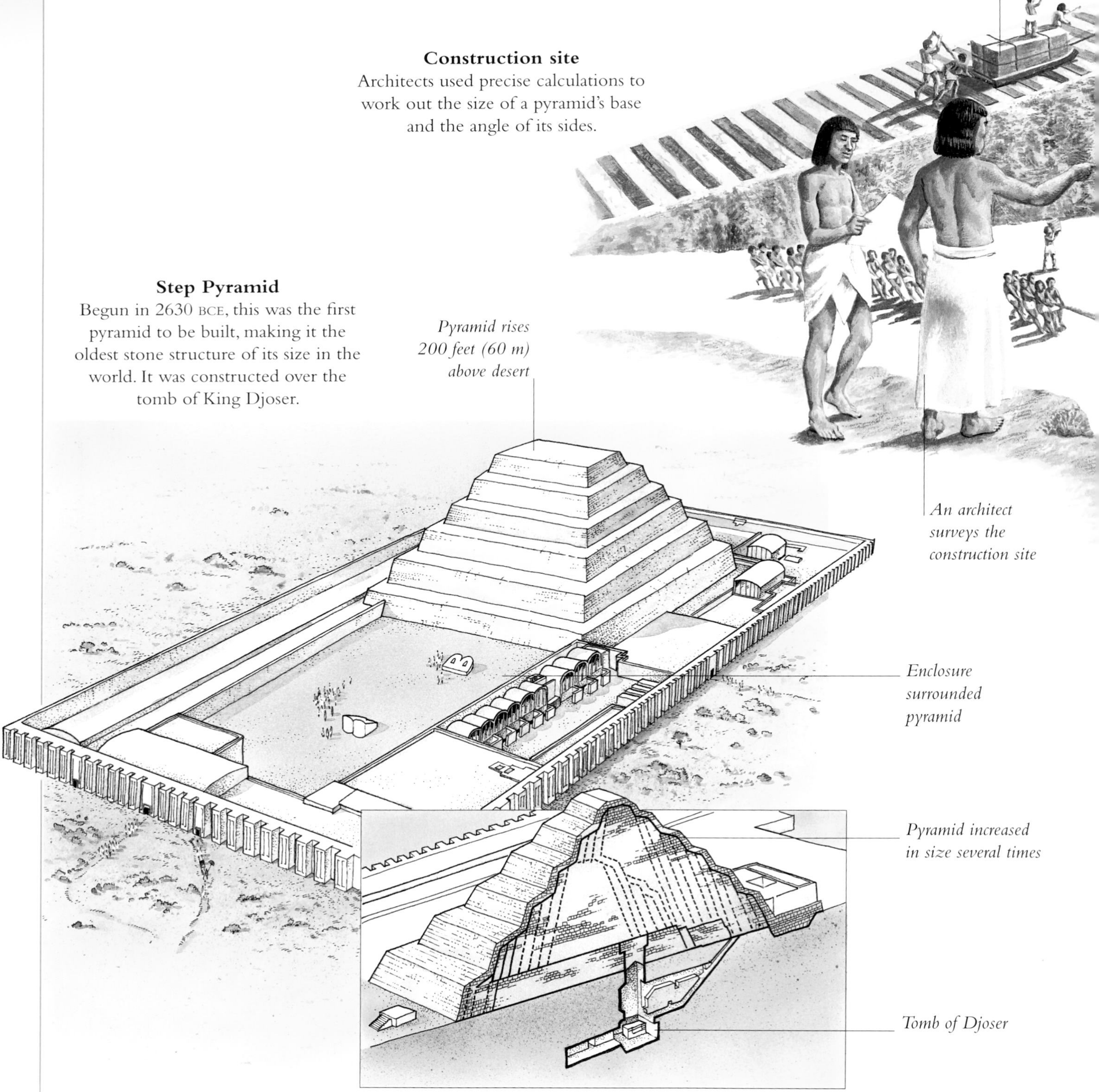
Stone being hauled up ramp
An architect surveys the construction site
Pyramid rises 200 feet (60 m) above desert
Enclosure surrounded pyramid
Pyramid increased in size several times
Tomb of Djoser

Construction site
Architects used precise calculations to work out the size of a pyramid's base and the angle of its sides.

Step Pyramid
Begun in 2630 BCE, this was the first pyramid to be built, making it the oldest stone structure of its size in the world. It was constructed over the tomb of King Djoser.

Hauliers
These men used ropes and brute force to move large blocks of stone to the construction site.

The Maidum Pyramid
This was a building disaster. A tower rising from a mound of rubble is all that remains of an early attempt to build a true pyramid. The outer casing was not well laid and had no proper foundations—as a result, the structure collapsed.

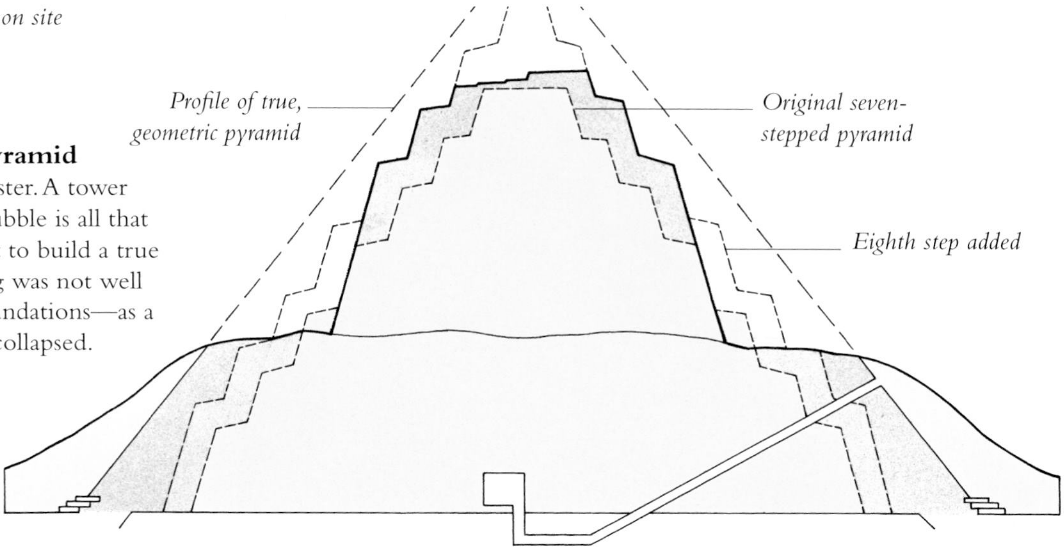

PYRAMIDS

As many as 100,000 laborers were used to build the Great Pyramid at Giza. To cut limestone slabs, workers hammered wooden wedges into the stone. The wedges were then soaked with water, which made them expand, splitting the rock. Builders also used copper pickaxes and chisels, granite hammers, and other stone tools. Pyramids were finished with a layer of limestone on the four sides and gold on the apex.

Work in progress
On this half-finished pyramid the central core and the stepped buttress walls are visible. Water is poured on the ropes and sledges to reduce friction while gangs of laborers haul limestone blocks up a ramp.

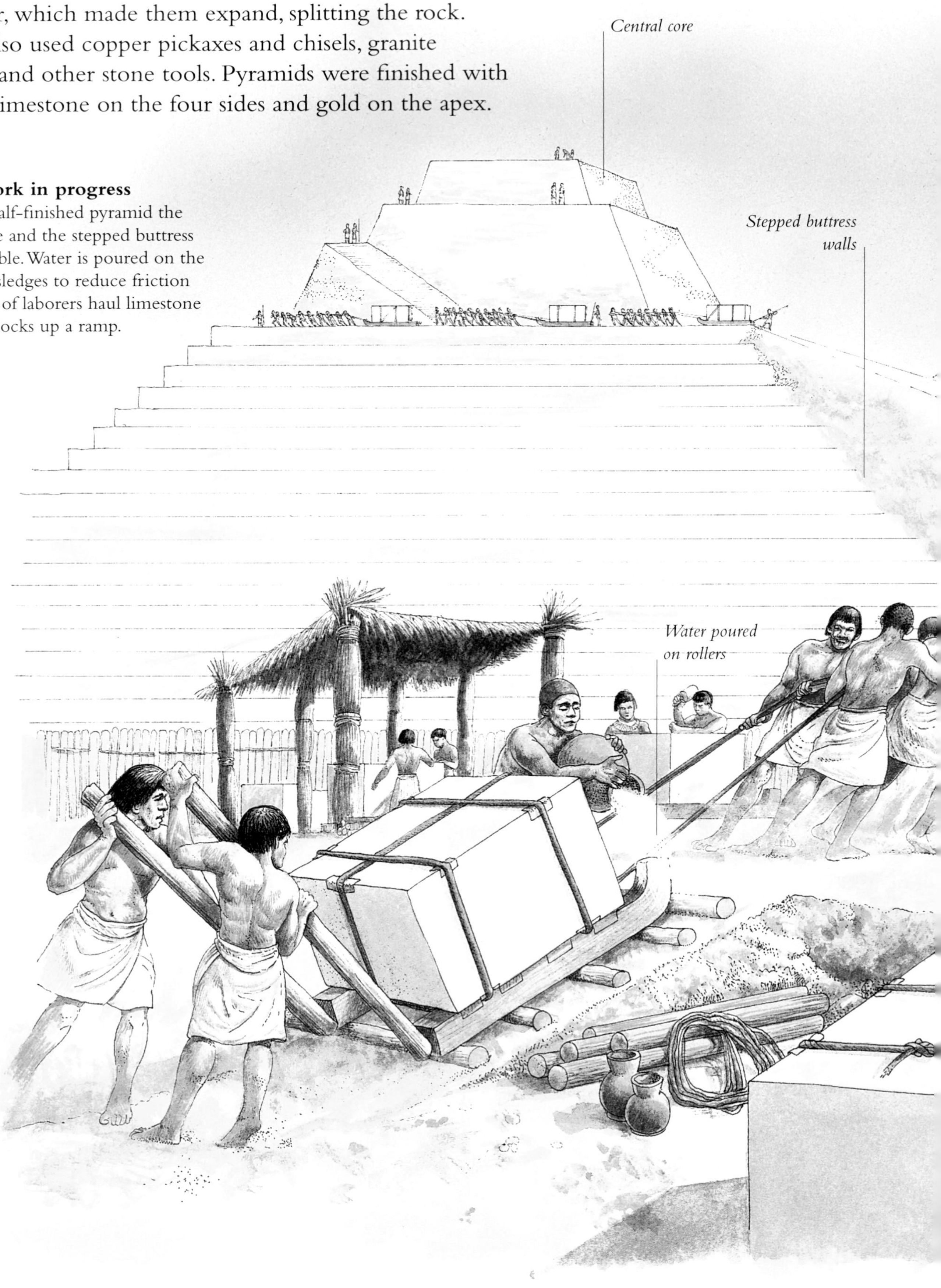

Rollers
Heavy sleds and blocks of stone were moved on wooden rollers, which had to be kept damp to reduce friction.

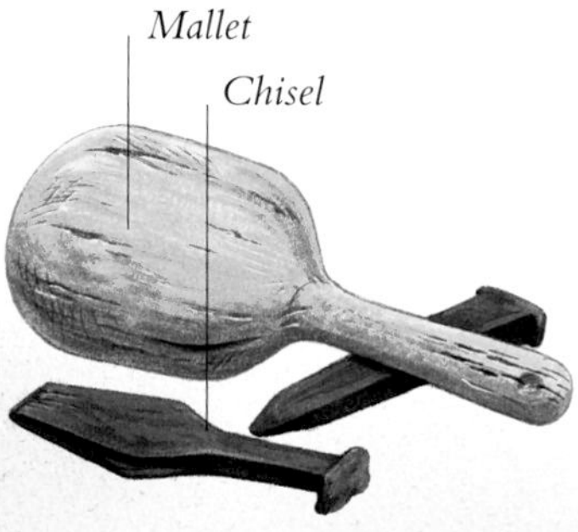

Stonemason's tools
Large chunks of stone were broken off by pushing wedges into crevices. Blocks were then shaped with a chisel and mallet.

Right angles
Stonemasons used right angles to make sure that the sides of the stone blocks were straight.

PYRAMIDS

Building the Old Kingdom pyramids was an enormous task. The Great Pyramid at Giza contains about 6.25 million tons (6.35 million tonnes) of stone, with individual blocks weighing 2–15 tons. To finish the pyramid during the reign of King Khufu (2589–2566 BCE), the blocks must have been produced at the rate of one every two minutes for 23 years. The stonemasons who quarried, shaped, and smoothed the blocks formed a highly skilled permanent workforce.

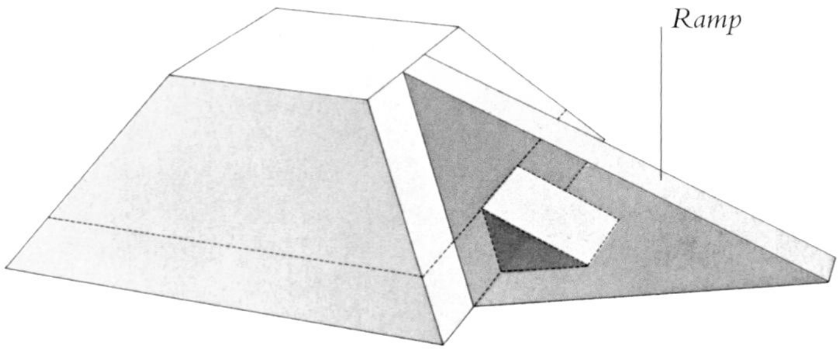

Building ramps
The best method of lifting heavy stone blocks to the required height on the pyramid was to drag them up ramps made of mud bricks and rubble.

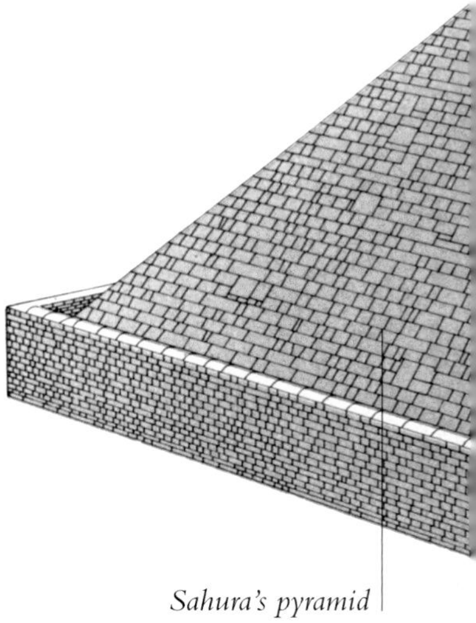

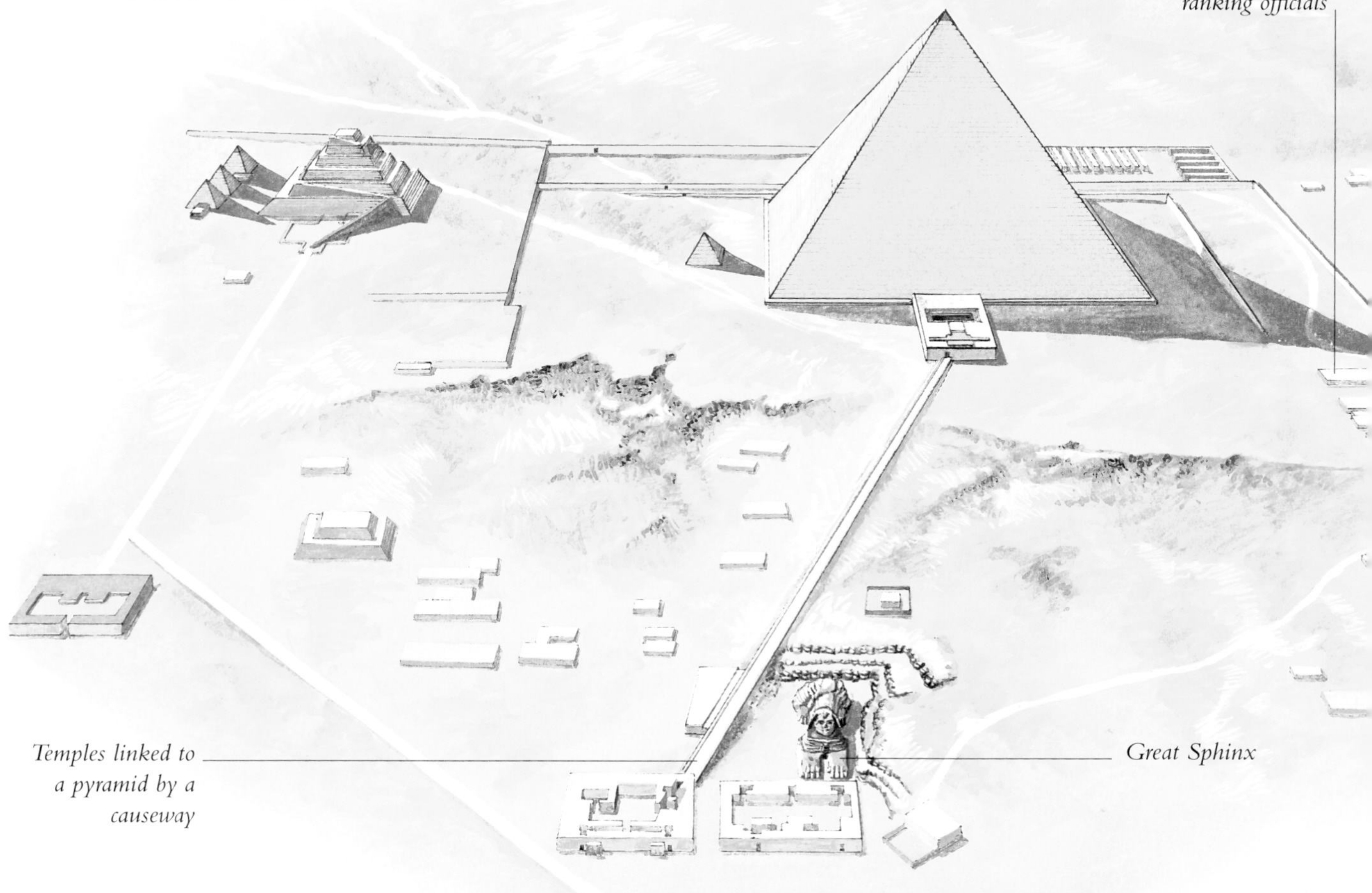

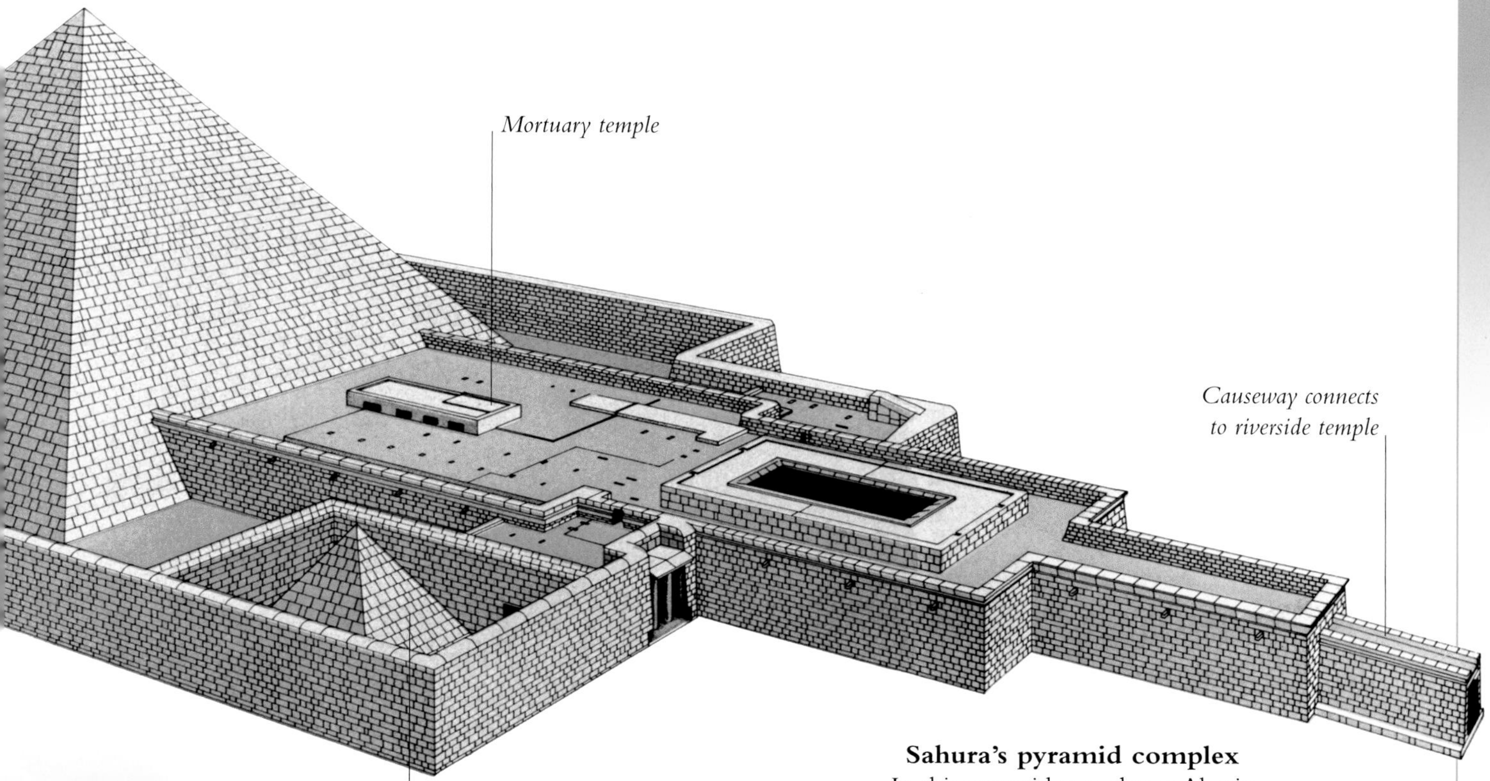

Sahura's pyramid complex
In this pyramid complex at Abusir, a causeway joins the riverside temple to the courtyard of the mortuary temple. There is one additional small pyramid.

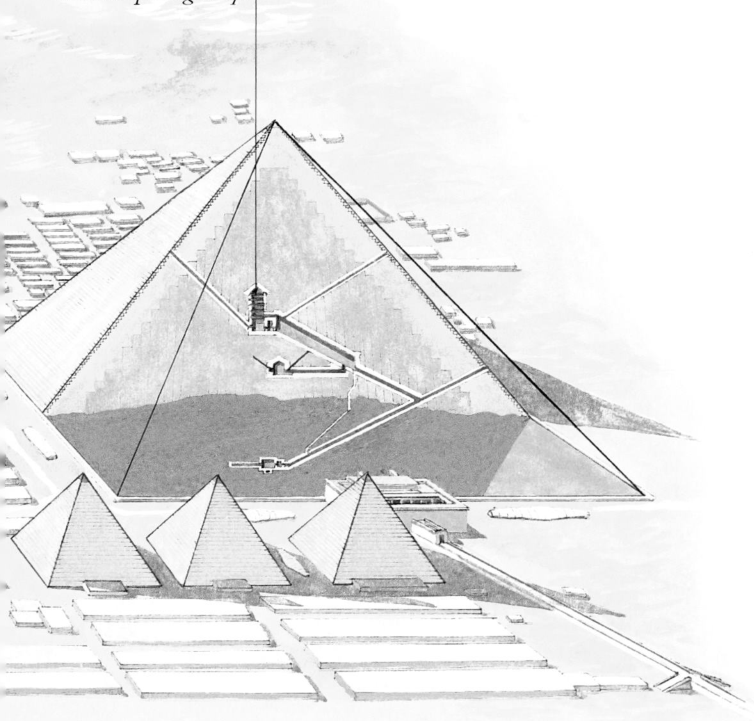

The Great Pyramid
The Great Pyramid at Giza was finished 4,500 years ago. It measures about 755 feet (230 m) on each side. A marvel of precision engineering, there is only an 8-inch (20 cm) difference between the longest and the shortest sides.

PYRAMID MEASUREMENT

The height of Khufu's pyramid equals the total length of the four sides of the base divided by 2 x pi (3.142). The ancient Egyptians probably did not have the knowledge to calculate this, so they may have arrived at these measurements by accident—for example, by measuring distances by counting the turns of a drum when rolled down the sides.

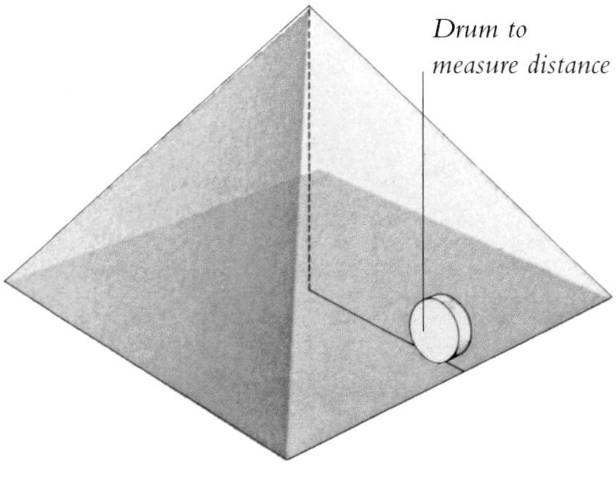

BOATS

Boats were the most important mode of transport in ancient Egypt, and the Nile was the civilization's highway. The earliest boats were small skiffs made from bundles of papyrus tied together with ropes. Skiffs were propelled by paddles or long poles. At least as early as the Old Kingdom (2575–2134 BCE), large boats were built from wood. For seagoing craft and the largest Nile boats, planks of cedar wood were imported from Lebanon.

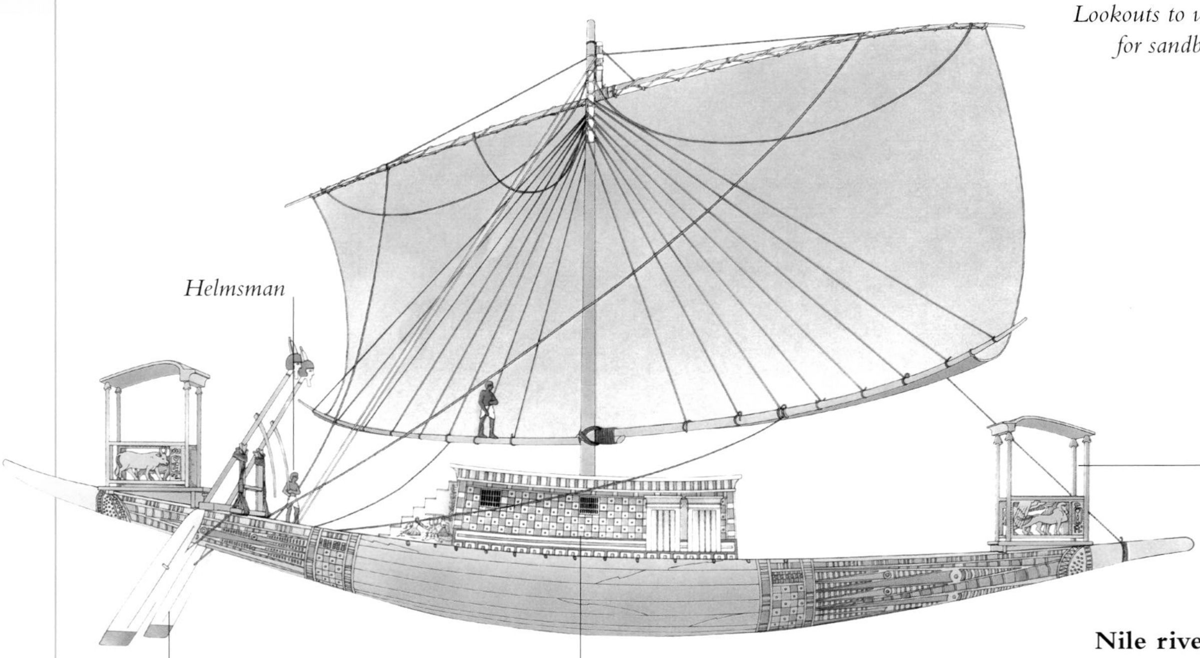

Nile river craft
By the time of the New Kingdom (1550–1196 BCE), the standard sail of a Nile-going boat was wider than it was tall, the cabin was in the center, and a helmsman stood in front of a rudder post to control the steering oars.

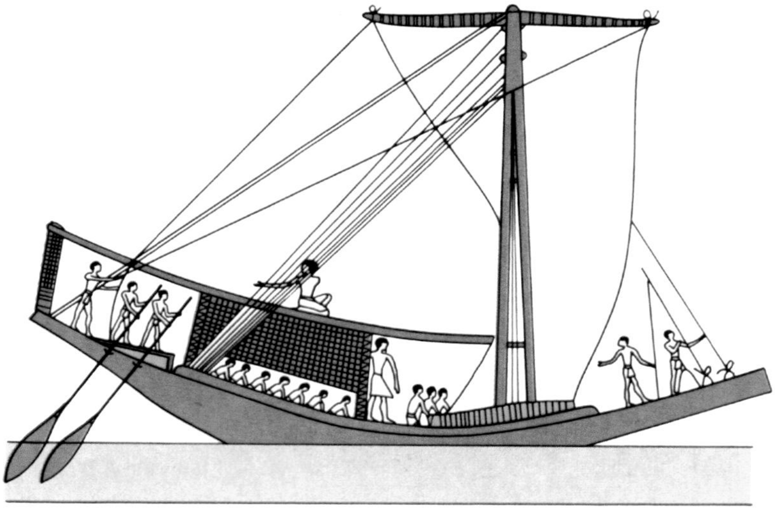

Technological advances
By the time of the Old Kingdom (2575–2134 BCE), the Egyptians were building sophisticated vessels with sails that could be raised and lowered, teams of rowers, and specialist helmsmen.

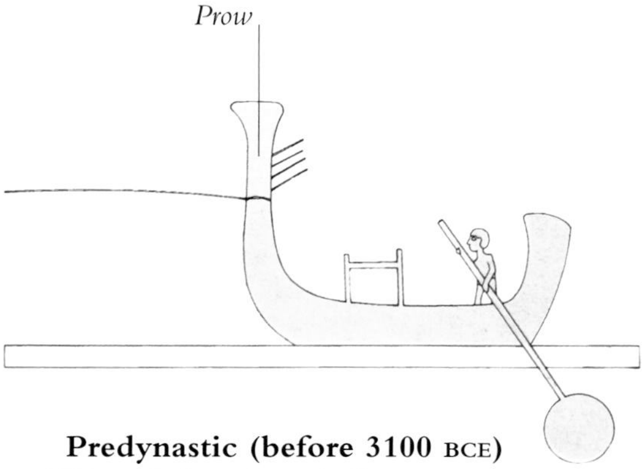

Predynastic (before 3100 BCE)
This early boat is made from papyrus, has a tall prow and stern, and one large steering oar.

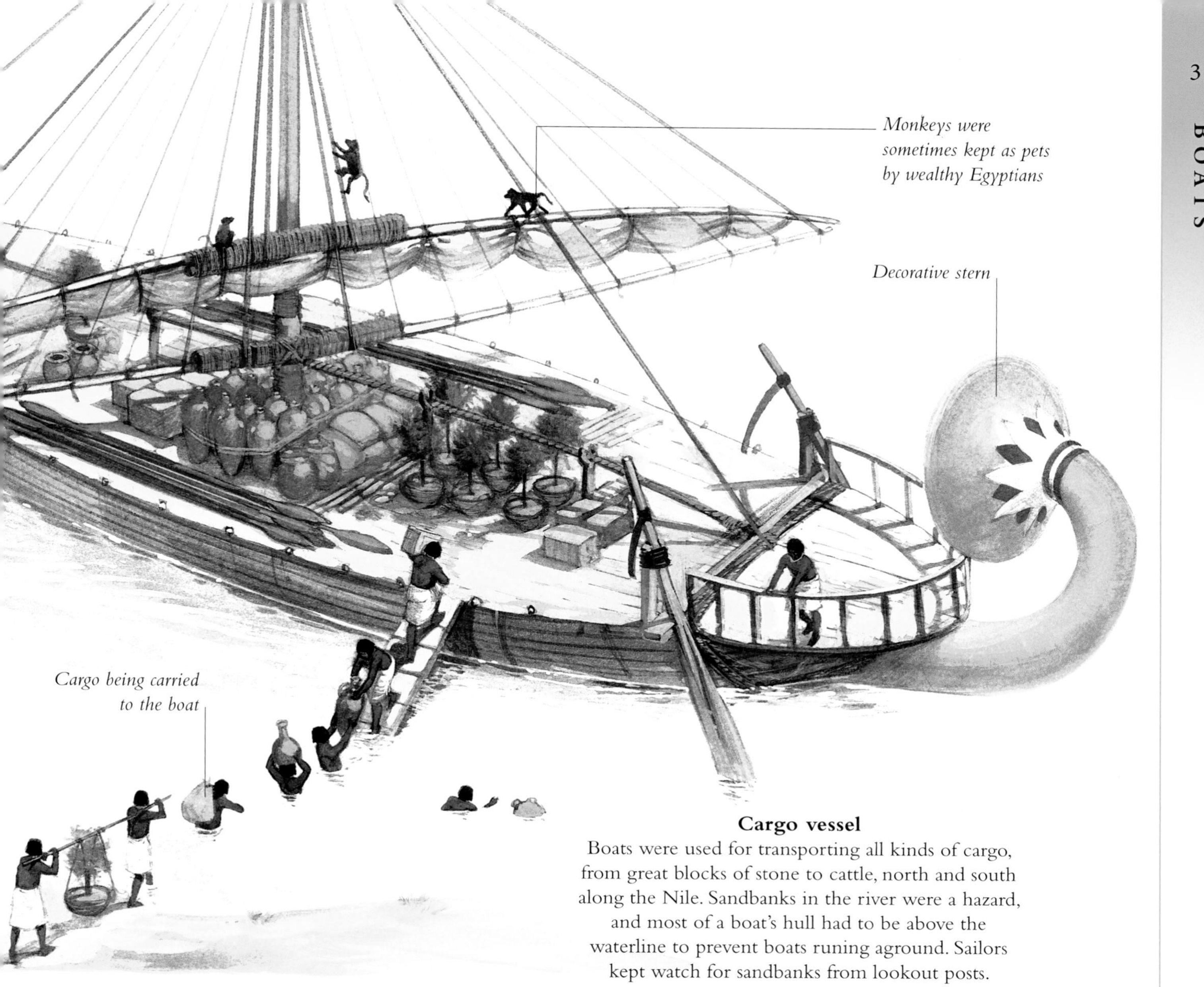

Cargo vessel
Boats were used for transporting all kinds of cargo, from great blocks of stone to cattle, north and south along the Nile. Sandbanks in the river were a hazard, and most of a boat's hull had to be above the waterline to prevent boats runing aground. Sailors kept watch for sandbanks from lookout posts.

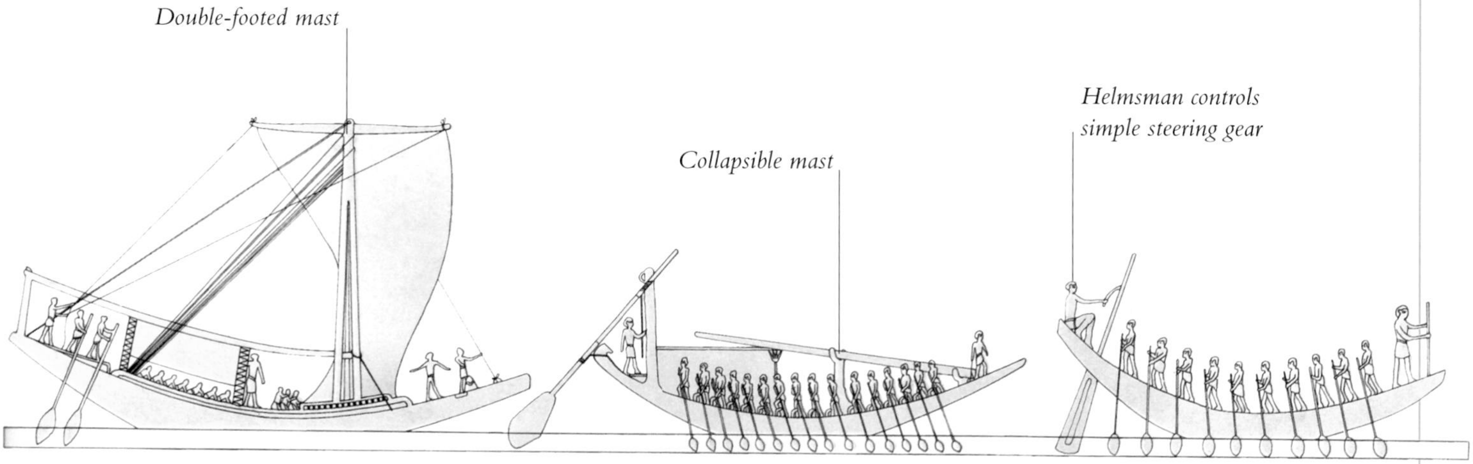

Old Kingdom (2575–2134 BCE)
Built from wood, this craft has a double-footed mast. It has steering gear and the sail is taller than it is wide.

Middle Kingdom (2040–1640 BCE)
The steering gear is more elaborate and the mast is collapsible. There is a bank of oars on each side.

Late Period (712–332 BCE)
This vessel has a very high stern with simple steering gear, and a lower prow.

WARFARE

There was no large permanent army in the Old Kingdom; troops were mustered as the need arose. The army was larger during the Middle Kingdom, and Nubian tribesmen were recruited as mercenary auxillaries. By the time of the New Kingdom (1550–1070 BCE), there was a large professional army with new and improved weapons. These included scimitars, bows with a greater range, and dagger blades cast in bronze.

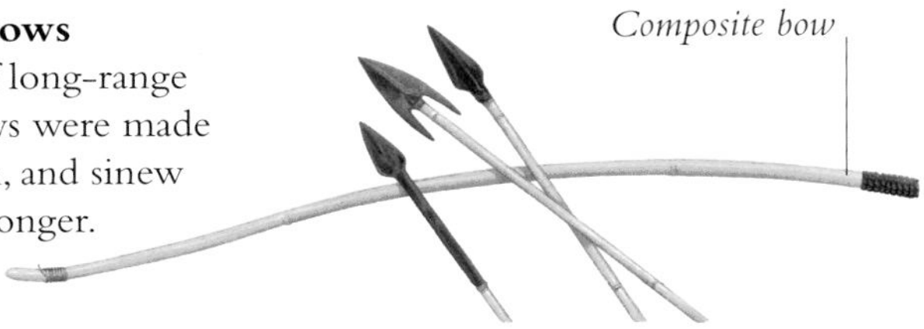

Bows and arrows
The bow was the chief long-range weapon. Composite bows were made of strips of wood, horn, and sinew to make them stronger.

Heavy infantryman
In the period of the New Kingdom, the Egyptian army was built around a core of heavy infantrymen. They wore a stiffened headdress, linen-padded body armor, and a large groin guard.

CHARIOT

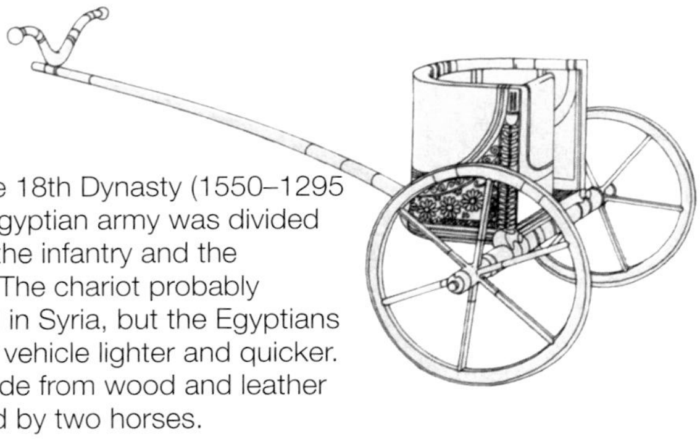

During the 18th Dynasty (1550–1295 BCE) the Egyptian army was divided between the infantry and the chariotry. The chariot probably originated in Syria, but the Egyptians made the vehicle lighter and quicker. It was made from wood and leather and pulled by two horses.

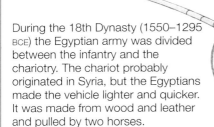

The army of Ramses II
A company of foot soldiers is drilled by its standard-bearer, while chariot horses are tethered in rows and, nearby, a chariot is being repaired. Meanwhile, the king's pet lion is taken for a walk.

Chariot charge
Chariots were introduced to Egypt by the Hyksos people. An archer shared the chariot's platform with the charioteer. Since there was so little space on the platform, the archer's bow was shorter than that used by ordinary soldiers.

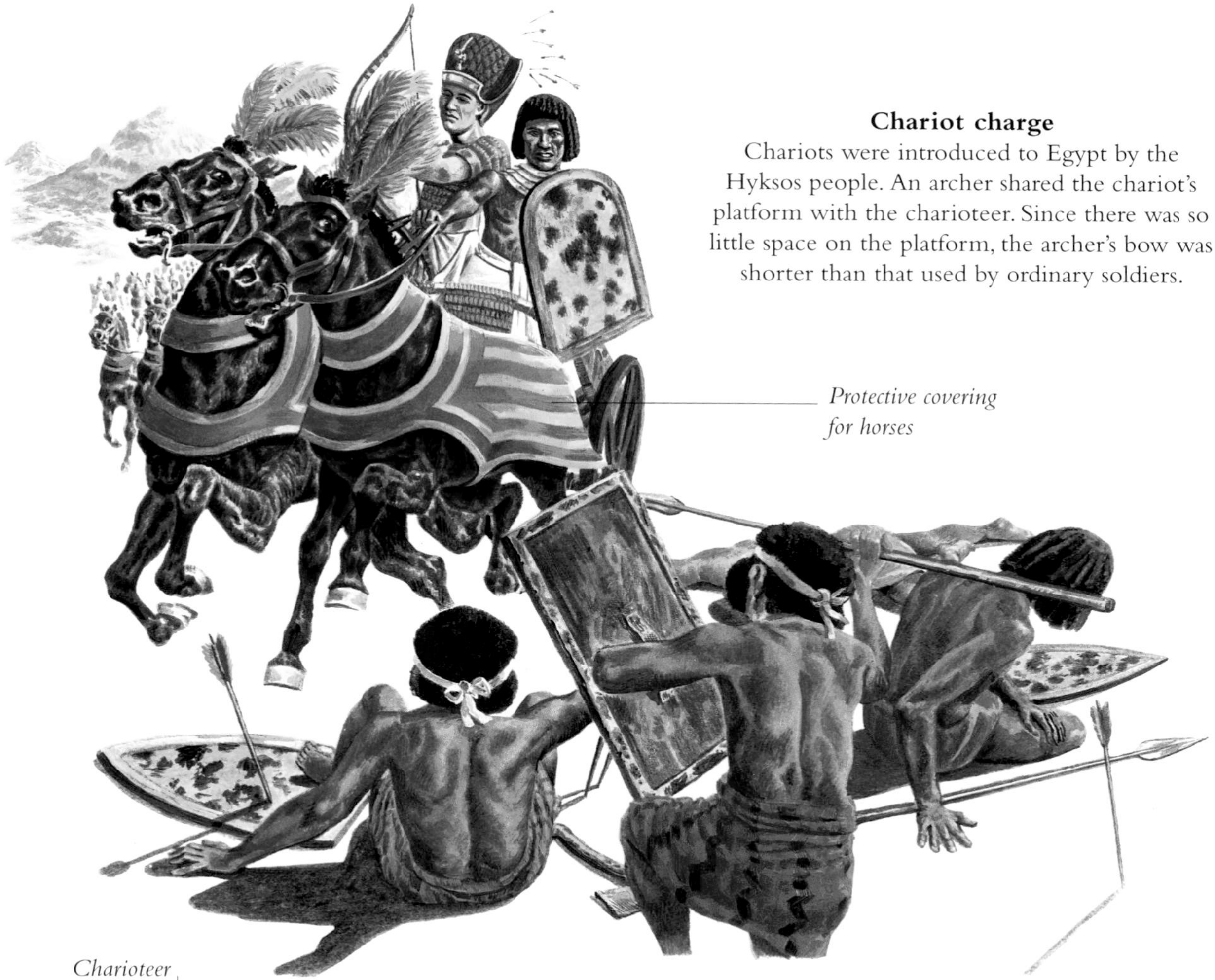

ART

Ancient Egyptian painters and sculptors were craftsmen, like stonemasons or carpenters. Most of the art that is exhibited in museums today was found in tombs, which painters decorated with scenes from the life of the dead person. From these paintings we can learn much about Egyptian societies. Sculptors made figures from stone, bronze, wood, and other materials. Although they did not have iron until about 1200 BCE, their copper or bronze tools were good enough to shape hard stone.

Colored stones
Besides the granite and limestone they used for building, the Egyptians used colored stones for making small sculptures.

Statue of Queen Nefertiti
Believed to have been crafted by the sculptor Thutmose, the representation of the chief wife of Akhenaten, is made from limestone covered in painted plaster.

Plaster and paint would once have covered the wood

Tomb statue
A tomb statue served as an extra body in case the mummy was destroyed. This statue of a chief priest was found at Saqqara.

String with weight attached to achieve a vertical line
Making a rough sketch on a pot

Painting a royal tomb
Painters in the royal tombs worked in teams and followed strict rules. They began by marking a grid pattern on the wall.

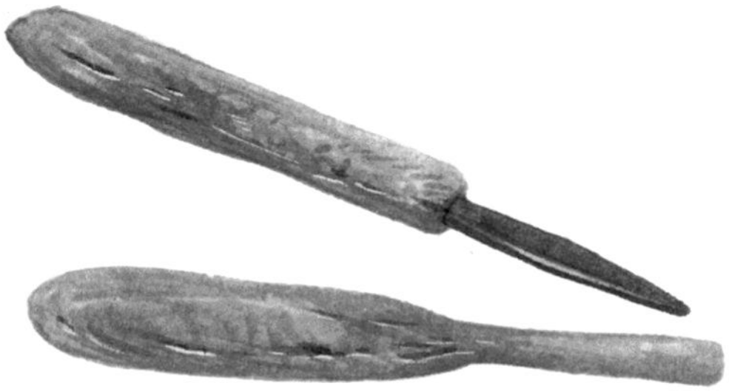

Sculptor's chisel
Sculptors shaped a stone by chipping away with a chisel and mallet. This kind of mallet is still used today.

Sphinxes
A sphinx was a mythical creature with the body of a lion and the head of a human. The famous Great Sphinx at Giza was sculpted from rock, but craftsmen often made small sphinxes to place in tombs.

Brushes
This brush is made from reeds with their ends split. Thinner brushes were used for detailed work.

DRAWING ON A GRID

Painters used squared grids to help achieve proper proportions for their figures from the beginning of the Middle Kingdom. The grid was drawn on the surface before a scene was sketched out and later colored in. Sometimes the grid lines were drawn using a straight edge. More commonly, a string was dipped in red paint and stretched out over the surface to be painted.

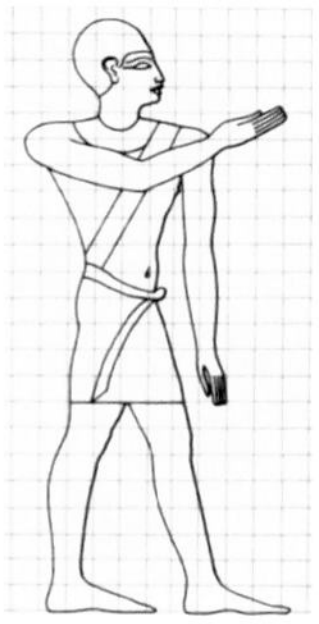

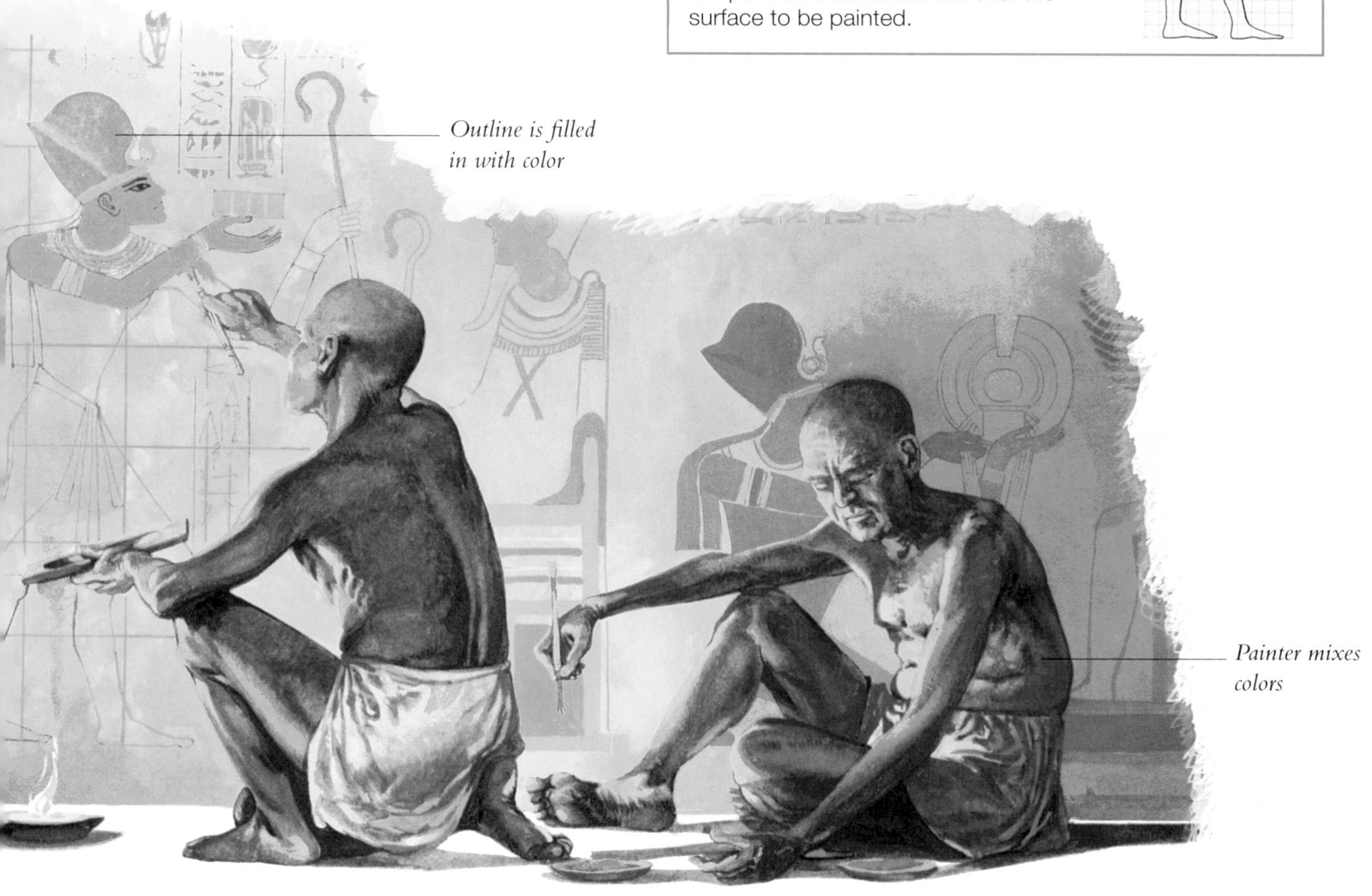

TEMPLES

Religion was a very important part of life for the Egyptians, who worshiped hundreds of different gods and goddesses. Temples served as places where deities could be worshiped, and they also often contained schools, workshops, and storehouses. As well as serving the gods and goddesses, priests taught and even helped with the harvest. The most important religious festivals were holidays.

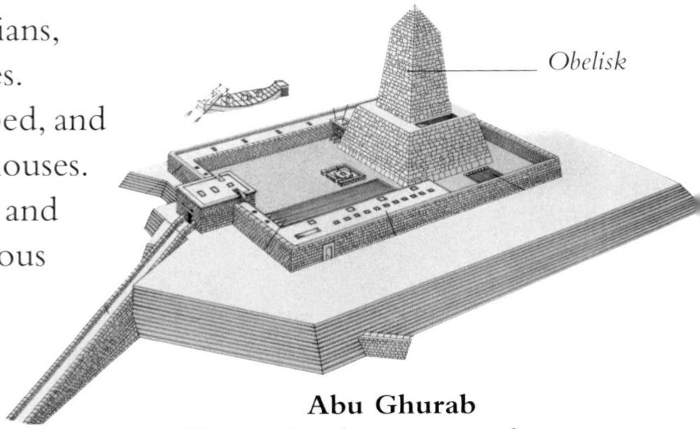

Abu Ghurab
Dominating the upper temple was a masonry tower, or obelisk, the symbol of the sun god Ra. The temple was built by King Neuserre some time after 2420 BCE.

Shrines
Each temple had a sanctuary containing the shrine of the temple's god. Priests were the only people allowed to enter the sanctuary. They had shaven heads and wore white linen robes.

Great Temple of Abu Simbel
Priests and a high official arrive for a festival of the sun god. The most important festivals here were on days when the Sun's rays shone through the entrance and along the temple's main axis to reach the sanctuary. The rock-cut facade has four enormous statues of the pharaoh Ramses II, who built the temple.

Inside the Great Temple at Abu Simbel
This cutaway diagram of Abu Simbel shows, from right to left, the terrace (1), great pillared hall (2), small pillared hall (3), and sanctuary (4).

Temple hall
The temple of a god consisted of a large, decorated hall, which any worshiper could enter, and a sanctuary; only priests were allowed to enter the sanctuary.

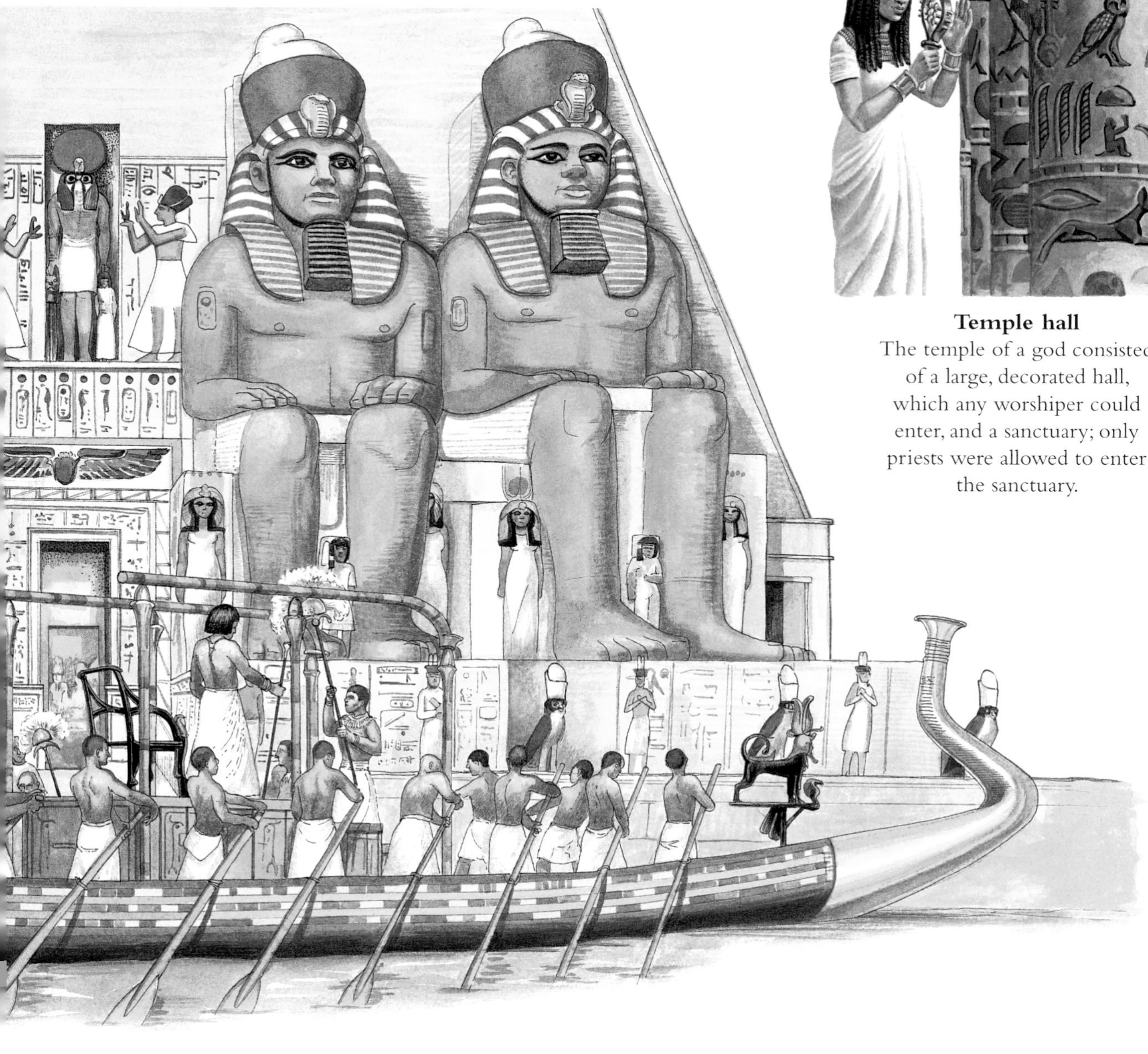

RULERS

The Egyptian king, or pharaoh, was considered to be a god as well as the country's ruler. Most, but not all, were men. A pharaoh's life was a long series of ceremonies, and everything he said or did was important. He owned the whole of Egypt and decided what was right and what was wrong. As a ruler, he was linked with the royal god, Horus, and sometimes he was seen as the sun god, Ra.

Nomarch

District governors
A district governor, or nomarch (seated, with staff), oversees a cattle census. Nomarchs ruled their districts (nome) on behalf of the pharaoh. Their most important functions included the upkeep of dykes and irrigation channels, and the distribution of food during times of famine.

King Na'rmer wielding a mace

Palette of Na'rmer
A late predynastic inscribed stone, dating from c.3000 BCE. It is thought to depict king Na'rmer unifying Upper and Lower Egypt.

Tribute brought to king on behalf of the ruler of a smaller country

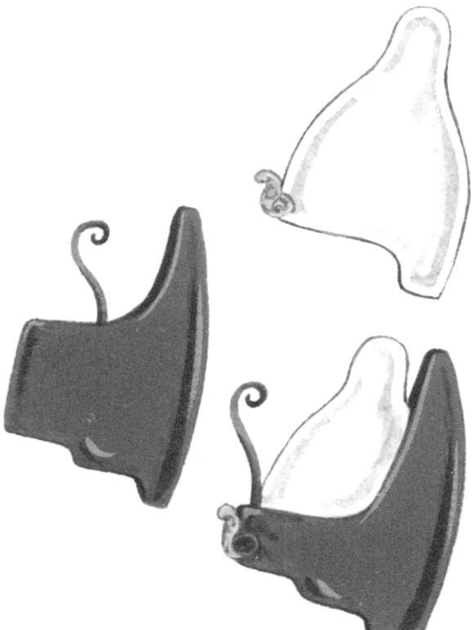

Hieroglyphs

In the picture-writing of ancient Egypt, hieroglyphs represented phenomena of the natural world, events, or gods. The scarab beetle represented the god Khepri, one of the sun gods. Many pharaohs incorporated his name into their own.

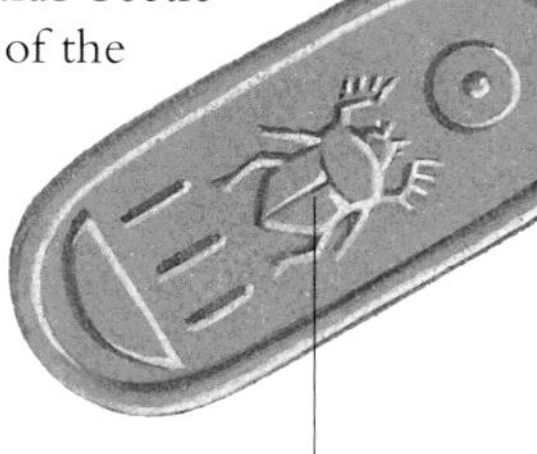
Scarab beetle

Royal crowns

Pictures of Egyptian kings show them wearing the red crown of Lower Egypt or the white crown of Upper Egpyt. Sometimes, they wear a combined crown, a sign that they ruled the whole country.

Scribes wrote down the king's wishes
The chief minister, or vizier, was the most powerful man after the pharaoh

The king and his attendants

The pharaoh was attended by scribes, courtiers, his family, priests, and sometimes the governors of Egyptian provinces.

TECHNOLOGY

The ancient Egyptians pioneered new technologies and they also used the knowledge of other peoples such as the Sumerians, Babylonians, and Assyrians. The Egyptians relied on math to count livestock and make accurate measurements of distance. They made paper from papyrus, created an accurate calendar, melted tin and copper to make bronze tools and weapons, and wove clothing with looms.

Cubit rod
Wooden measuring rods like this one were produced in ancient Egypt to standardize units of measurement. It is exactly one cubit long and is subdivided into smaller units called "hands."

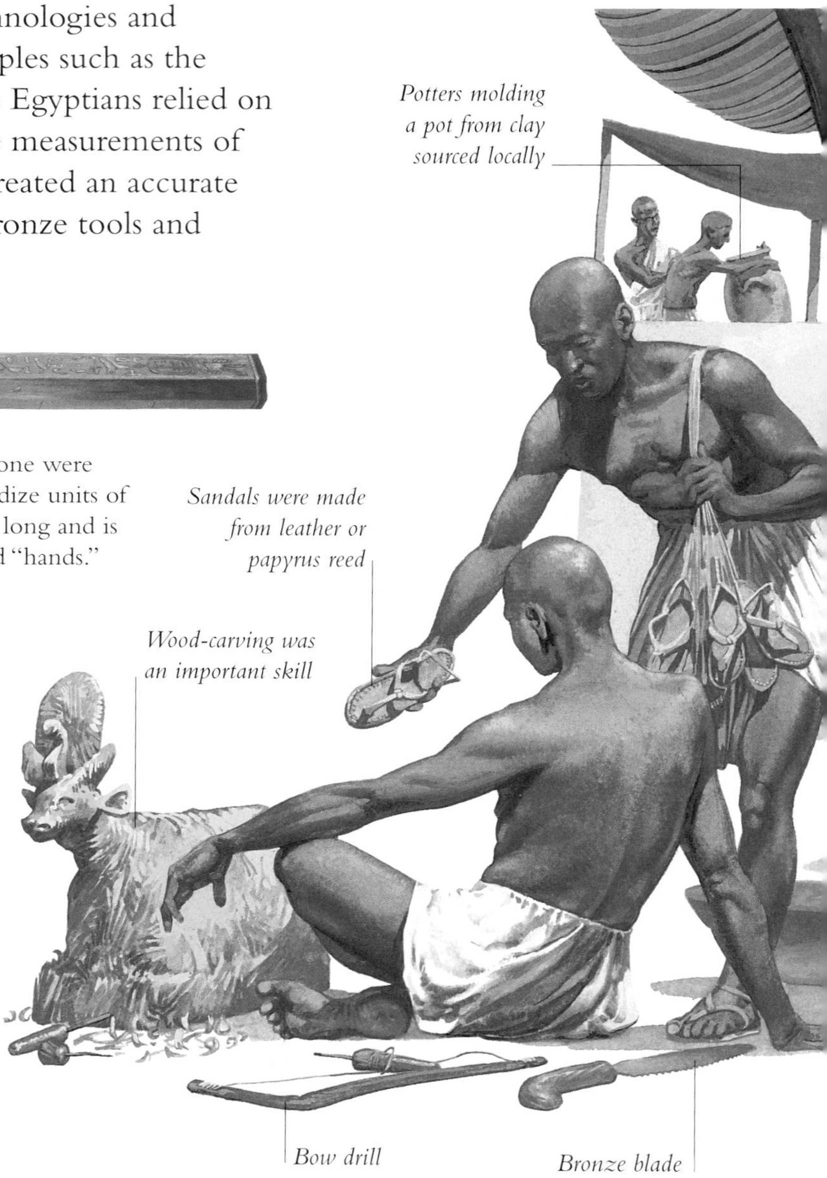
Potters molding a pot from clay sourced locally
Sandals were made from leather or papyrus reed
Wood-carving was an important skill
Bow drill
Bronze blade

Water clock
The Egyptians measured time by letting water drip out of a bowl.

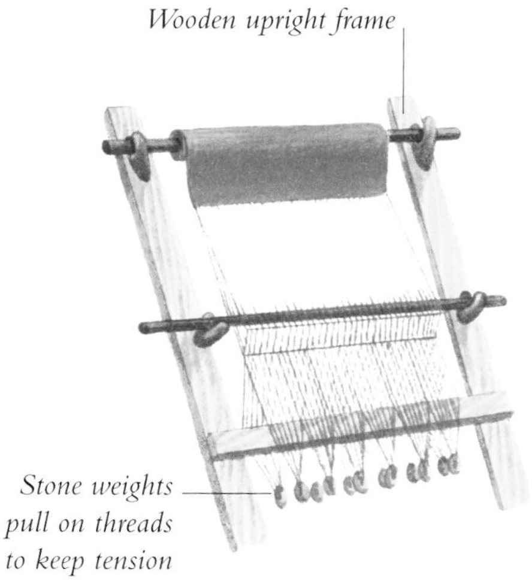
Wooden upright frame
Stone weights pull on threads to keep tension

Vertical loom
This replaced the horizontal loom for weaving in the New Kingdom. The cross-thread was pushed back and forth between the vertical threads, then pushed up into place.

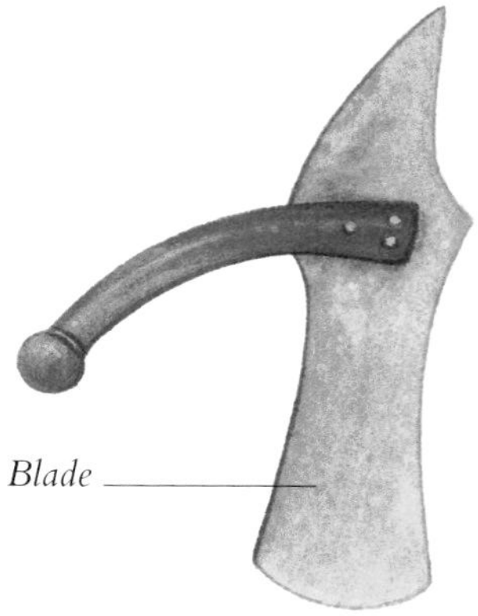
Blade

Razor
The Egyptians believed in personal hygiene and were also convinced that to be clean-shaven was a religious duty.

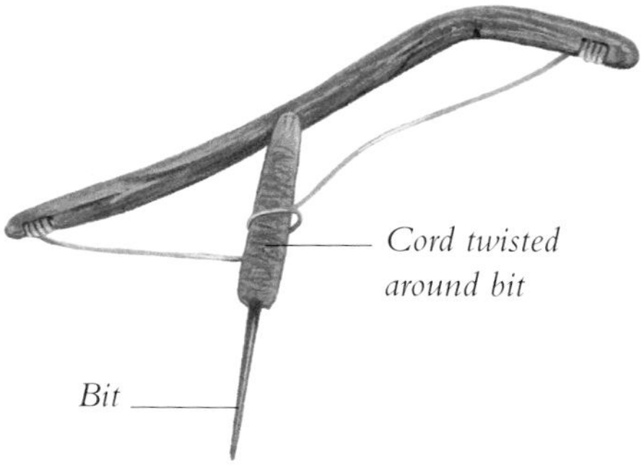
Cord twisted around bit
Bit

Bow drill
A carpenter pressed down on the bit with one hand and, with the other, moved the bow back and forth.

Craftsmen
Egyptian potters, shoemakers, carvers, jewelers, and other craftsmen were highly skilled. They produced finely crafted artefacts with only simple tools. Fathers passed down their skills to their sons.

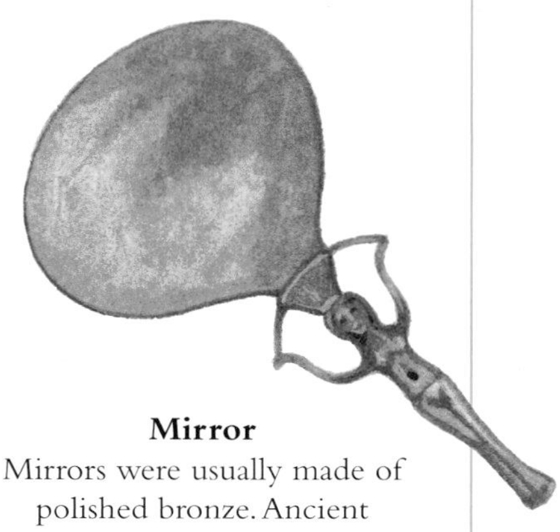

Mirror
Mirrors were usually made of polished bronze. Ancient Egyptians' glass was not pure enough for mirrors.

MEASUREMENT

The basic unit of length was the cubit, which was based on the distance between the middle finger and the elbow, and standardized at 20.6 inches (52.4 cm).

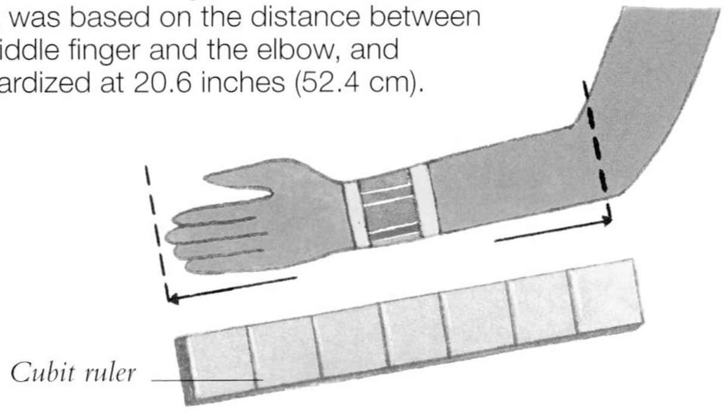

The calendar
By charting the movements of the Sun, Moon, and stars, the Egyptians worked out their calendar. For example, their new year began when the star Sirius appeared. The year had 365 days and three seasons of four months.

AGRICULTURE

Crops grew well in the fertile soils either side of the Nile. Cereals, vegetables, dates and other fruit, vines, and olives were grown for bread, beer, animal fodder, wine, and oil. The Egyptians' three seasons were based on the growing seasons. Akhet (June to September) was when the river flooded and no farming was done. Peret (October to February) was the growing season; and shemu (March to May) was the harvest.

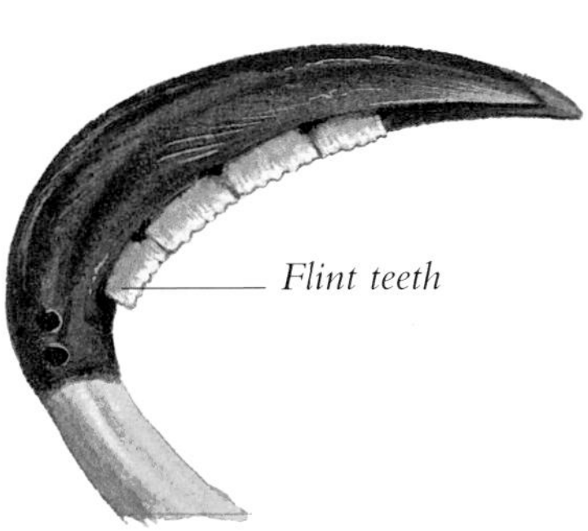

Sickle
At harvest time grain was cut by hand using wooden sickles with sharp flint teeth.

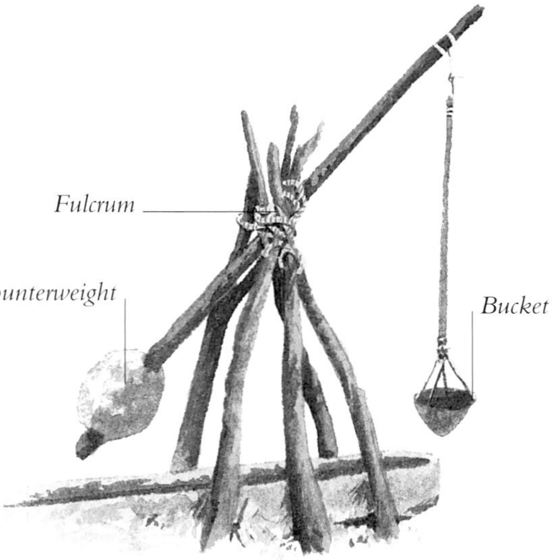

Irrigation with a shaduf
This ingenious fulcrum mechanism was used to raise water from irrigation canals and tip it onto the growing crops.

Harvest time
The harvest season ran from March to May and was a time of great activity. Women and children were heavily involved, as well as men.

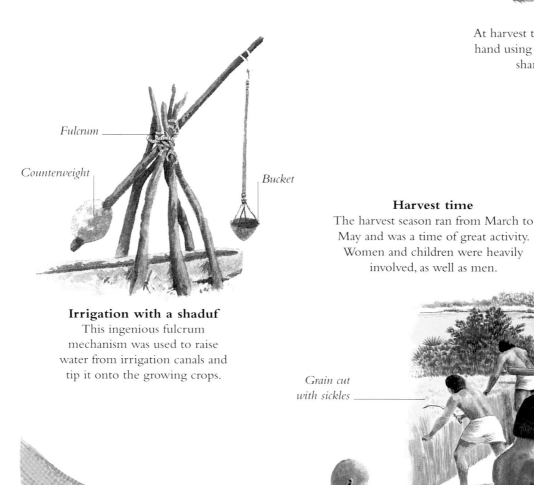

Flax linen
Fibers from the stem of flax (a plant with blue flowers) were used to make linen thread. Nearly all ancient Egyptian clothes were linen.

Wooden plow
The soil left behind when the Nile receded was easy to turn with wooden plows pulled by people or oxen.

Making wine
Grapes were crushed by trampling, and the juice was drained off and stored in pottery jars to ferment into wine.

CITIES

Egypt was a farming country, but it also had large cities. These often began as religious centers and grew bigger. Memphis and Thebes were the largest of the cities. Thebes may have had a population of 80,000 people in 1000 BCE, making it the largest city in the world at that time. Ordinary people lived in simple houses with high walls and small windows; because of the heat, they were designed to keep sunlight out.

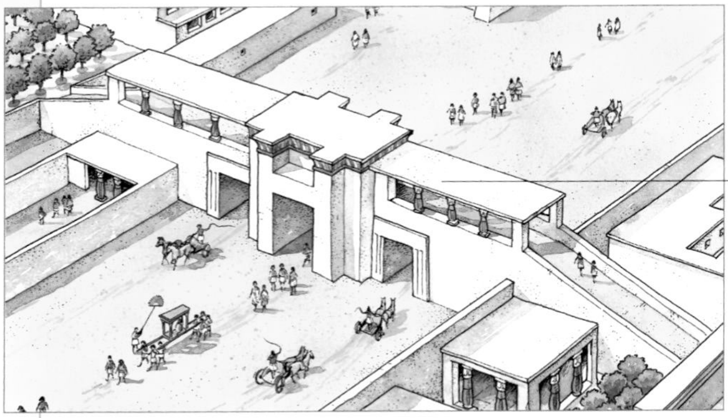

El-Amarna

The pharaoh Akhenaten started to build a new capital at El-Amarna in about 1349 BCE, but the city was abandoned after his death about 15 years later.

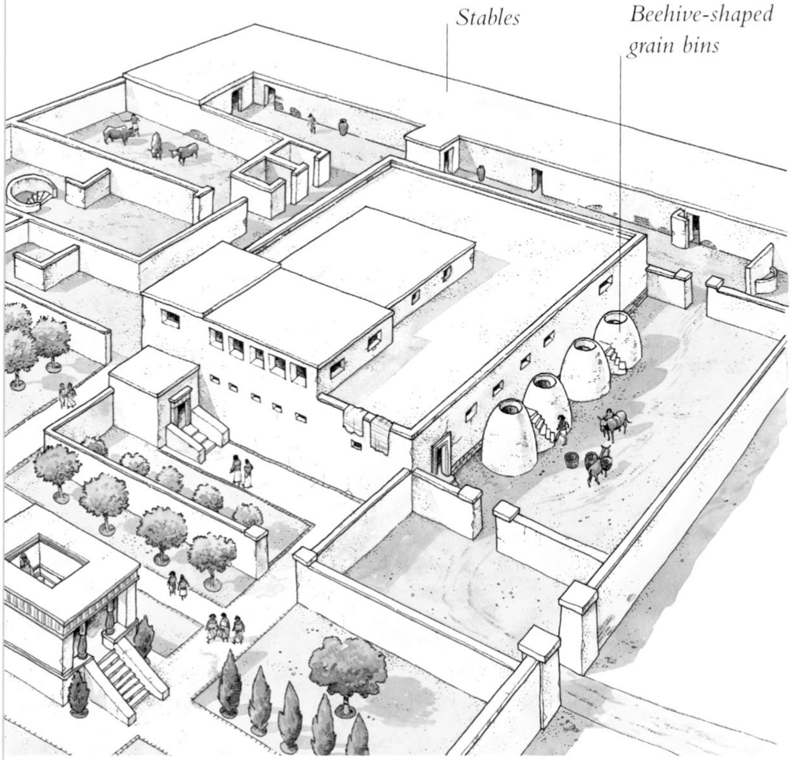

An official's villa

This reconstruction of the villa of an important official in El-Amarna shows gardens for growing fruit and vegetables, grain bins, a cattle yard, and stalls and stables for chariot horses. Each villa had a shrine.

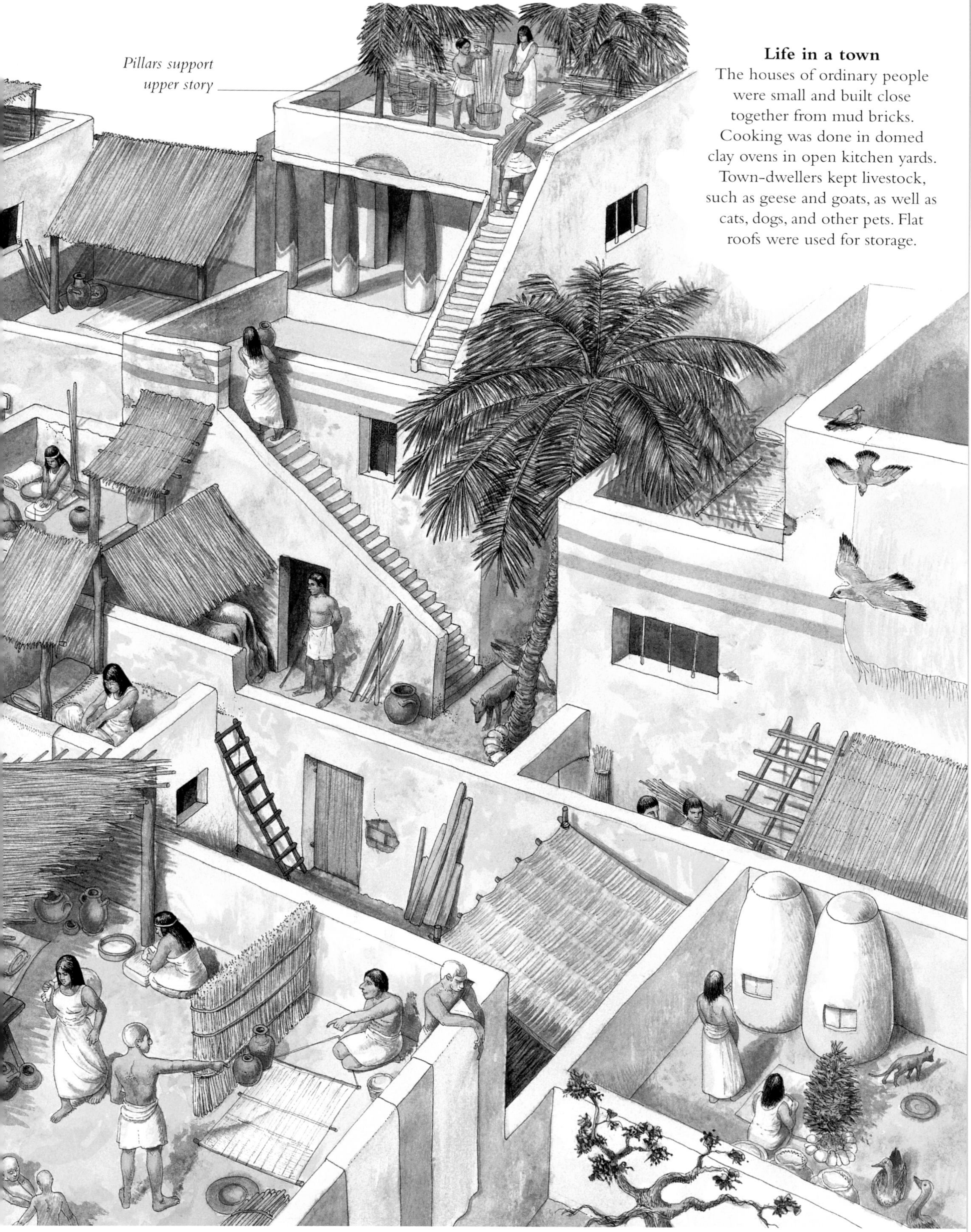

Life in a town
The houses of ordinary people were small and built close together from mud bricks. Cooking was done in domed clay ovens in open kitchen yards. Town-dwellers kept livestock, such as geese and goats, as well as cats, dogs, and other pets. Flat roofs were used for storage.

Phoenician traders
The kingdoms of ancient Mesopotamia traded with the civilizations of the eastern Mediterranean.

ANCIENT MESOPOTAMIA

Often called the "Cradle of Civilization," ancient Mesopotamia was one of the first regions where people made the shift from a nomadic hunter-gatherer lifestyle to settled agriculture. Living on the fertile floodplains of the Tigris and Euphrates rivers (the name "Mesopotamia" is ancient Greek for "between the rivers"), the people of Mesopotamia built some of the world's first cities and had the earliest-known written language.

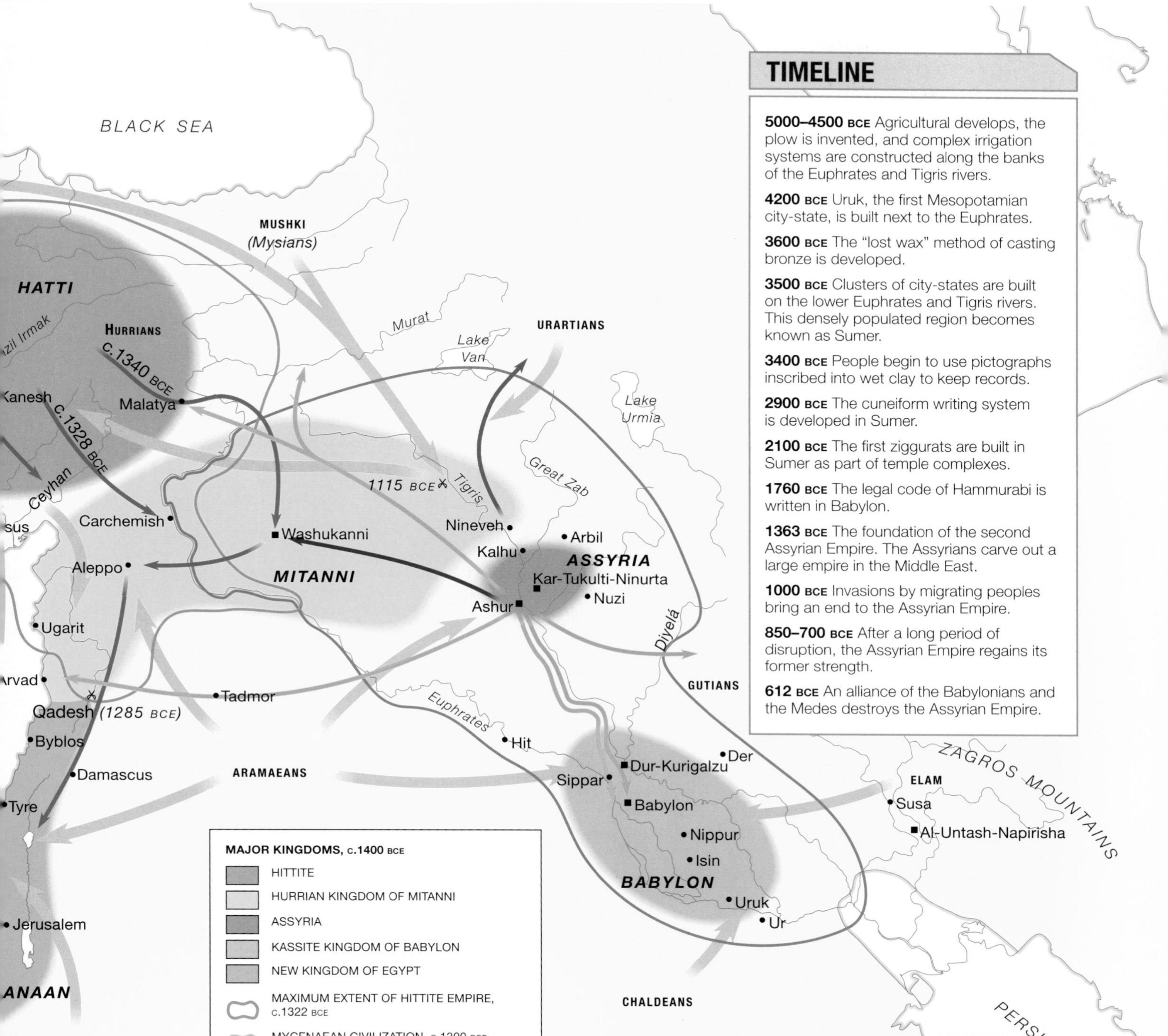

TIMELINE

5000–4500 BCE Agricultural develops, the plow is invented, and complex irrigation systems are constructed along the banks of the Euphrates and Tigris rivers.

4200 BCE Uruk, the first Mesopotamian city-state, is built next to the Euphrates.

3600 BCE The "lost wax" method of casting bronze is developed.

3500 BCE Clusters of city-states are built on the lower Euphrates and Tigris rivers. This densely populated region becomes known as Sumer.

3400 BCE People begin to use pictographs inscribed into wet clay to keep records.

2900 BCE The cuneiform writing system is developed in Sumer.

2100 BCE The first ziggurats are built in Sumer as part of temple complexes.

1760 BCE The legal code of Hammurabi is written in Babylon.

1363 BCE The foundation of the second Assyrian Empire. The Assyrians carve out a large empire in the Middle East.

1000 BCE Invasions by migrating peoples bring an end to the Assyrian Empire.

850–700 BCE After a long period of disruption, the Assyrian Empire regains its former strength.

612 BCE An alliance of the Babylonians and the Medes destroys the Assyrian Empire.

Cylinder seals
Important people in Mesopotamia carried carved cylinders that pressed a unique mark into the clay seals which identified their property.

URUK

Uruk was one of the mightiest cities in Sumer, southern Mesopotamia, between 4000 and 3000 BCE. Uruk developed from two older settlements—Kullaba and Eanna—where there were temples to the sky god, Anu, and the goddess of love, Inanna. An important religious site grew up at Uruk, centered on the two temples. Gilgamesh, hero of the great Sumerian story *The Epic of Gilgamesh,* was said to be a king of Uruk.

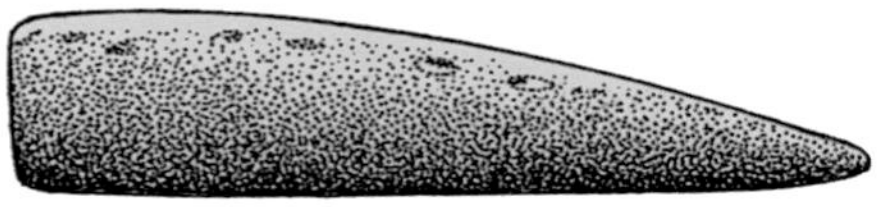

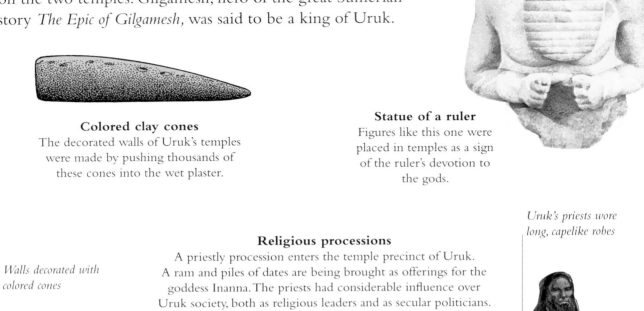

Colored clay cones
The decorated walls of Uruk's temples were made by pushing thousands of these cones into the wet plaster.

Statue of a ruler
Figures like this one were placed in temples as a sign of the ruler's devotion to the gods.

Religious processions
A priestly procession enters the temple precinct of Uruk. A ram and piles of dates are being brought as offerings for the goddess Inanna. The priests had considerable influence over Uruk society, both as religious leaders and as secular politicians.

Walls decorated with colored cones

Uruk's priests wore long, capelike robes

The Warka vase
Probably carved around 3000 BCE, this vase was found in the temple treasury at Uruk. The carvings depict offerings being brought to the goddess Inanna during an elaborate ceremony. The ruler of Uruk is depicted to the left of the goddess on the top layer of the vase.

HOUSES AND DAILY LIFE

Most of what we know about daily life in ancient Mesopotamia comes from the village of Tell Madhhur in eastern Iraq. Excavations here revealed 12 houses from around 4000 BCE, including one particularly well-preserved home whose rooms contained pots, cooking utensils, and agricultural tools. The house is thought to have been filled in with earth after having been badly damaged in a fire.

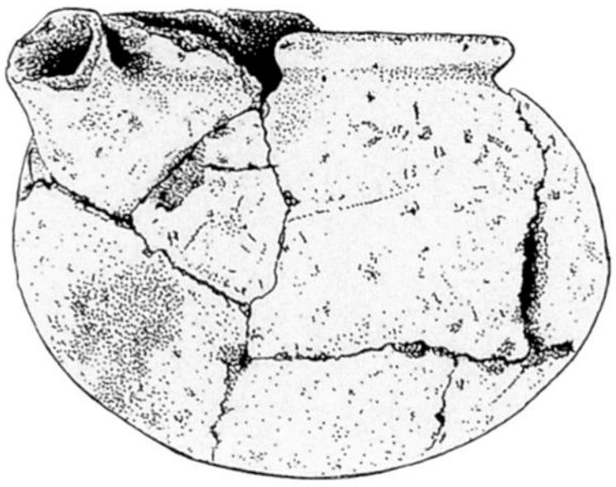

Pouring jar
This spouted jar, used for storing and pouring liquids, was found in the kitchen area at Tell Madhhur.

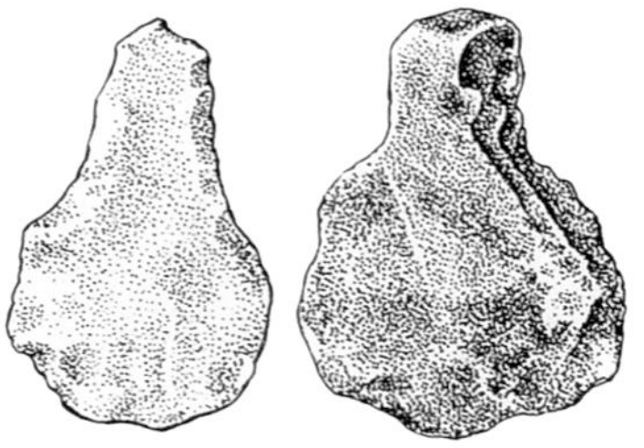

Stone tools
These carefully shaped stones were probably the blades of hoes used for turning over topsoil before planting seeds.

Painted cup
The pottery found at Tell Madhhur included everything from large grain storage pots to this small painted cup.

Making pots
As Mesopotamian society evolved, distinct trades like potters or carpenters began to appear. Using a wheel or wooden molds, a skilled potter could make larger and finer vessels than it was possible to make by hand.

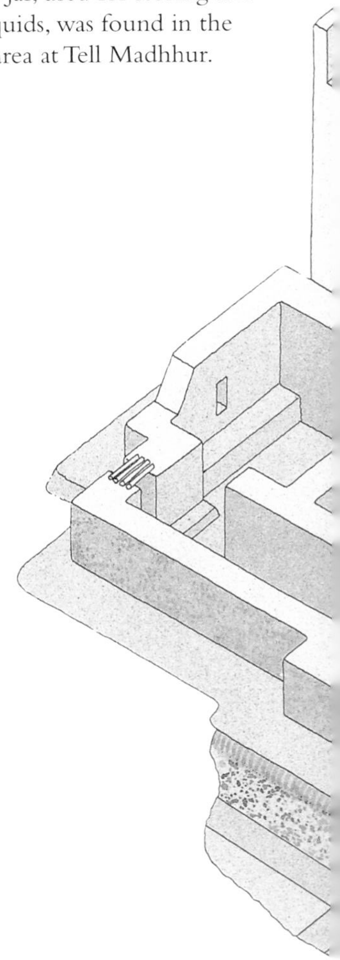

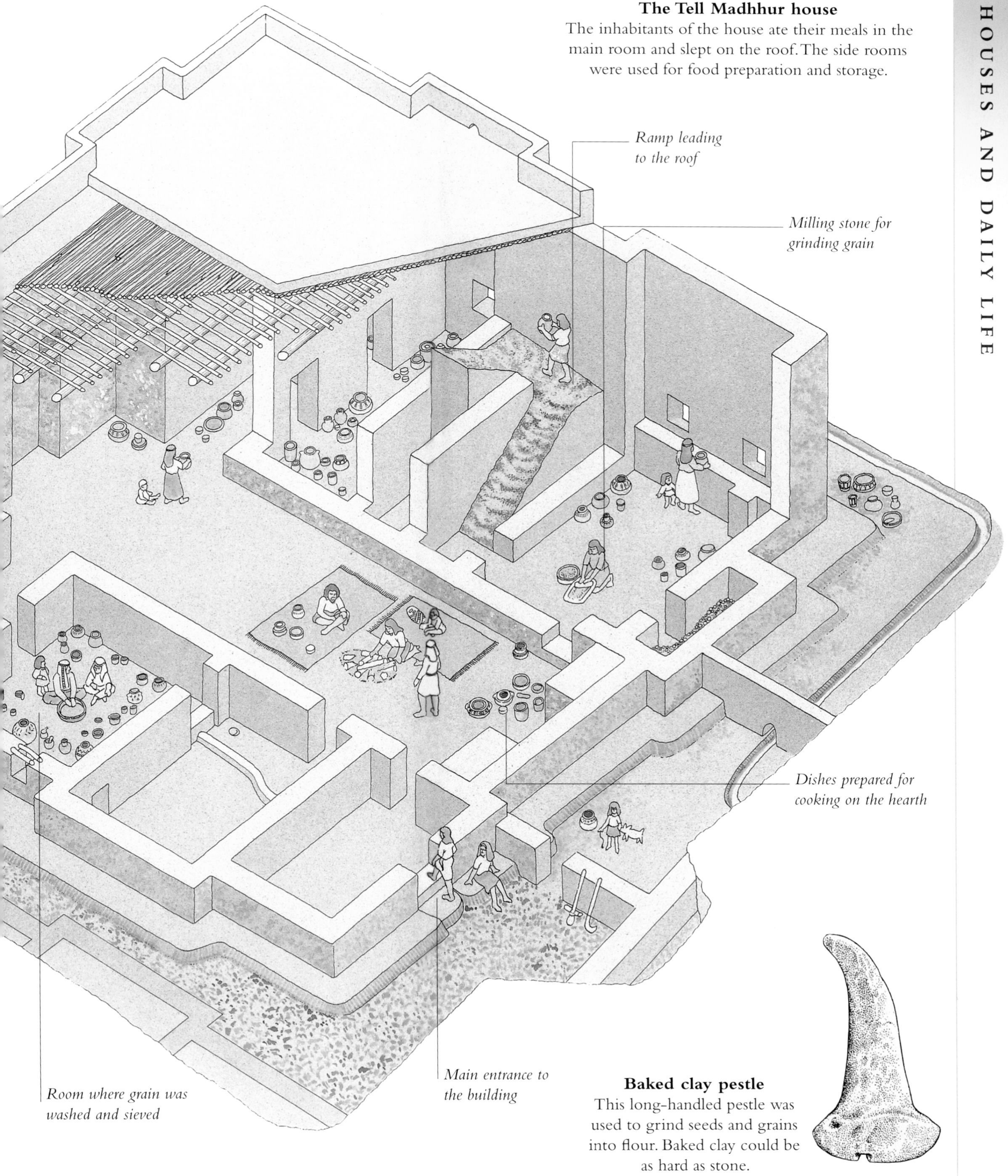

The Tell Madhhur house
The inhabitants of the house ate their meals in the main room and slept on the roof. The side rooms were used for food preparation and storage.

Baked clay pestle
This long-handled pestle was used to grind seeds and grains into flour. Baked clay could be as hard as stone.

WRITING AND SEALS

The world's earliest writing system, known as cuneiform, comes from Uruk and has been dated to around 3300 BCE. Cuneiform was developed from an earlier Mesopotamian system of clay tokens and personal property markers called cylinder seals. Cuneiform was originally used by institutions such as temples to keep detailed records of their possessions, but was later adapted for legal and literary uses.

Decorative seals
Some seals were highly ornate, carved from lapis lazuli and mounted on gold swivels.

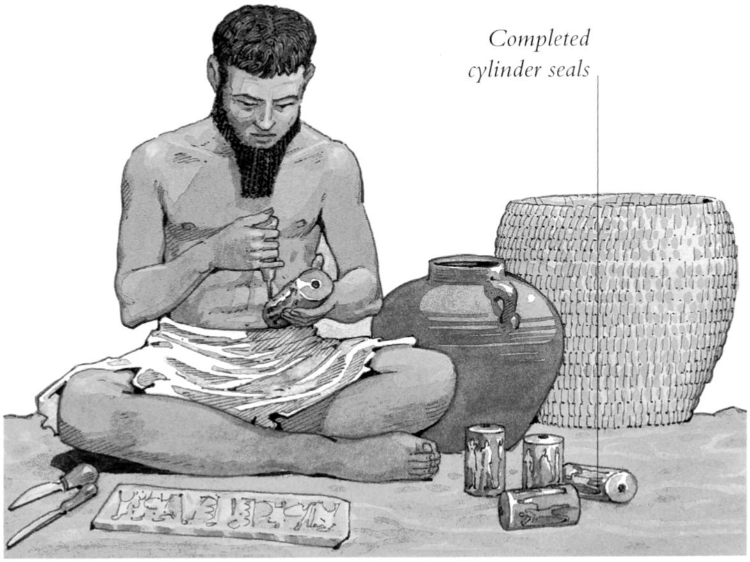

Carving the seals
Cylinder seals were made by cutting stone with flint or copper tools. When the cylinder had been shaped, the artist would carve the scene or inscription.

Cylinder seal designs
The carved designs on cylinder seals were unique to their owner. They often showed scenes from daily life, mythological beasts, or images of the gods.

How seals were used
Cylinder seals were used to mark ownership of property. In the case of a storage jar, impressions were made on a lump of clay attached to a string that tied down the cover. Seals were also used as a kind of signature on clay tablet legal documents.

Seals as jewelry
Cylinder seals were status symbols in ancient Mesopotamia, showing off the owner's wealth and importance. They were often worn as jewelry.

Keeping records
Writing was developed as a way of keeping records of produce and accounts of trade. Here a scribe notes the quantities of food delivered to a temple.

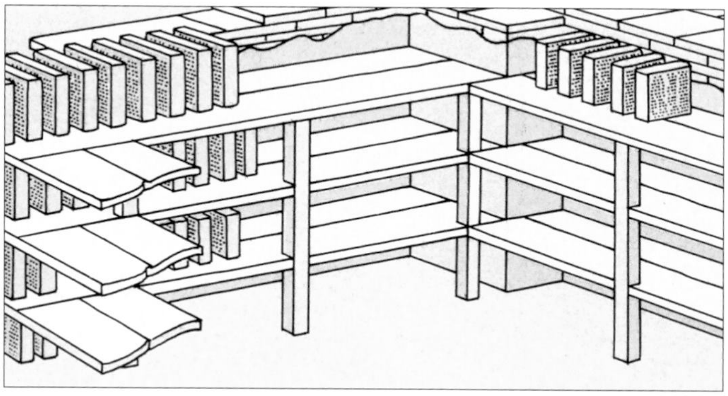

The archive room of Ebla
The king of Ebla's clay tablet archive was discovered in 1967. It is filled with administrative records from his rule.

Cuneiform
Cuneiform was written by pressing a sharpened reed into wet clay to make a series of wedge-shaped impressions.

TECHNOLOGY AND TRADE

The interconnected societies of ancient Mesopotamia were responsible for numerous technological innovations, including the first known use of the wheel, ceramics, and metal tools. They were also the first to develop the complex economic and social structures needed for large urban communities to thrive.

The merchant's personal cylinder seal

A merchant camp
A wealthy Mesopotamian merchant watches as his scribe conducts an audit of the goods that have just arrived from Iran. He will sell some of these items in Mesopotamia and send others on for sale farther west.

Clay mold, formed around a wax model that was then melted
Molten metal is poured into the mold
Once cooled, the mold is smashed

"Lost wax" casting
The Mesopotamians invented a new method of casting that made it easier to make large numbers of metal objects.

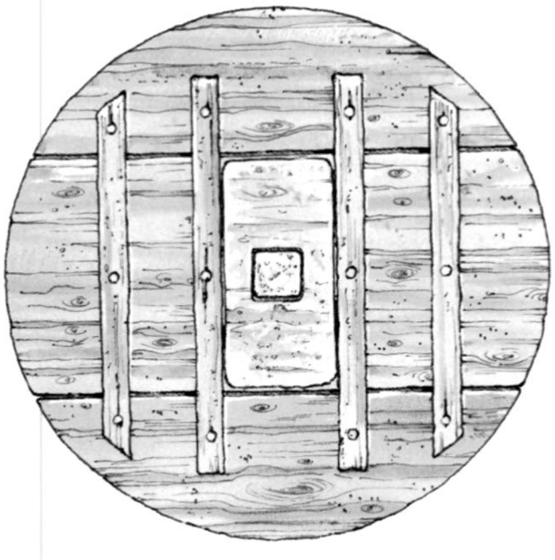

The wheel
Mesopotamian wheels were solid, made from several thick planks of wood cut into a circle.

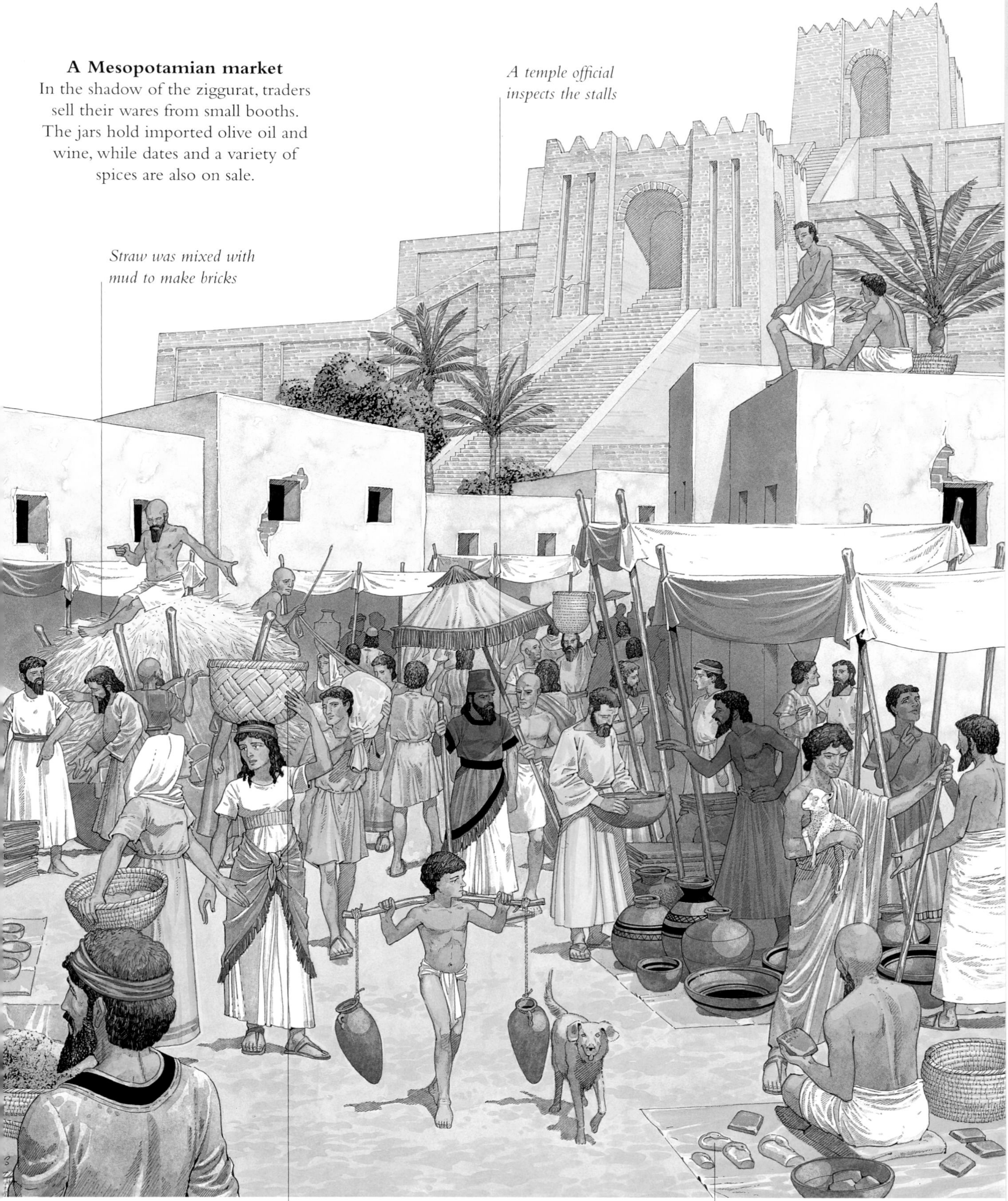

A Mesopotamian market
In the shadow of the ziggurat, traders sell their wares from small booths. The jars hold imported olive oil and wine, while dates and a variety of spices are also on sale.

ZIGGURATS

Ziggurats—enormous stepped temples—were first built in Mesopotamia around 2000 BCE. These man-made sacred mountains looked very impressive rising over the flat Mesopotamian plains and are thought to have inspired the biblical story of the Tower of Babel. The exterior walls of most ziggurats were made of kiln-baked mud bricks, which were more resistant to water damage than sun-dried bricks.

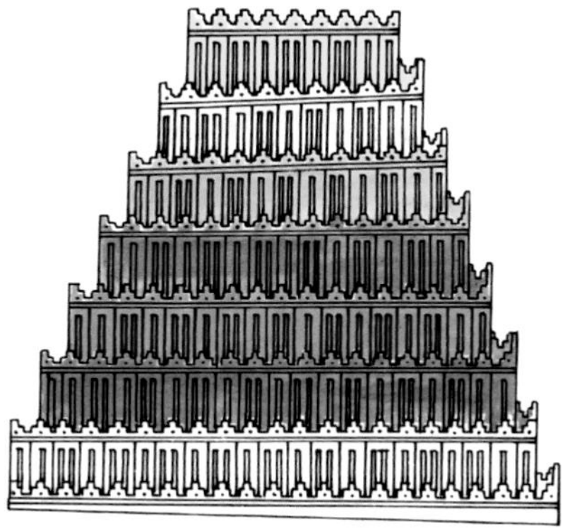

Dur-Sharrukin
This ziggurat had a spiral path that wound around the outside. Each level was painted a different color.

Step pyramids
Ziggurat-like structures can be found all over the world. This is the result of ancient engineers thinking alike, rather than as a result of any direct influence.

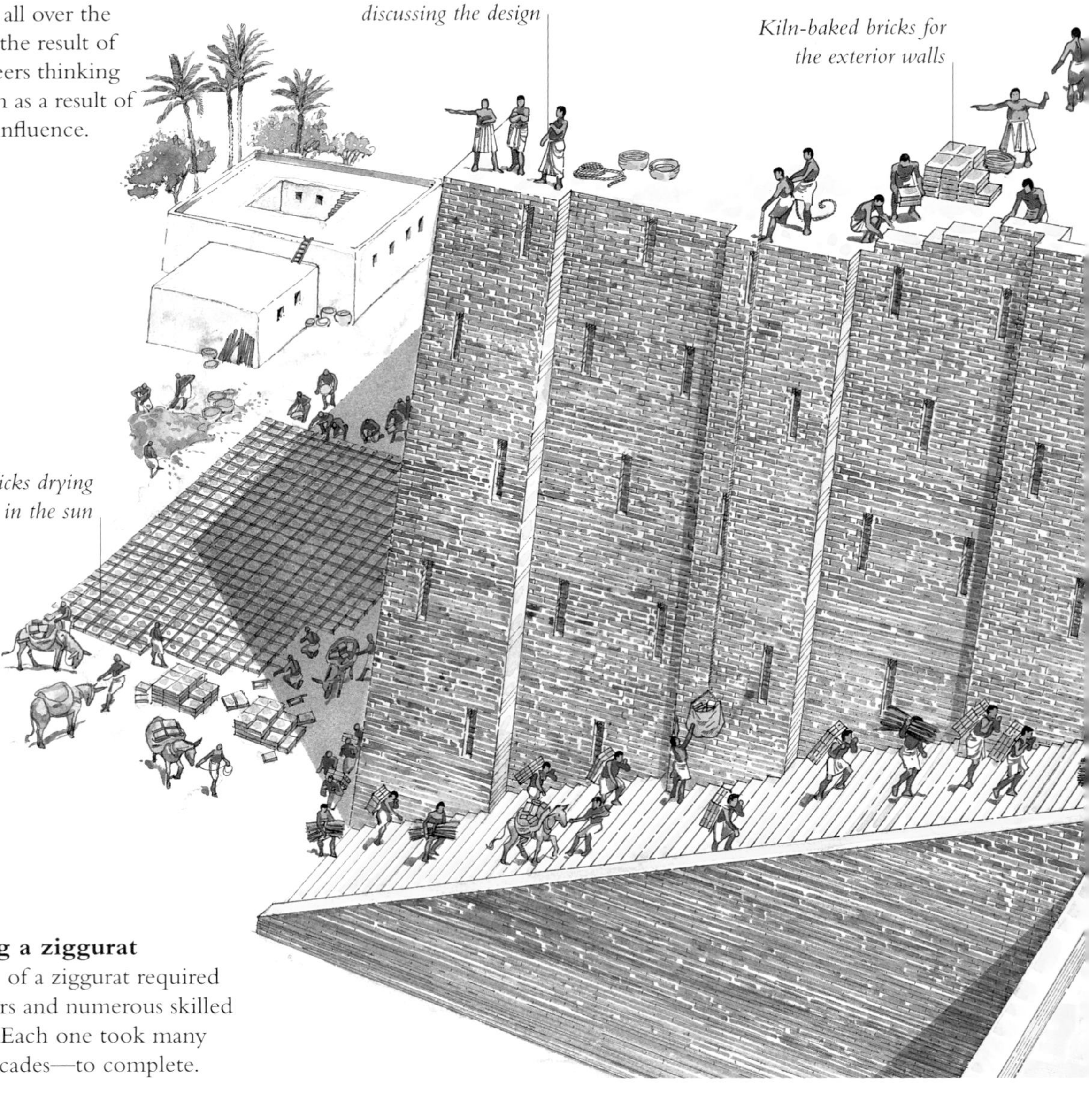

Building a ziggurat
The construction of a ziggurat required hundreds of laborers and numerous skilled master builders. Each one took many years—even decades—to complete.

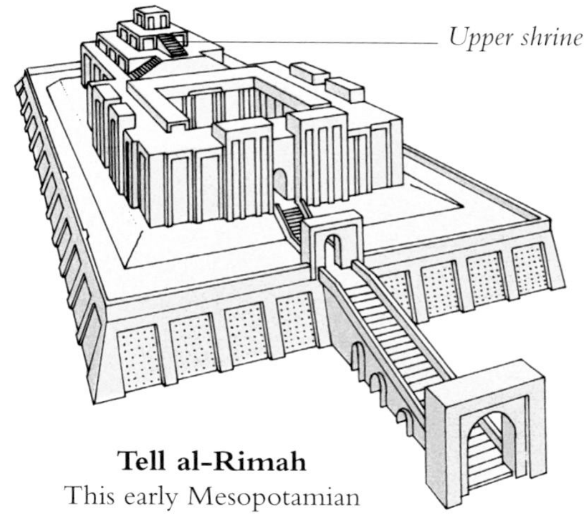

Tell al-Rimah
This early Mesopotamian ziggurat had a small shrine on the roof of the main temple.

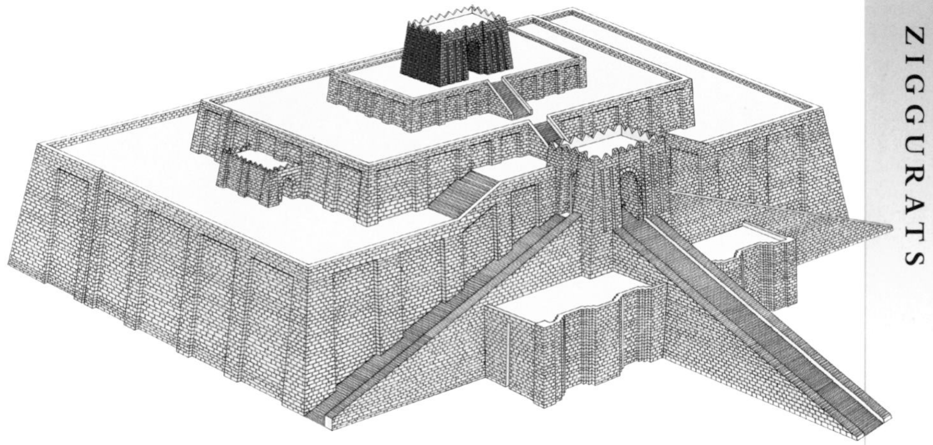

The ziggurat of Ur
Built by King Ur-Nammu, this ziggurat was a symbol of the city and often appeared on official seals.

ASSYRIA

In around 1200 BCE Mesopotamia entered a 300-year-long dark age. The reason for this collapse is not clear, but both human and environmental factors seem to have been involved. Toward the end of this period a new society, the warlike Assyrian Empire, came to dominate Mesopotamia. At the peak of its power, under King Shalmaneser III, the Assyrian Empire stretched from the Tigris River to the Mediterranean coast.

Archers
New bow designs made archery more effective.

King Tiglath-pileser
This section of a large wall relief comes from the palace complex in the city of Kalhu. It depicts one of Assyria's warrior kings.

Siege warfare
The Assyrians were experts in siege warfare. Here one of Tiglath-pileser's armies is storming a city gate using wooden siege towers. The smaller siege engine carries a bladed battering ram.

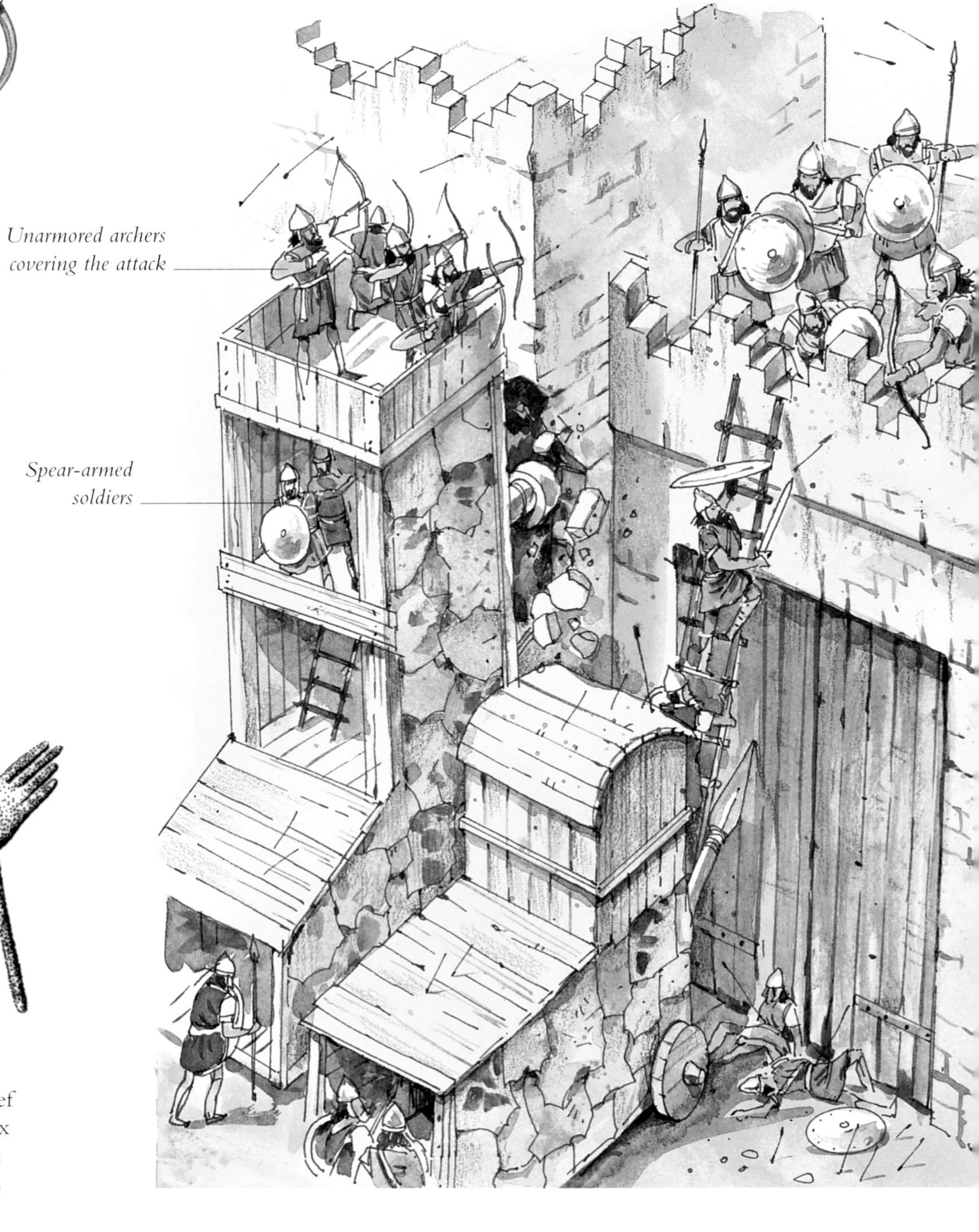

Bronze lion
Many small sculptures like this one were made by the Assyrians for use as standardized weights.

Siege engines
This relief, which once decorated one of the gates of the Assyrian city of Balawat, shows a group of archers riding a siege engine toward the gates of a city.

Shields were usually made from hardened leather stretched over a wicker frame

Charioteer
The charioteers were the elite force of the Assyrian army during the reign of Shalmaneser. There were usually three members of a chariot crew: the driver, the spear-wielding warrior, and the shieldman.

BABYLON

"Babylon surpasses in splendor any city of the known world," wrote the Greek historian Herodotus, who visited Babylon in around 450 BCE. The city was the capital of the Babylonian Empire established during the rule of King Nebopolassar and later his son Nebuchadnezzar (605–562 BCE). These wealthy rulers undertook a massive building program that included the Etemenaki ziggurat and the famous Hanging Gardens.

The Ishtar Gate
A royal procession enters Babylon through the Ishtar Gate. It was faced with blue glazed bricks and decorated with bulls and dragons, symbols of the gods Adad and Marduk.

Babylon at its height
At the time of Nebuchadnezzar the Euphrates River flowed through the city, dividing it into two sections. The eastern half was the older of the two, home to the king's palace and the Ishtar Gate.

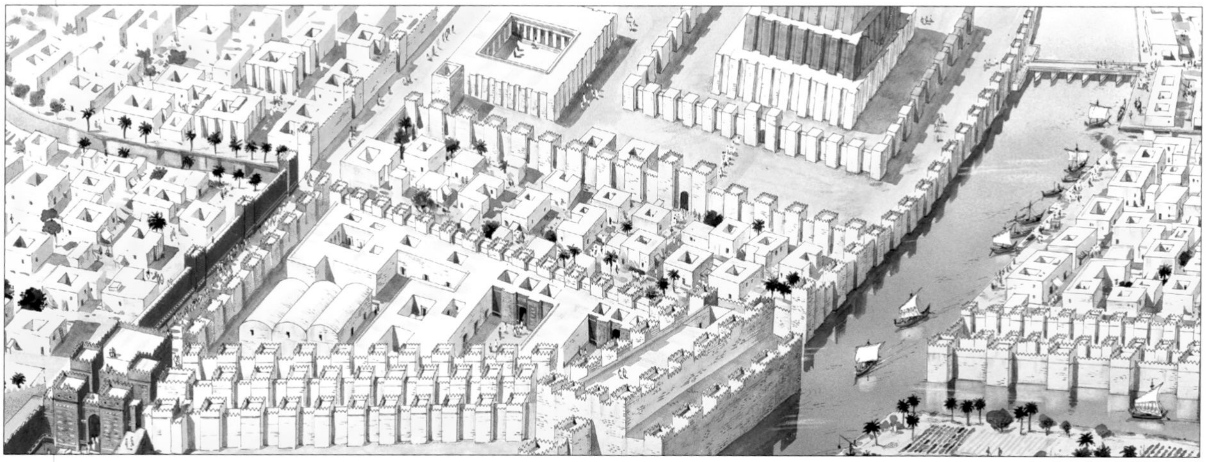

The Hanging Gardens
It is said that Nebuchadnezzar built a great "mountain" in his capital and covered it with lush gardens. No one really knows how they were constructed or irrigated.

Nebuchadnezzar
Nebuchadnezzar and his wife relax in the Hanging Gardens of Babylon. The king and queen wear blue and gold garments.

ANCIENT GREECE

The ancient Greek civilization, which developed from the ninth century BCE, was one of the most remarkable in history. Greek achievements in science, the arts, literature, philosophy, and politics still influence the modern world. Yet this was not a peaceful period of history: there was almost constant warfare between Greece's rival city-states.

Education
Greek society valued education highly. School students wrote on wax tablets in class. There were different teachers for music, reading, and sport. Teachers were not well paid.

TIMELINE

1650 BCE The Mycenaean civilization emerges in mainland Greece.

1200 BCE After expanding to cover much of the eastern Mediterranean, the Mycenaean civilization collapses, plunging Greece into a "dark age."

900 BCE The first city-states appear in Greece.

776 BCE The first known Olympian Games is held to honor the Greek god Zeus.

750 BCE The first war galleys equipped with rams are built.

730 BCE The Greeks adapt the Phoenecian alphabet to their language.

534 BCE The first festival of theater, held in honor of the god Dionysius, is organized in Athens.

509 BCE Athens introduces a democratic government.

490–479 BCE The allied city-states of Greece fight off Persian invasions, defeating the invaders at Marathon (490 BCE), Salamis (480 BCE), and Platea (479 BCE).

457–445 BCE The First Peloponnesian War is fought between the city-states of Athens and Sparta.

450–400 BCE The golden age of Greek theater. Playwrights Aeschylus, Sophocles, and Aristophanes compose dozens of plays, many of which are still performed today.

447 BCE Construction begins on the Parthenon temple at the Acropolis of Athens.

431–404 BCE The Second Peloponnesian War, marked by long sieges and naval battles, is fought between the empires of Athens and Sparta.

338 BCE Philip II of Macedon establishes his control over all of Greece.

334–330 BCE Alexander the Great, son of Philip II, invades Persia.

327–323 BCE Alexander the Great pushes his armies as far as the Indus Valley, but later dies from wounds sustained in battle in Babylon.

300–200 BCE Greek city-states go into decline.

146 BCE Greece becomes a province of the Roman Empire.

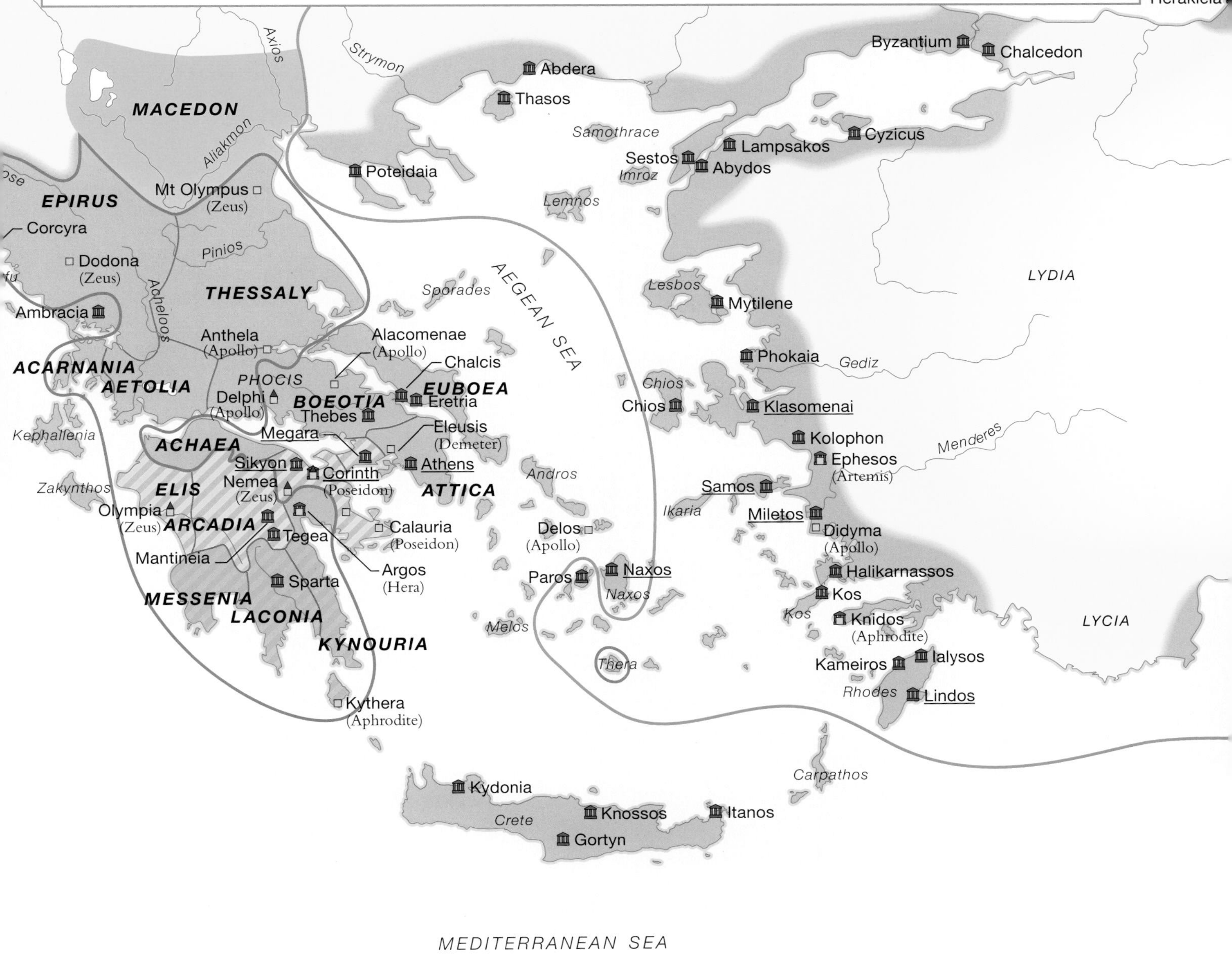

RELIGION

The ancient Greeks believed in many gods, powerful figures who could help or harm people. The most important of them—including the supreme god, Zeus, and his wife Hera, Aphrodite, and Poseidon—lived on Mount Olympus, in northern Greece. People could visit temples individually to ask for help from their chosen god. The gods were best approached by making offerings of wine and animal sacrifices.

Burnt offerings
Sacrificed animals were often burnt or cooked on an altar.

Aphrodite
The goddess of love, Aphrodite, was considered to be one of the most important Greek deities. Her birth is depicted in this sculpted relief.

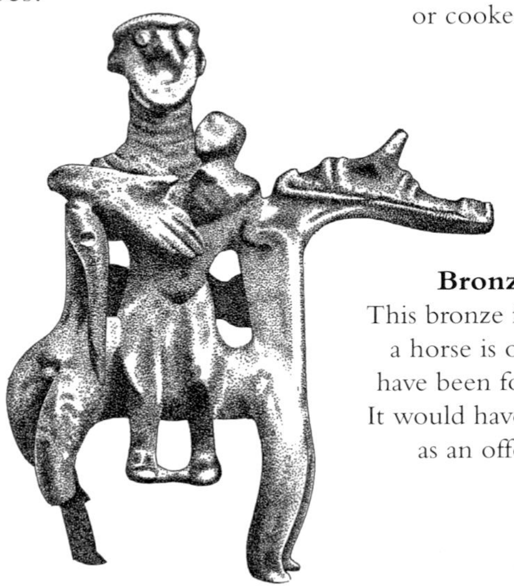

Bronze offering
This bronze figure of a man on a horse is one of many that have been found at Olympus. It would have been taken there as an offering to Zeus.

Apollo
The god of music and healing was considered to be youthful and energetic.

Athena
Athenians believed the goddess of wisdom and war had brought olives to their city.

Religious processions
Priests and priestesses led processions of people bearing offerings for the gods. These events were colorful, loud, musical occasions. Offerings included wine, and animals for sacrifice.

Asklepios
Asklepios was the god of healing, and many temples were dedicated to him. People who were unwell visited the temples and asked Asklepios to help them.

The myth of King Pentheus
Greek myths were famous for their violence and tales of revenge. Pentheus, the mortal ruler of Thebes, waged war against the god Dionysos. In revenge, the god's female followers (the Maenads) tore him to pieces.

TEMPLE OF ZEUS

The Temple of Zeus was built at Olympus between 472–456 BCE. It had a giant, seated figure of Zeus as its centerpiece. The wooden framework of the 43-foot (13 m) tall sculpture was covered with ivory plates and gold panels. The temple was destroyed by an earthquake in the sixth century CE, but excavations have uncovered its remains.

WORK AND TRADE

Farmers grew barley, olives, and vines for making bread, olive oil, and wine. They also grazed sheep and goats. In Athens and other cities, workers crafted tools and weapons from iron, tin, and copper, much of which was imported. Slaves were used for most of the toughest work in mines. There were also many craftsmen making products such as pots, jewelry, and leather shoes. The Greeks traded with people in Egypt, Persia, Cyprus, Italy, Libya, Syria, and Carthage.

Potter's wheel keeps the pot turning as it is being shaped

Pottery

Pottery was a major industry in Athens and in other Greek cities. Both men and women made pots, which were used as storage jars or painted and displayed.

Amphora of wine
Knives for gutting fish

Street life

With no mechanized transport, Greeks carried many burdens—including amphoras of wine and baskets of bread—on their backs.

Sea trade
Cargo ships imported and exported food and drink in massive quantities. Athenians exported much of their olive oil and wine. Copper and tin were imported from Cyprus, Syria, and elsewhere. Slaves were also brought to Athens by boat.

The pharos at Alexandria
The world's first lighthouse was built in the harbor at Alexandria, a city founded by Greeks on the Egyptian coast.

Archimedes' screw
First used to pump water out of ships, this device is a large screw inside a cylinder. It was later used to draw water from rivers to irrigate crops.

ART AND MUSIC

Greek civilization saw huge developments in several areas of the arts, notably architecture, sculpture (both large and small), painting, pottery design, and coin design. Music was an important feature of religious festivals, banquets, weddings, and funerals. Three instruments were especially favored: the lyre, a sophisticated instrument called a kithara, and a double-pipe instrument called the aulos.

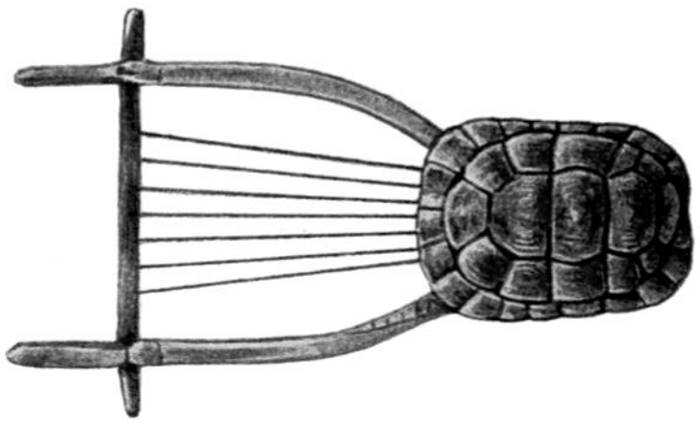

Tortoiseshell lyre
Any educated man was supposed to be able to play this instrument. The hollow side of the tortoiseshell was covered by ox skin.

Pipes
Pipes were made from wood or bone. Musicians usually competed with each other at festivals.

Kithara
This was a particularly grand form of lyre used at large music festivals.

A sculptor's workshop
A sculptor chisels the figure of a horse from a block of marble. Ropes will later be attached to the projections at the end of the block so it can be lifted into its final position.

HOPLITE WARFARE

The Greek hoplite was the most feared soldier in the lands around the eastern Mediterranean Sea between the 7th century BCE and the 4th century BCE. No foreign force could come to terms with these well-trained men with spears and shields. Hoplites usually had to pay for their own equipment so the poorer soldiers fought almost naked apart from their spear and shield. Wealthy hoplites also had impressive body armor.

Bronze helmet
This helmet protected the cheeks as well as the forehead and top of the head. It would once have had a high crest to make the hoplite look more terrifying in battle.

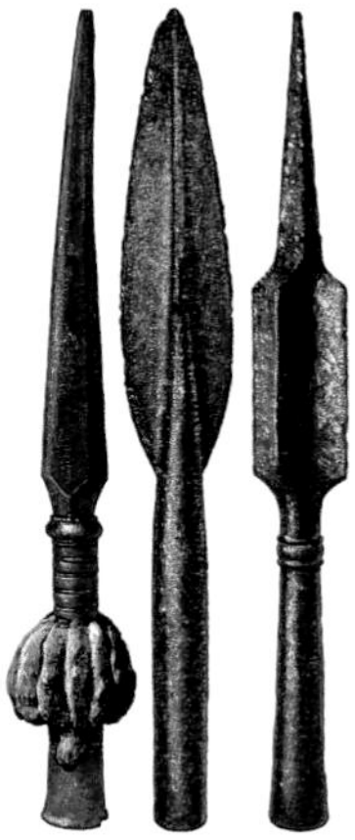

Spear tips
A hoplite's spear had an iron tip at one end and a bronze butt-spike at the other end.

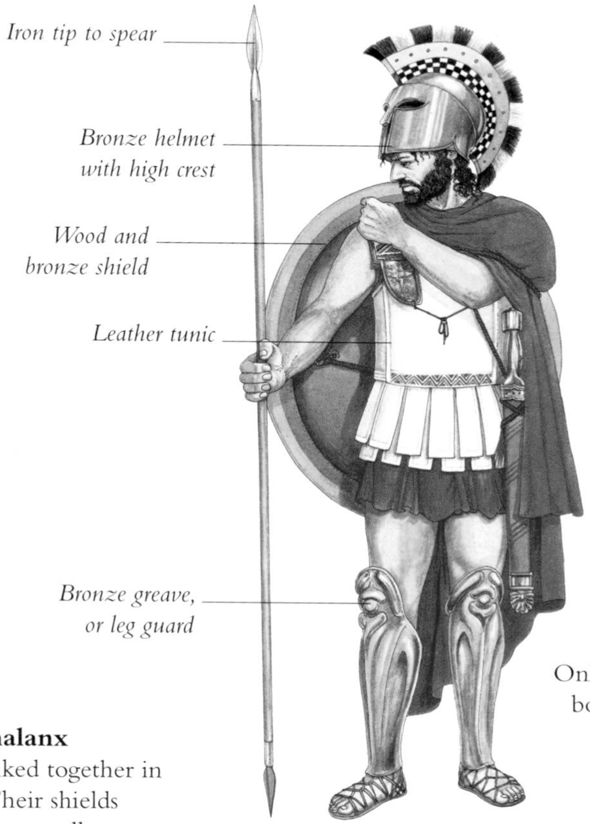

Hoplite dress code
Only wealthy hoplites had full body armor and weaponry.

A fighting phalanx
Greek soldiers fought linked together in rows, or phalanxes. Their shields overlapped to form a wall.

SIEGE WARFARE

By the fifth century BCE, it was not just fortresses that were defended by walls. Entire cities were given walled protection, and there was constant technological progress in weaponry. As cities became better defended, so the means to attack them became more ingenious and deadly. In particular, siege machines became bigger and stronger.

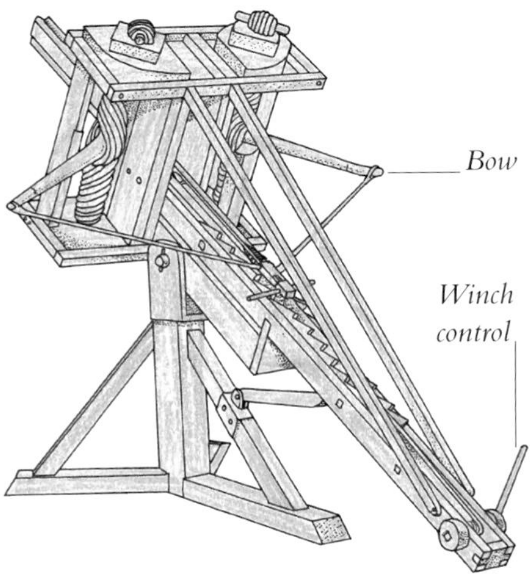

Catapult
Arrows over 6 feet (2 m) long could be shot from catapults such as this. The winch pulled the flexible bow back to ensure it shot its arrow with the maximum power.

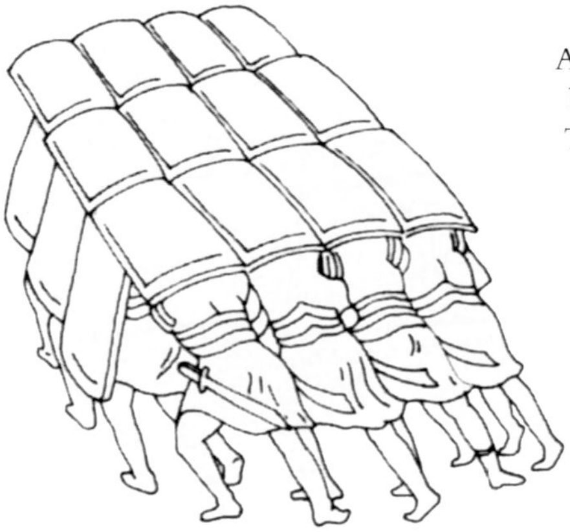

Tortoise of shields
On a single order, a small unit of soldiers could form a "tortoise" of shields overhead and to protect them against volleys of missiles.

Catapults in towers
Catapults mounted at several levels in the tower of a defensive wall made it very difficult for attackers to approach.

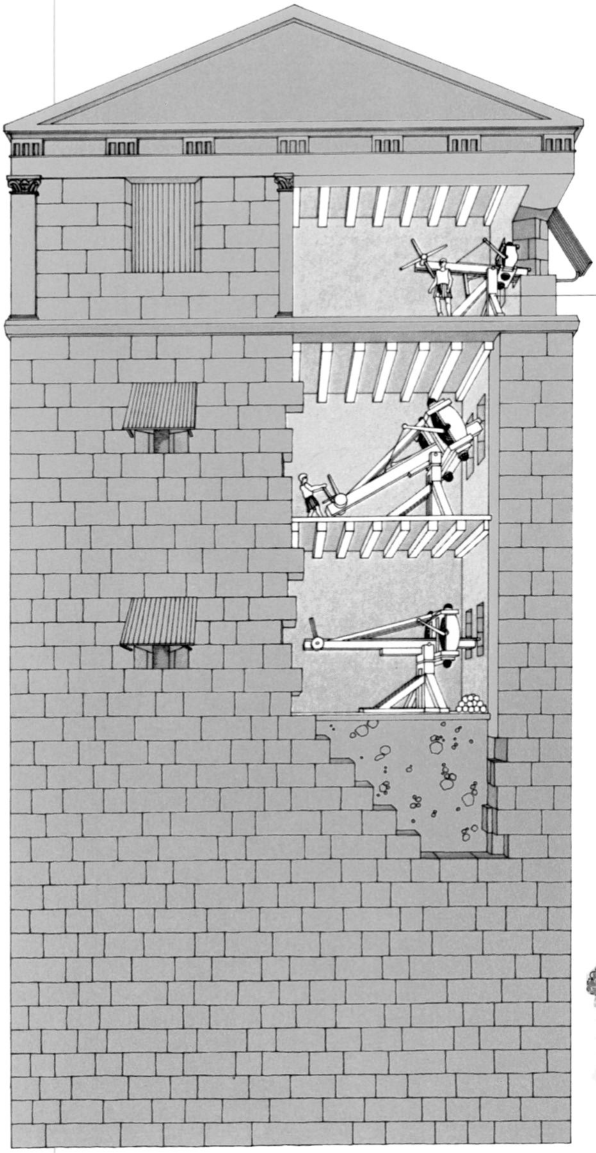

Mobile battering ram

Soldiers inside this wheeled hut could drive the ram forward and backward by turning winches. Padding around the outside offered protection against missile attack.

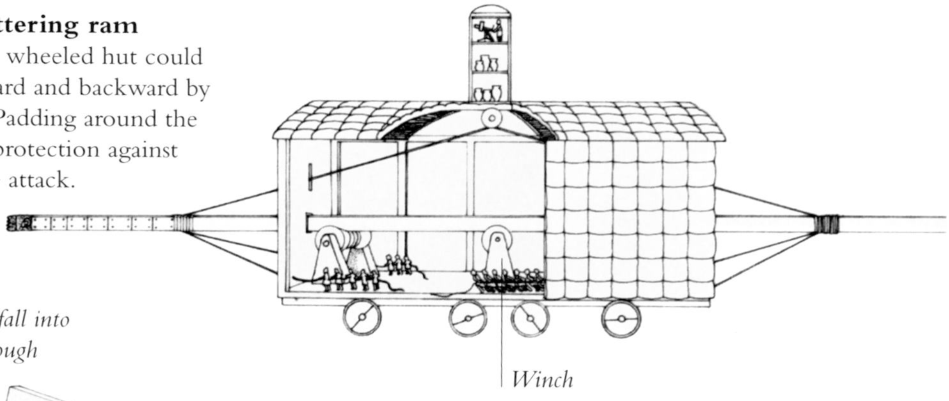

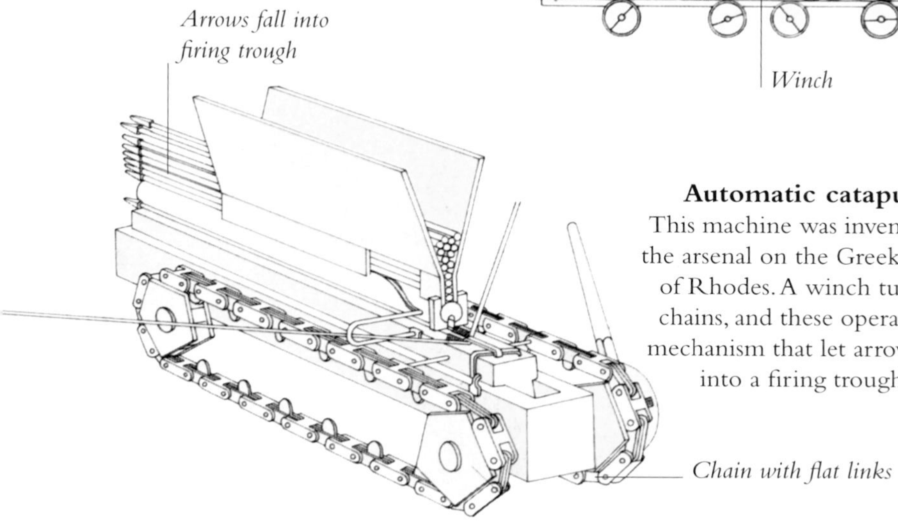

Automatic catapult

This machine was invented at the arsenal on the Greek island of Rhodes. A winch turned chains, and these operated a mechanism that let arrows fall into a firing trough.

Siege machine

This cutaway diagram of a wheeled siege machine shows how catapults are stationed on seven levels.

The Siege of Plataia

In 429 BCE, Thebans and Spartans launched an assault on Plataia, a city allied with Athens. The besiegers used siege machines and battering rams, and hurled burning wood into the city, but it was two years before Plataia was finally destroyed.

TRIREMES AND NAVAL WARFARE

By the fifth century BCE, the trireme was the primary warship for the Greeks and their enemies in the eastern Mediterranean. In 480 BCE, an estimated 40,000 Persians died when their fleet of 1,200 triremes was battered by the Greeks. Most of the crew were organized in three banks of rowers on either side of the vessel. Each trireme aimed to sink as many enemy ships as possible by ramming them in the side. The stamina of the rowers and the ability to maneuver at speed were crucial.

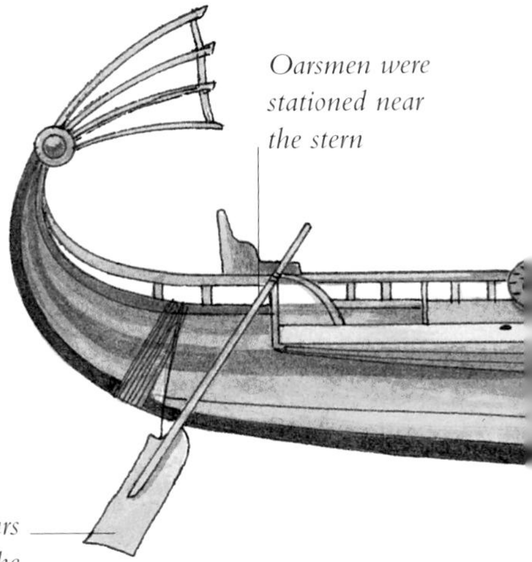

Oarsmen were stationed near the stern

Two oars controlled the vessel's direction

Trireme design

Many triremes are known to have been about 121 feet (37 m) long. With a flattish keel and a shallow draft (amount of the hull below the waterline), the vessels were easy to beach.

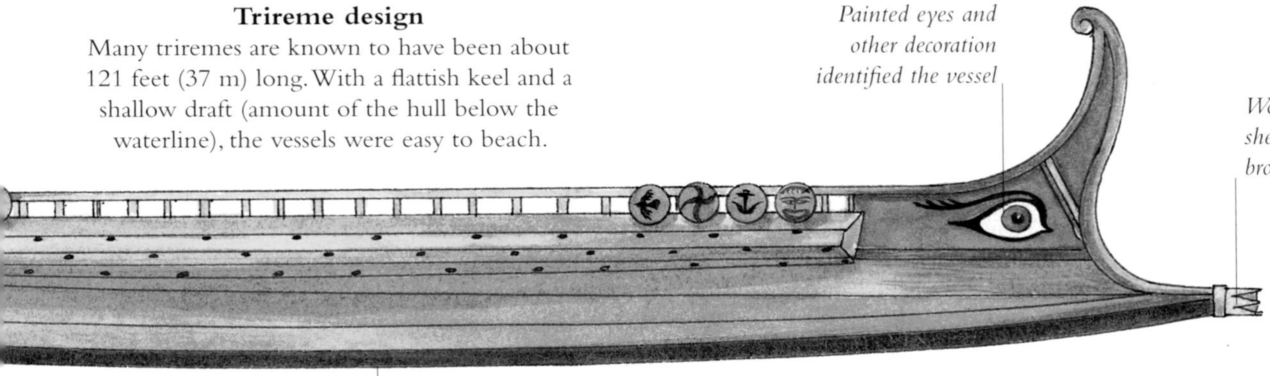

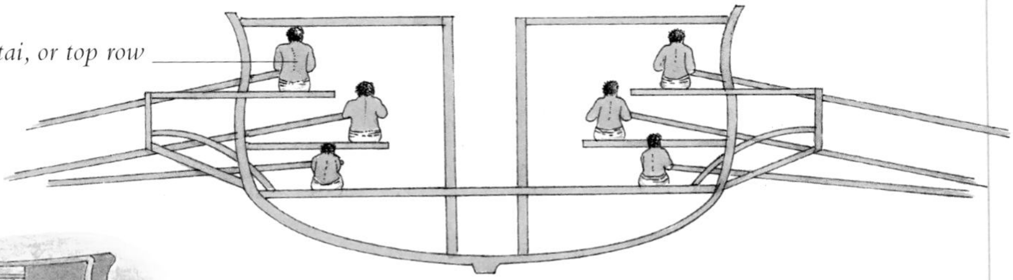

Banks of rowers

A trireme needed 170 men to row it. There were three banks of rowers on each side.

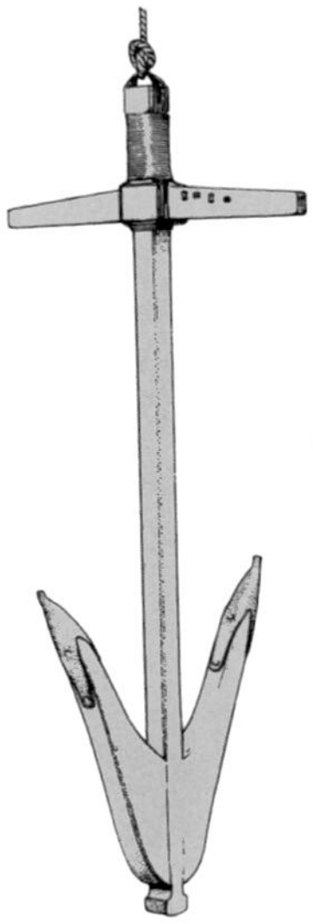

Anchor

This is a relatively sophisticated example. Early anchors were probably just stones tied to a rope.

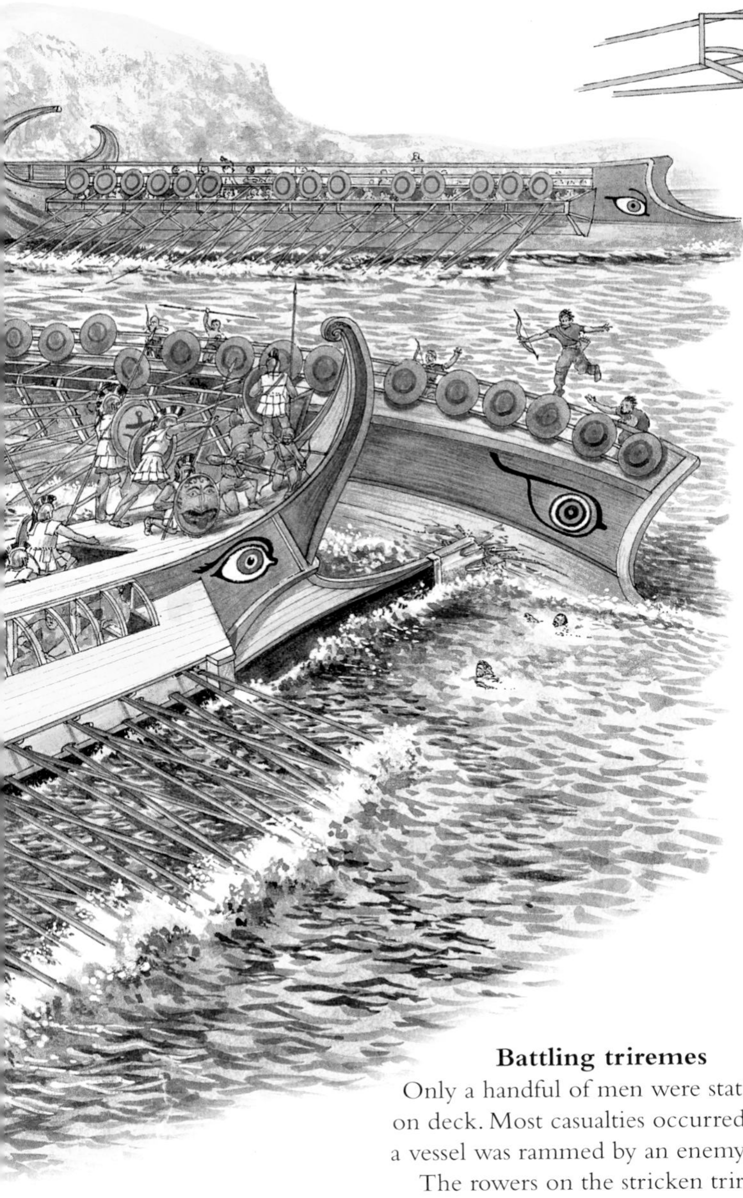

Battling triremes

Only a handful of men were stationed on deck. Most casualties occurred when a vessel was rammed by an enemy vessel. The rowers on the stricken trireme would be thrown into the sea.

Coin

Coins were used to commemorate naval victories. This example depicts the bow of a trireme.

DAILY LIFE

Unless they were very wealthy, most ancient Greek men worked on the land or in workshops. The wealthy had slaves to do their chores. Men were expected to play a role in the public life of their city, but women generally led domestic lives as wives and mothers. The city-state of Sparta was an exception: there, women were more active outside the home. The Greeks were religious people and also knew how to enjoy themselves. Festivals were popular, and the Olympic Games took place every four years.

Farming

Most Greeks worked on the land. The soil was poor and the work was hard. Crops were sown in December and harvested in May. Vineyards were grown on terraces cut into hillsides.

Olympic Games

Competitive sports were common in Greece. Every four years from 776 BCE, the best Greek athletes competed to honor Zeus at Olympus. In these first Olympic Games, all athletes competed naked.

Olive trees grow well in dry soil

Spartan training
In Spartan society, boys were encouraged to play rough games from an early age. Those who showed signs of weakness or cowardice were scorned and made fun of.

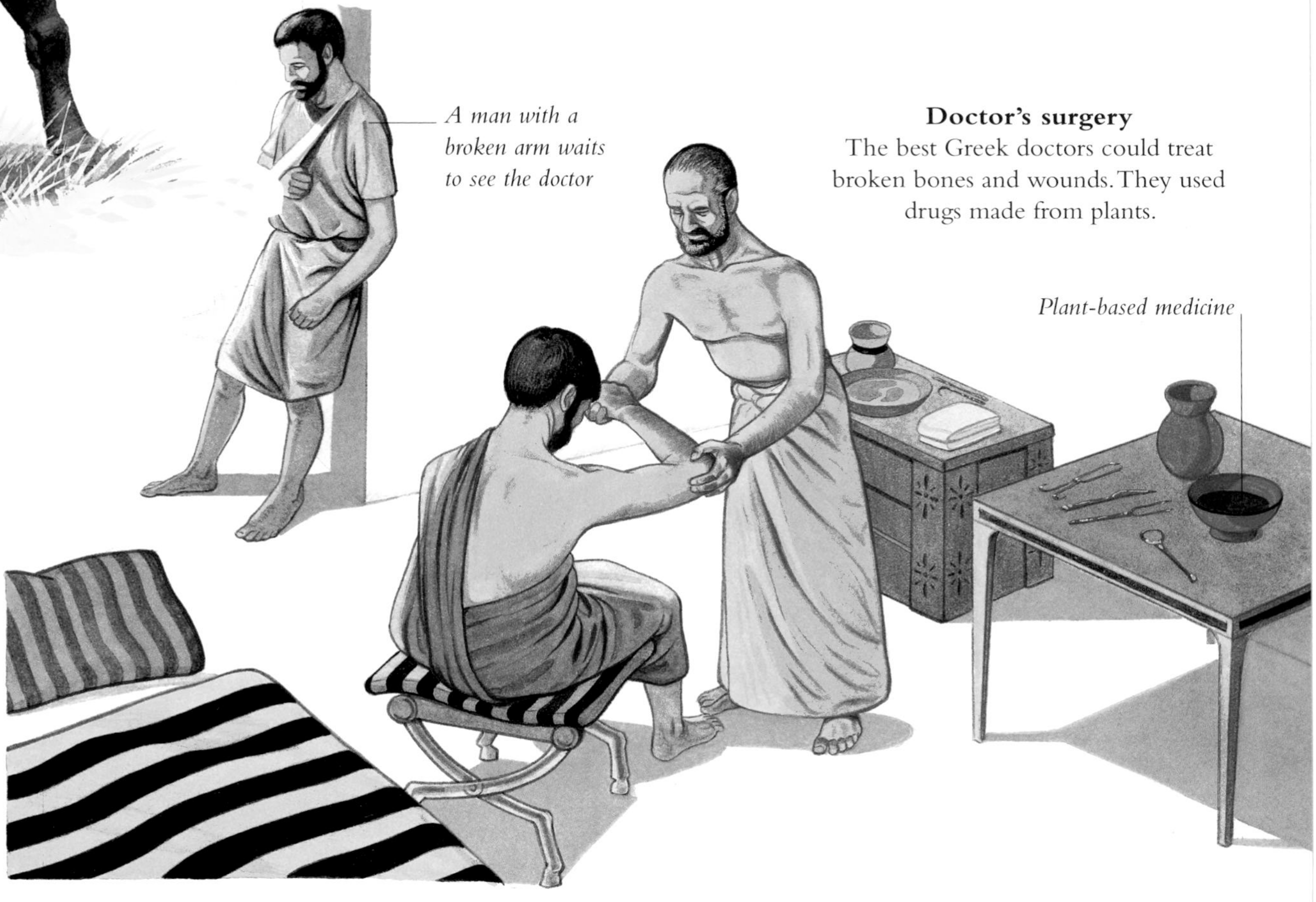
A man with a broken arm waits to see the doctor
Plant-based medicine

Doctor's surgery
The best Greek doctors could treat broken bones and wounds. They used drugs made from plants.

THE ACROPOLIS

Most Greek cities had an acropolis, or fortified "high place" or citadel. In Athens, the large rocky outcrop above the city was used to honor the patron goddess, Athena. The Parthenon is the largest building within the walled citadel, but other fine buildings include the Temple of Victory and the Erechtheion temple.

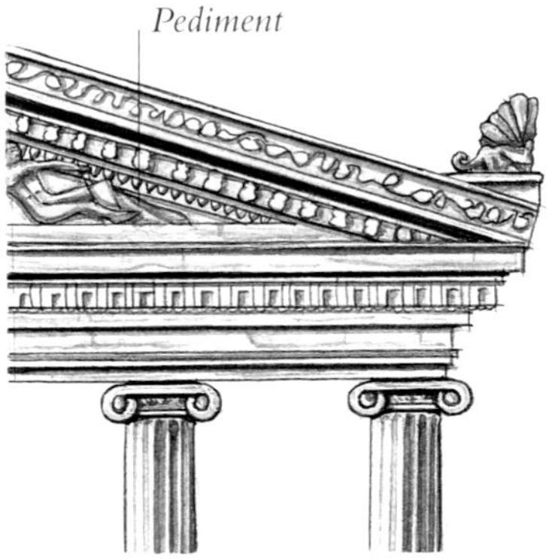

Ionic order
This column style was common in the Greek cities of what is now Turkey.

Doric order
This style was used for the columns of the Parthenon. It was generally common in the Greek cities of what is now Italy.

Walled citadel
The original wall around the hilltop was built in the Mycenean period in c.1200 BCE. Fragments of this wall still exist, but it was mostly destroyed by the Persians in 480 BCE. The Athenians rebuilt the wall after the Persians left.

COLUMNS

These are the three kinds of columns used in Greek temples. The plain Doric style was used in the Parthenon. The Ionic column, with its rams horn curls, was used in the Temple of Victory, which is also in the Acropolis. Corinthian columns are the most elaborate of the three styles.

Parthenon

Dedicated to the goddess Athena, this magnificent stone temple was built between 447–438 BCE. It once housed a large statue of Athena, made of gold and ivory on a wooden core. The Parthenon combines elements of the Doric and Ionic architectural orders.

Parthenon frieze

This wall carving, or frieze, can be seen inside the Parthenon. It shows the Panathenaeic festival.

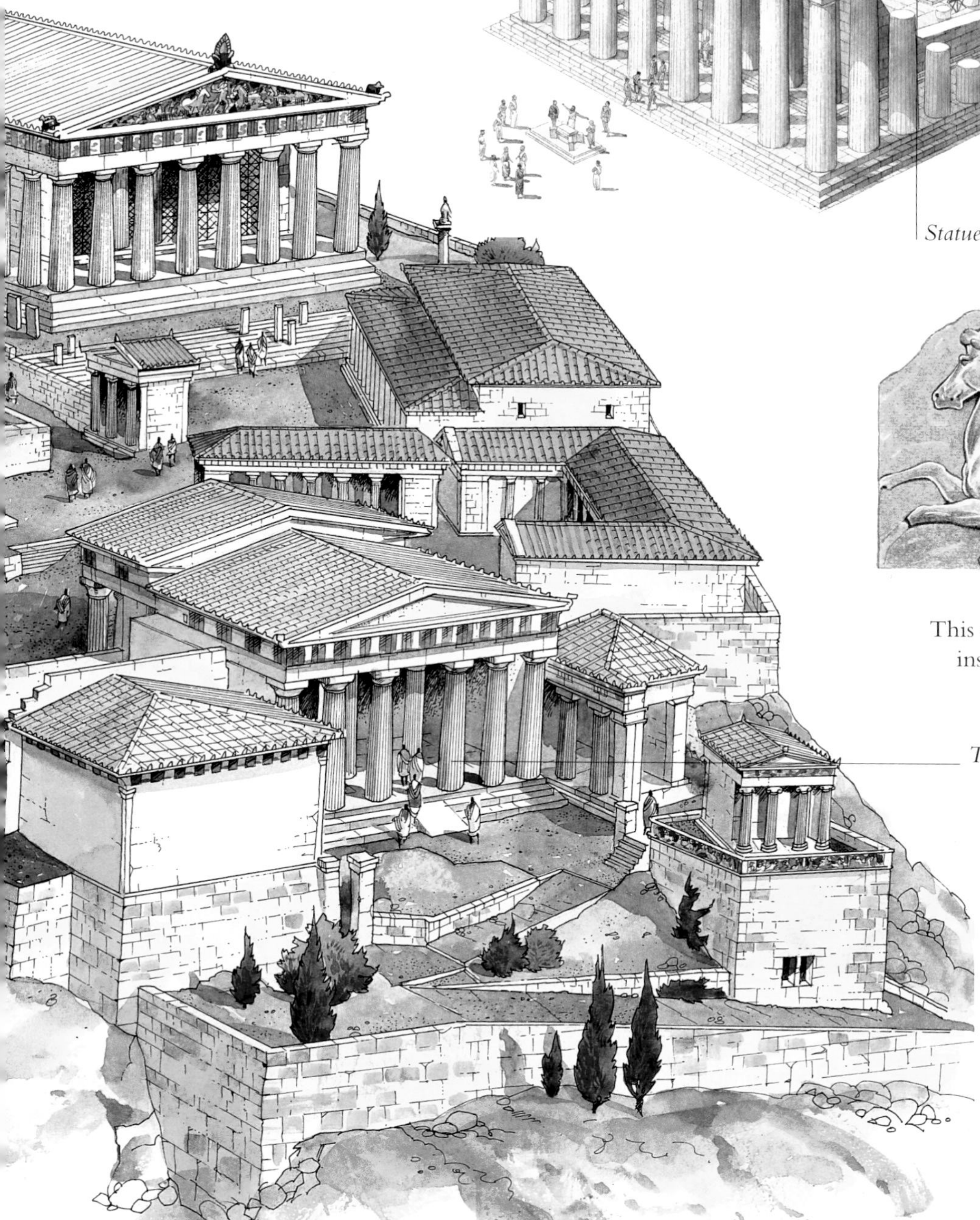

LIFE AT HOME

Most houses—for rich and poor alike—were built from mud bricks and had small windows and a tiled roof. Furniture was simple. Richer people had mosaics on the floors and a cooling central courtyard surrounded by several rooms. In Athens, at least, the women spent most of their lives in the home, spinning, cleaning, and cooking. Wealthy households had slaves to do these chores.

Domestic goddess
Hestia was the goddess of the home and family. Any new arrival in a home—a bride or a baby, for example—was walked around a fire lit in her honor to receive Hestia's protection.

Entertaining aristocrats
A poet sings verses while playing a lyre, as two wealthy men drink from hand-painted pottery. Slaves serve olives and wine.

The house of a rich man
This reconstruction is based on the house of a wealthy man at Olynthos, in northeast Greece. The floor mosaic and the wood used for the balcony overlooking the courtyard would have been too expensive for most Greeks.

An Athenian kitchen
The woman mixing in the foreground has the short hair of a slave. In the background, another woman is weaving. Clothes were usually made at home.

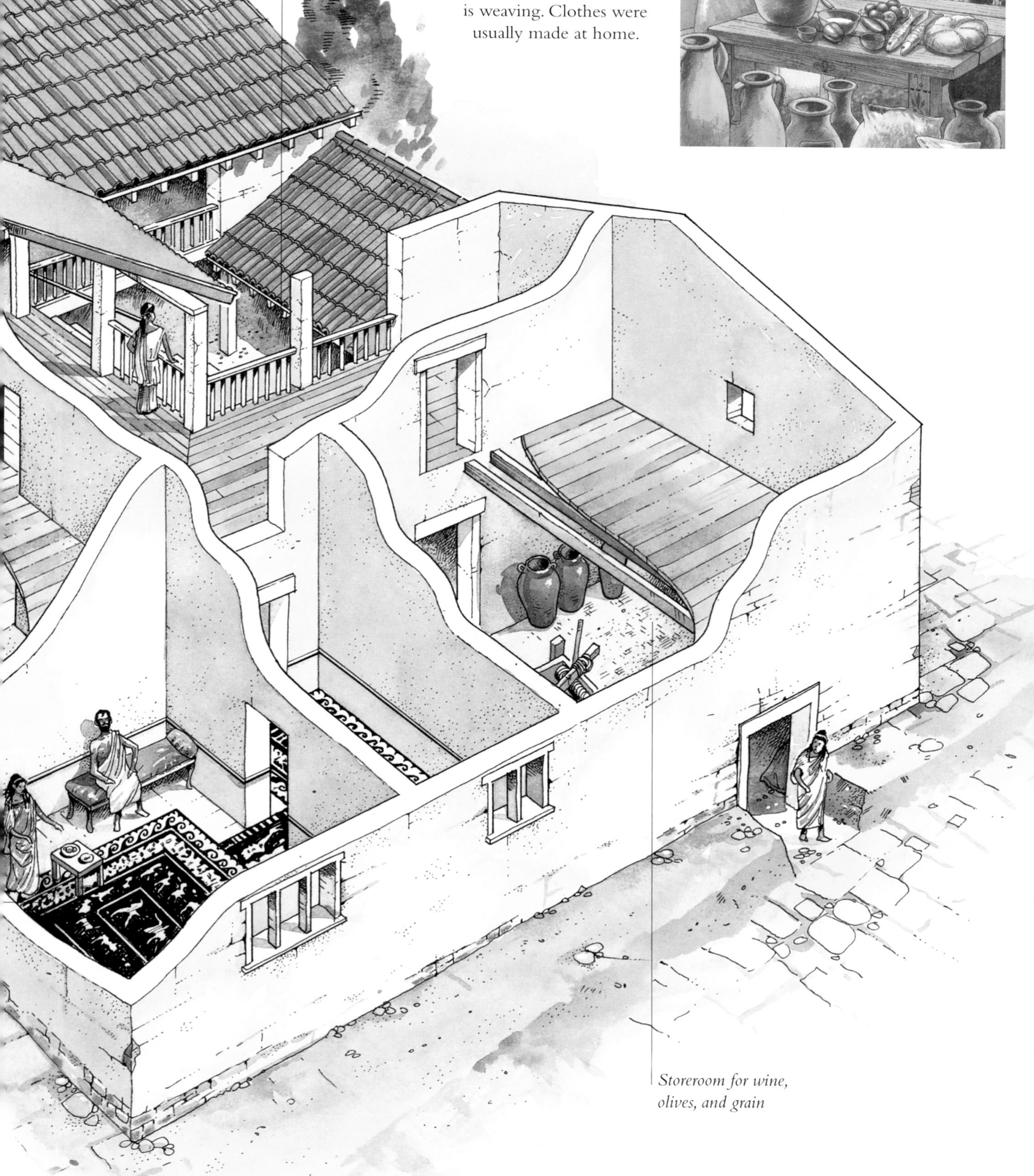

THEATER

Drama was one of the Greeks' greatest inventions, and it was most popular in Athens. The dramatic action usually took the form of either a comedy or a tragedy. What happened during a tragedy was not violent—though the actors often wore fearsome masks—but often told of violence offstage. Comedy was very often about life in Athens at the time. Famous people, including politicians, were teased, often about their love-lives.

Theatrical mask
By swapping masks—which were sometimes designed to frighten the audience—one actor could quickly portray a number of different characters.

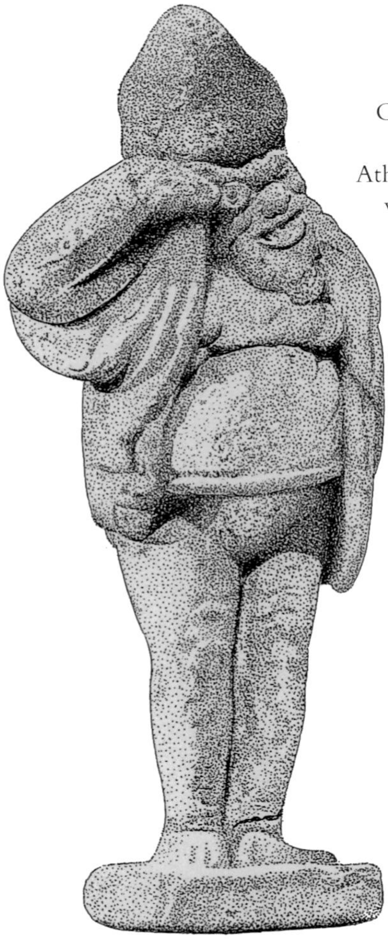

Comedy
Comic servants and slaves were favorite figures in Athenian comedy. Their roles were usually predictable.

Theater design
Theaters were built on hillsides and were shaped like horseshoes, with steps cut into the slope to provide seating.

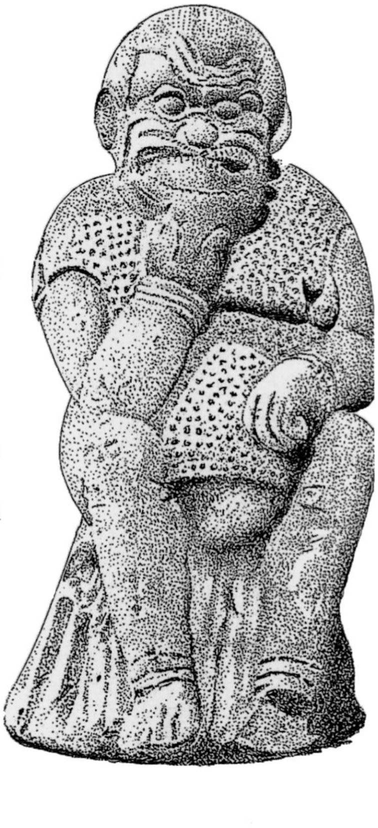

Figurines
Many figurines depict comic slave and servant characters wearing grotesque masks and padded costumes.

Actors preparing
This contemporary painting shows two actors getting ready to go on stage. One is holding the mask of Dionysus, the god of wine, while the other is already wearing the mask of a woman.

Tickets
These metal tokens are probably theater tickets. The letters refer to sections of benches.

Masquerades
Sometimes actors would dress up as animals and put on a comedy show.

ATHENS

From the eighth century BCE, city-states began to emerge throughout Greece. From the 470s BCE, after the defeat of the Persian invasions, Athens became the most powerful city not just in Greece but throughout the Mediterranean. It had the fine temples of the Acropolis, a large agora, or market, theaters, and thousands of houses. The city-state of Athens, which included the surrounding plains of Attica, probably had a population of about 250,000 at this time, but that number included many slaves.

Athenian pottery
By the fifth century BCE, Athenian pottery was the best in the Greek world, often featuring painted scenes from myths about gods and goddesses.

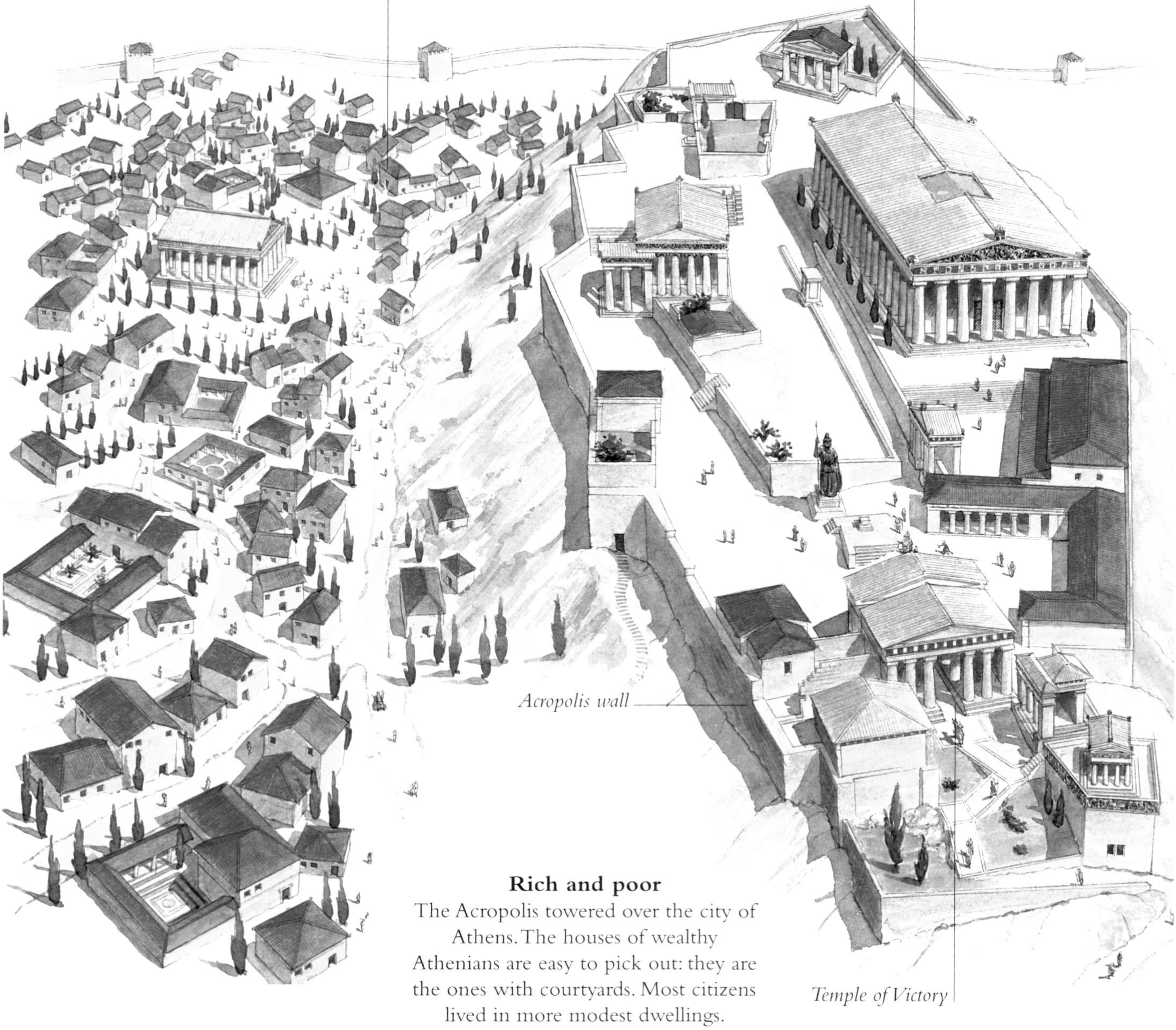

Rich and poor
The Acropolis towered over the city of Athens. The houses of wealthy Athenians are easy to pick out: they are the ones with courtyards. Most citizens lived in more modest dwellings.

DEMOCRACY

Athens involved large numbers of its citizens in running its affairs. This system of government, where decisions are made by the people—not just by one ruler or a small group—is called democracy. About 30,000 people could vote, but women, children, foreigners, and slaves were excluded. Decisions were made at an assembly, which met on a hill called the Pnyx about 40 times a year. Up to 8,000 citizens attended these assemblies.

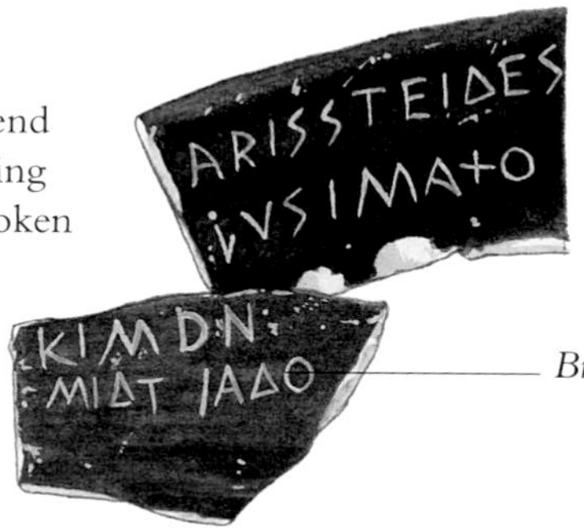

Ostraka
Athenians could vote to send citizens into exile by writing their names on pieces of broken pottery called ostraka.

Voting counters
Bronze wheels were used as voting counters. Some had solid axles, others were hollow. One meant a "yes" vote and the other a "no."

The assembly
In debates on Pnyx hill, citizens over the age of 50 had a right to be heard first. Great Greek orators and debaters spoke there, including Pericles, Aristides, and Demosthenes.

MACEDON

In the fourth century BCE, the Greek kingdom of Macedon, northeast of the Greek mainland, was ruled by King Philip II. Philip was very ambitious and he used the gold mined in Macedon to build and pay his army. He saw the decline of other Greek city-states and took advantage, defeating a combined army of Thebes and Athens at Chaironeia in 338 BCE. When Philip was murdered two years later, his son Alexander (who was to become known as Alexander the Great) took the throne and led a great army to war against Persia, to the east.

Defeating the Persians
Alexander's great military campaign, which ended up covering most of the known world, started as an invasion of Persia. His well-trained troops crushed the Persians at the battle of Gaugamela in 331 BCE.

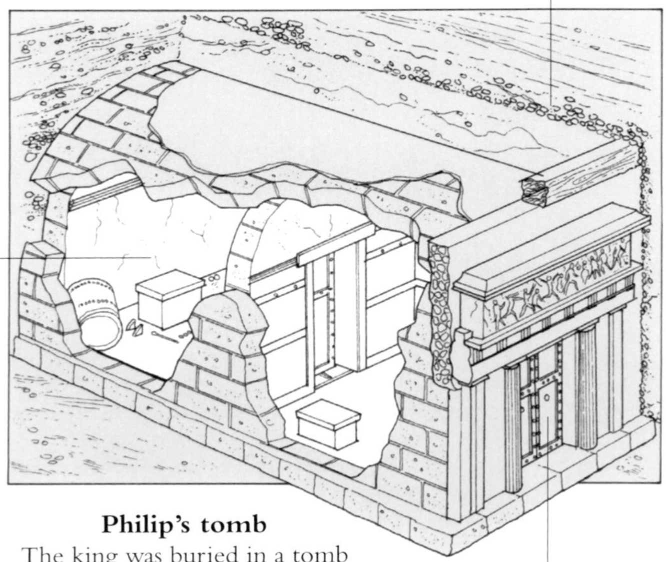

Philip's tomb
The king was buried in a tomb in his native Macedon. The entire structure was buried under a mound of earth called a tumulus.

Philip
Philip of Macedon spent years planning the invasion of Persia that his son would later carry out.

PIKEMEN OF MACEDON

Philip's main force in battle was heavily armored infanty. They fought much like hoplites but used a longer, heavier spear called a pike, or sarissa.

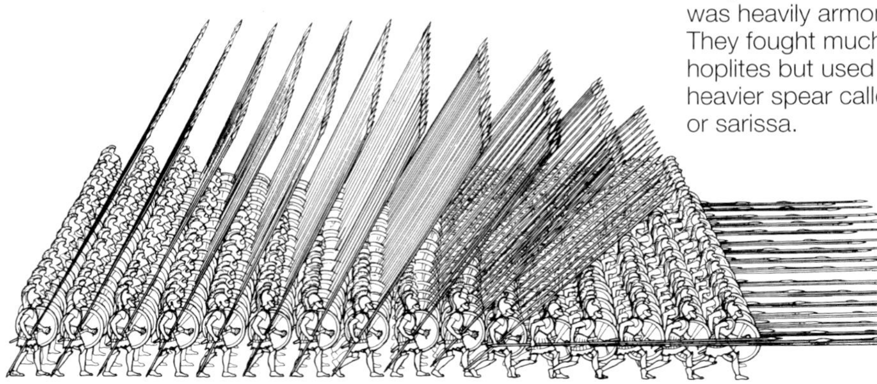

Persian soldiers wore thick cloth hoods called kyrbasia

Fighting elephants
After conquering lands far to the east of Macedon, Philip's son Alexander the Great finally reached northern India. There, his soldiers encountered the fearsome war elephants of King Poros.

Alexander the Great
The Macedonian armies of Philip II and Alexander the Great successfully combined massed ranks of infantry with the intelligent use of cavalry.

ANCIENT ISRAEL

The Israelites arrived in Canaan (the hill country west of the Dead Sea) some time around 1200 BCE. Over the next 200 years they gradually expanded their kingdom, culminating in King David's transfer of his capital from Hebron to Jerusalem in 995 BCE. Under King David and his son, Solomon, Jerusalem became the center of the Israelite nation and the Jewish faith, home to the First Temple and the Ark of the Covenant (a chest said to contain the tablets of the Ten Commandments).

Solomon's temple
Constructed some time in the 10th century BCE, Solomon's Temple was said to have housed the Ark of the Covenant.

Old Testament Jerusalem
The city of King David stood on a ridge overlooking the Kidron River. The city shown here includes the strengthened walls added by Hezekiah around 700 BCE.

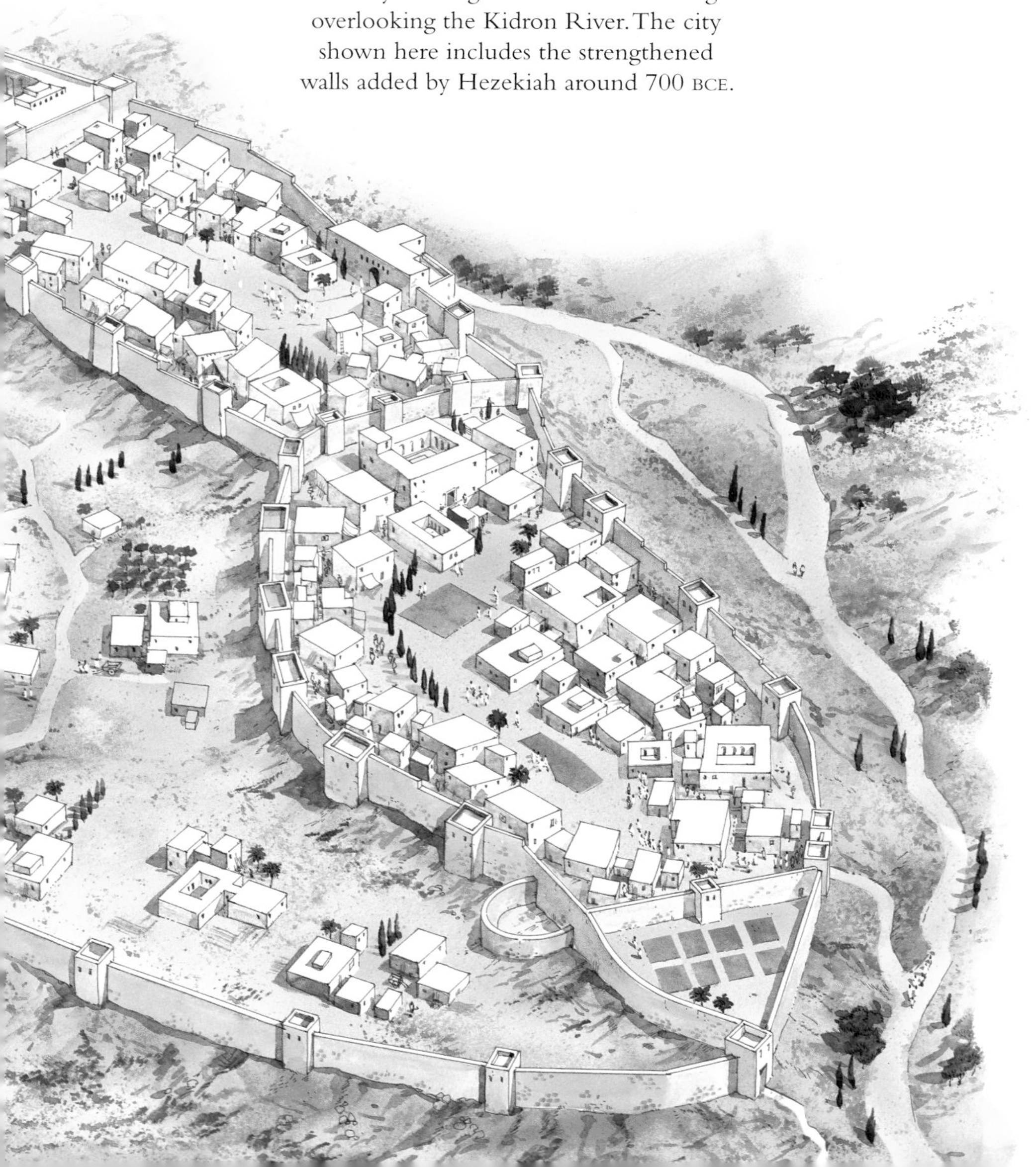

TIMELINE

1020 BCE The various Hebrew tribes living in the hill country near the Jordan Valley are united under King Saul.

1000 BCE King David captures Jerusalem from the Canaanites and makes it the capital of the kingdom of Israel.

958 BCE King Solomon begins a period of major construction in Jerusalem, building the First Temple and a large palace.

928 BCE The Hebrew kingdom is divided into the states of Israel and Judah.

720–700 BCE The kingdoms of Israel and Judah are conquered by the Assyrian Empire.

597 BCE Israel is conquered by Babylon as the Assyrian Empire collapses.

586 BCE The Babylonians destroy Solomon's Temple in Jerusalem and take large numbers of Hebrews to Babylon, where they are forced into slavery.

64 BCE Israel and Judah are incorporated into the Roman Empire. The local Jewish political elite, led by King Herod, is recruited to rule the region.

20 BCE Herod rebuilds the Temple in Jerusalem as part of a major building project that includes new fortifications and a grand palace. During the same period, he also oversees the construction of a new port—Caesarea—on the coast.

66–73 CE The Zealot Revolt—a Jewish uprising against Roman rule—is brutally suppressed by the Roman administration. Herod's Temple (the Second Temple) is demolished.

ASSYRIA
Aleppo
Ugarit
Qarqar (854 BCE)
Hamath
ARAM
CYPRUS
Arvad
Tadmor
Riblah
MEDITERRANEAN SEA
Byblos
ARAM-ZOBAH
PHOENICIA
Sidon
Damascus
Tyre
Dan
ARAM-DAMASCUS
Hazor
Acco
Megiddo
Beth-shean
SYRIAN DESERT
Samaria
Shechem
Joppa
KINGDOM OF ISRAEL
AMMON
Rabbah
Eltekeh (701 BCE)
Gezer
Jerusalem
Ashkelon
Bethlehem
Lachish
Gaza
MOAB
INDEPENDENT OF ISRAEL, 843 BCE
Arad
PHILISTIA
Salt Sea (DEAD SEA)
KINGDOM OF JUDAH
EGYPT
EDOM
INDEPENDENT OF JUDAH, 843 BCE
Ezion-geber
BORDER OF FORMER KINGDOM OF SOLOMON
GREATEST EXTENT OF THE KINGDOM OF ISRAEL
GREATEST EXTENT OF THE KINGDOM OF JUDAH
BORDER OF STATE GAINING INDEPENDENCE FROM KINGDOMS OF ISRAEL OR JUDAH
KINGDOM OF EGYPT, 924 BCE
ASSYRIAN EMPIRE, 722 BCE
BABYLONIAN EMPIRE, 597 BCE
CAMPAIGNS IN ISRAEL AND JUDAH
PHARAOH SHOSHENQ I OF EGYPT, 924 BCE
KING SENNACHERIB OF ASSYRIA, 701 BCE
0 50 100 150 KM
0 50 100 MILES

JOSHUA AND DAVID

The creation of ancient Israel was defined by two important Israelite leaders. The first was Joshua, appointed by Moses to lead the Israelites into Canaan. He led his people in a highly successful campaign against the Canaanites, securing a foothold for the Israelites in the region. The second was David, who defeated the Philistines and conquered a large empire that stretched from Damascus to the Gulf of Aqaba.

King David's city
The already-ancient city of Jerusalem was rebuilt by King David, who added a fortified citadel to its northern end and strengthened its defenses.

The Canaanites
The Canaanites had a large and well-equipped army. Joshua made sure that he went into battle against them only on terrain where their chariots could not be used.

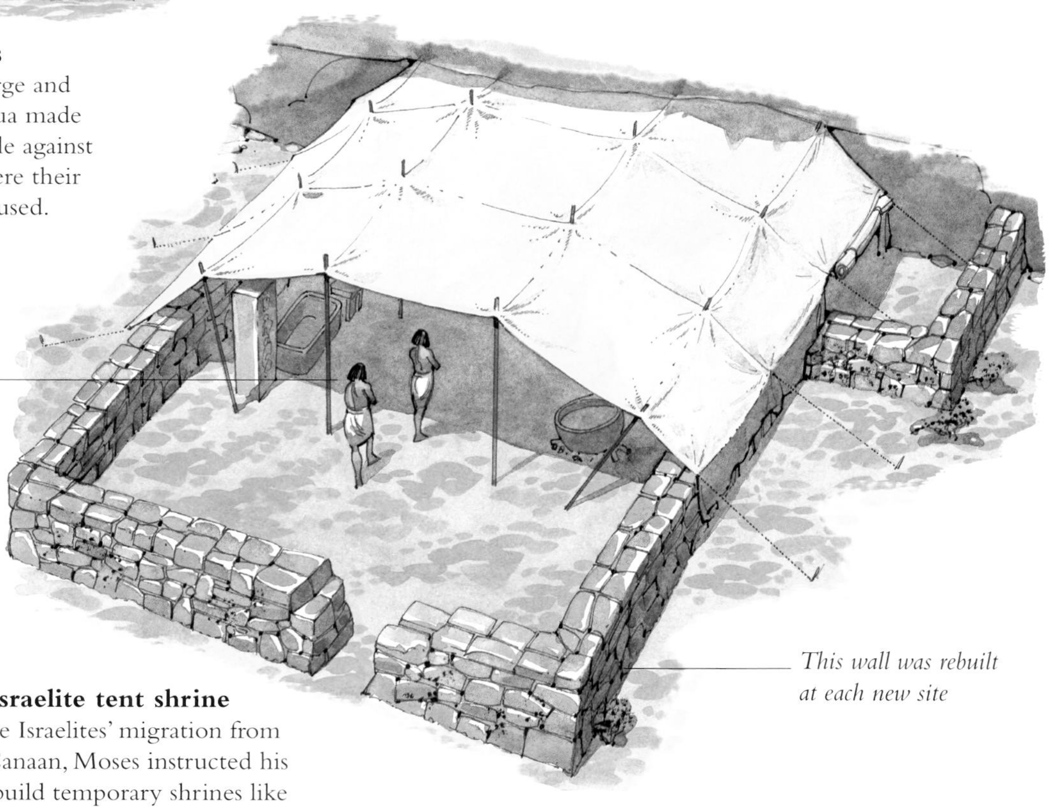

An Israelite tent shrine
During the Israelites' migration from Egypt to Canaan, Moses instructed his people to build temporary shrines like this one for religious ceremonies.

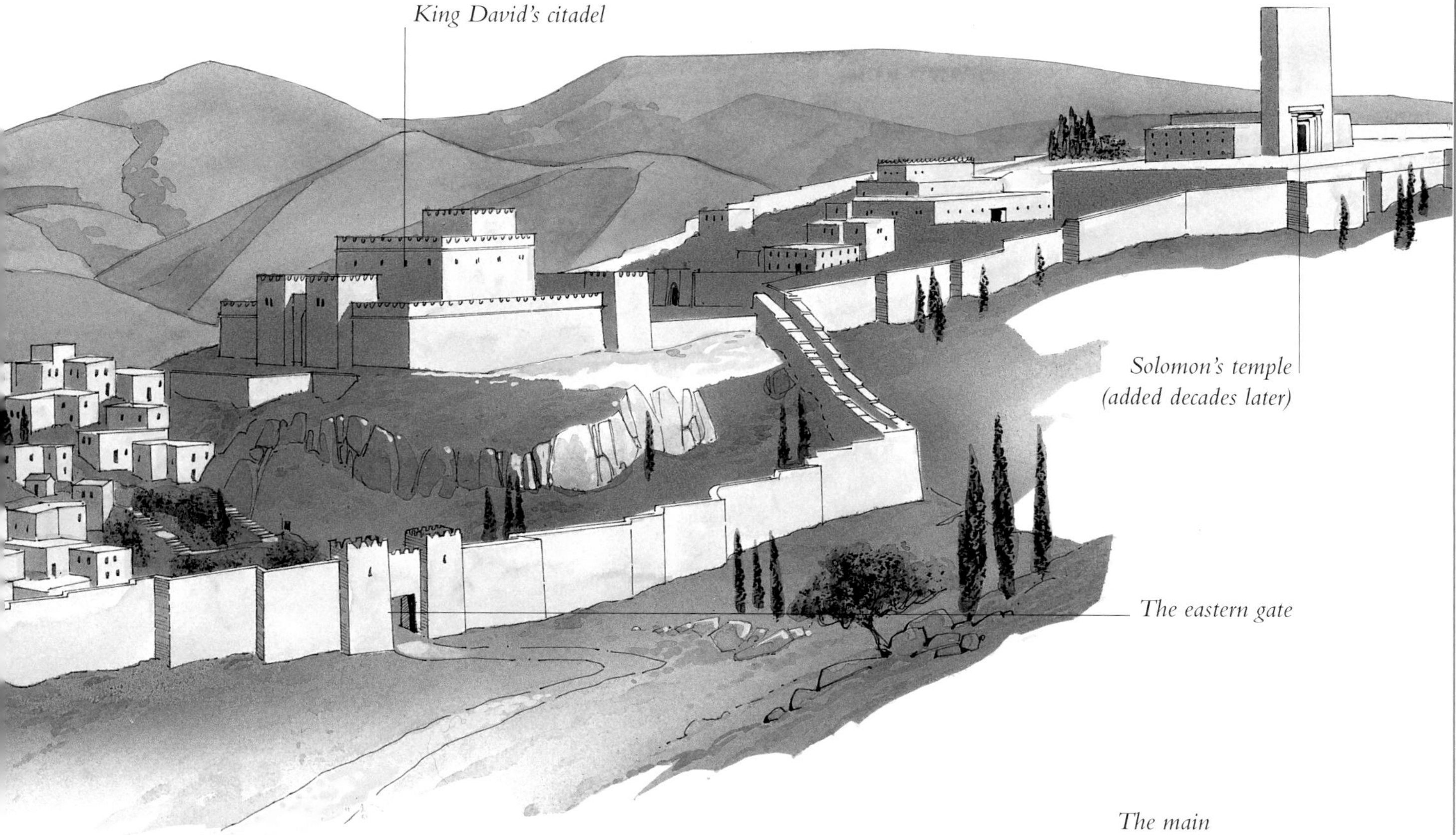

Solomon's temple
The plan of the building resembled Phoenician architecture. It was rectangular with a porch flanked by a pair of bronze columns. The temple forecourt held a huge bronze water basin, used for rituals.

ROMAN RULE

In 63 BCE, the Roman general Pompey conquered Israel and made the country part of the Roman Empire. The Romans ruled Israel (which they called Judea) through Jewish representatives, the best known of whom was King Herod. Roman rule brought prosperity to some in Judea—particularly Herod and his inner circle—but was widely resented by the Jewish population, who rose up in rebellion several times.

Israelite fishing boat
This type of fishing boat would have been used on the lake known as the Sea of Galilee, where conditions were mild.

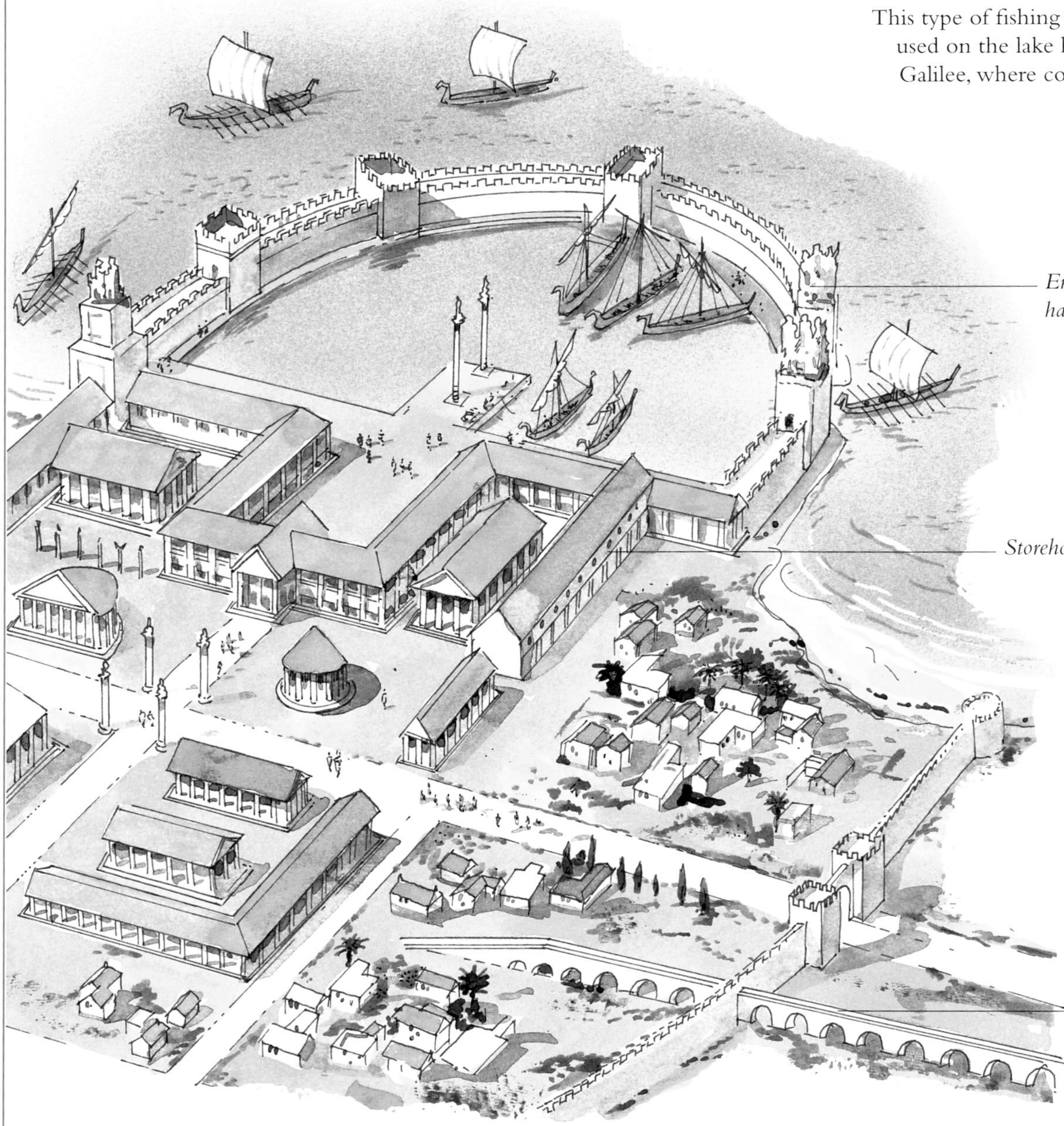

Caesarea
Herod constructed an artificial harbor at Caesarea to improve his kingdom's links to the rest of the Roman Empire.

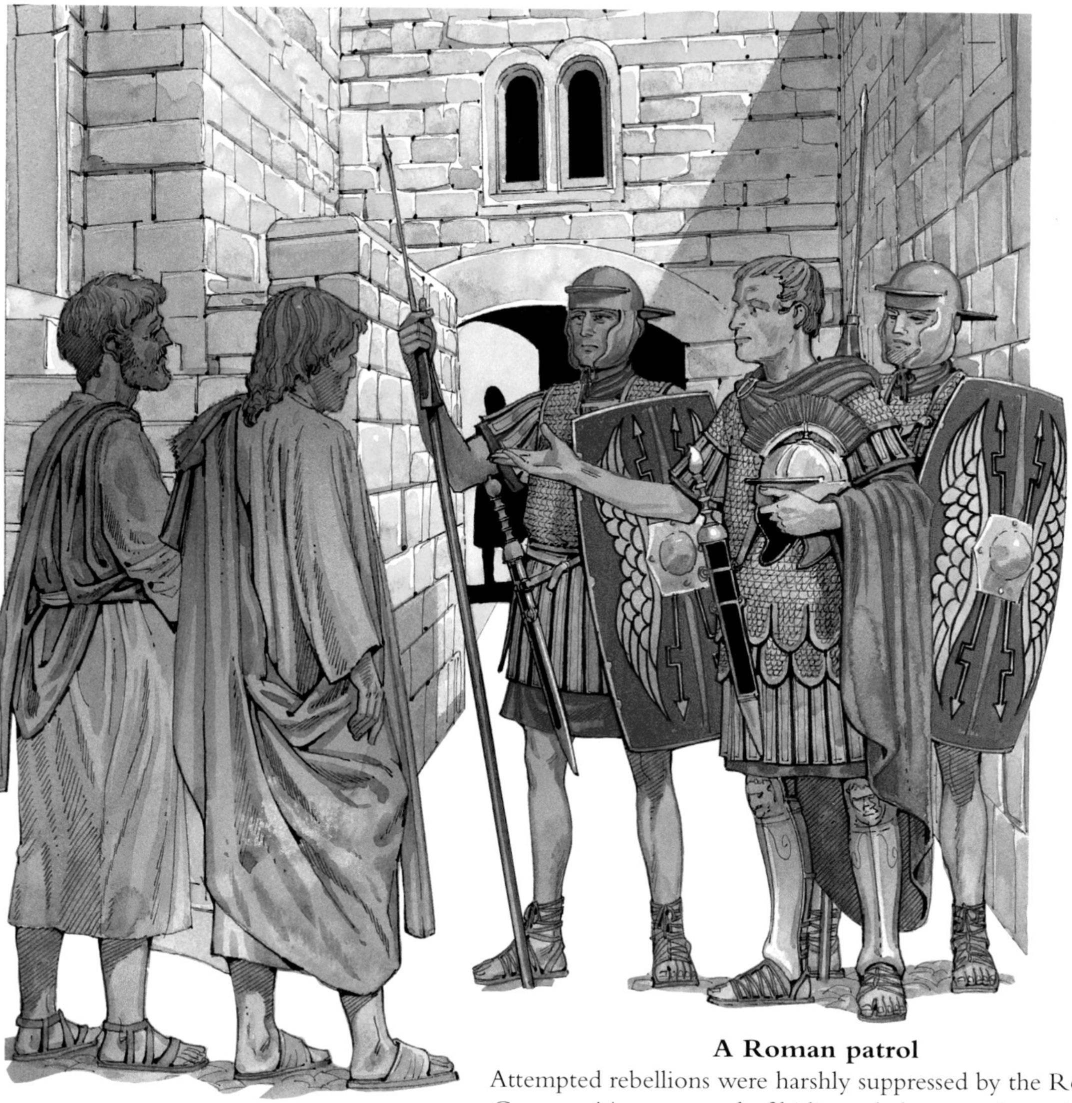

A Roman patrol
Attempted rebellions were harshly suppressed by the Romans. Communities suspected of hiding rebels were often subjected to curfews and random arrests.

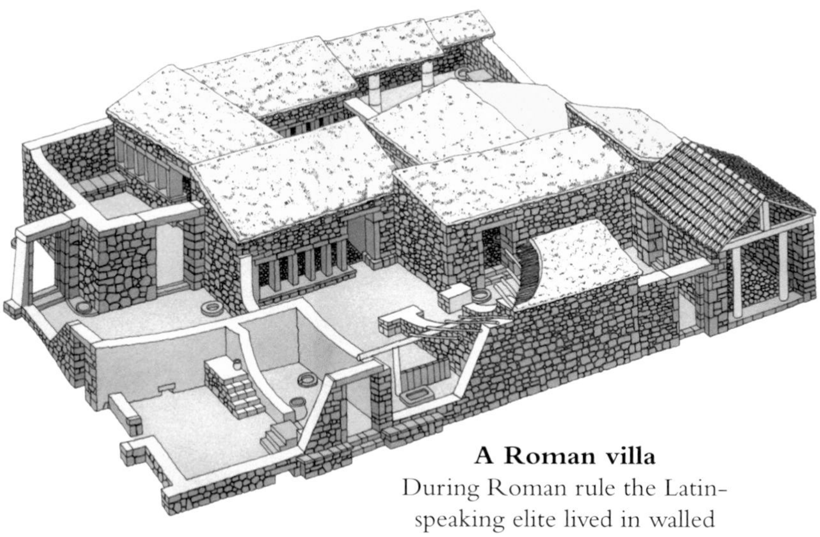

A Roman villa
During Roman rule the Latin-speaking elite lived in walled compounds and villas like this one, often with armed guards.

Carpenters
The period of Roman rule saw a boom in major construction projects, so carpenters and stonemasons prospered.

HEROD'S JERUSALEM AND THE TEMPLE

Through manipulation of Rome's shifting political groups, Herod managed to become one of the most powerful governors in the empire during his rule (37–4 BCE). The prosperity of Judea during this period allowed him to undertake numerous monumental construction projects. These included palaces, fortresses, and, most famously, rebuilding the temple at Jerusalem.

The largest tower in the palace was called the Phasael Tower
Central courtyard

FRONT OF THE TEMPLE

This sketch, produced by a historian in 1956, represents the most likely appearance of the Second Temple during the time of Herod. As no detailed paintings or carvings survive, reconstructions have to be based on patchy and incomplete contemporary descriptions.

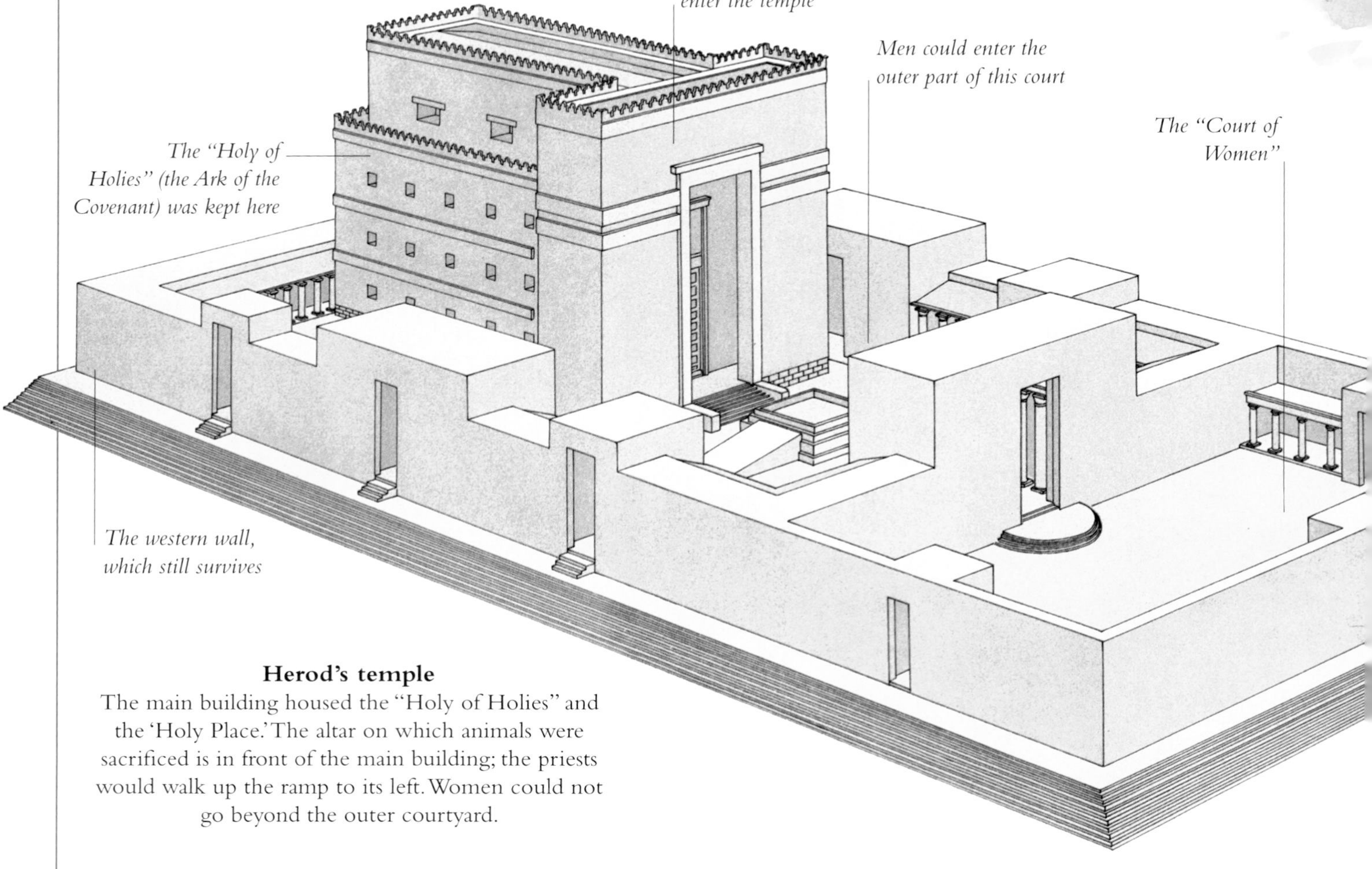
Only priests could enter the temple
Men could enter the outer part of this court
The "Court of Women"
The "Holy of Holies" (the Ark of the Covenant) was kept here
The western wall, which still survives

Herod's temple

The main building housed the "Holy of Holies" and the 'Holy Place.' The altar on which animals were sacrificed is in front of the main building; the priests would walk up the ramp to its left. Women could not go beyond the outer courtyard.

Herod's palace
Herod's upper palace in Jerusalem was built on the summit of the western hill overlooking the temple area. The palace was built in the Greco-Roman style, with large reflecting pools, open courtyards, and many elaborate mosaic floors.

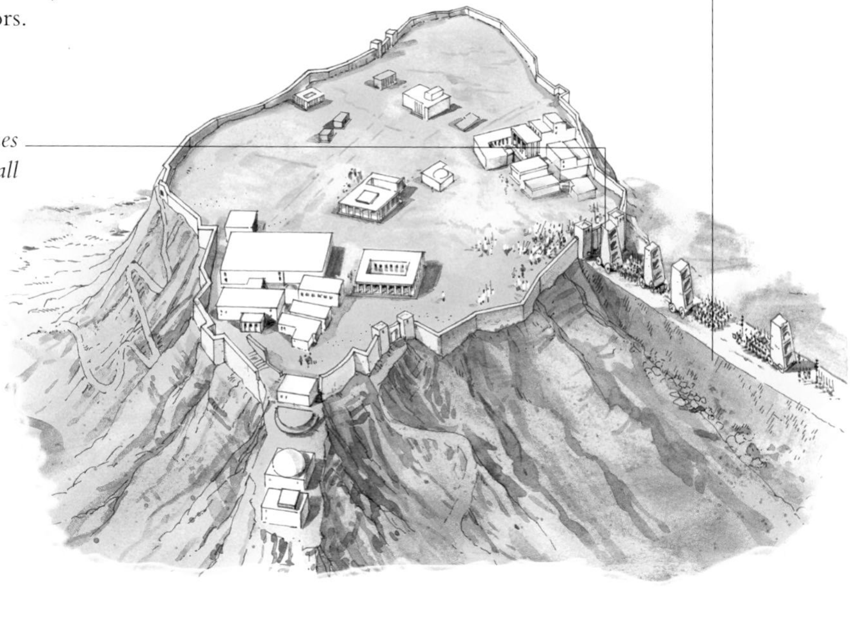

Masada
The fortress of Masada was built by Herod as a palace. During the Jewish Revolt (67–73 CE) Masada was the last Jewish fortress to fall to the Romans.

ROMAN EMPIRE

According to legend, the settlement of Rome was founded in 753 BCE. It was ruled by kings until 509 BCE, when the monarchy was overthrown and the Roman Republic was founded. By the second century CE, Rome had transformed itself from a minor city-state into the major power in the western world. Its empire stretched from Britain to North Africa and West Asia.

TIMELINE

753 BCE Traditional date for the foundation of the city-state of Rome by the brothers Romulus and Remus. Archeological evidence suggests the city was already established by this point.

753–509 BCE Rome is ruled by hereditary monarchs.

509 BCE King Tarquin II is overthrown, marking the beginning of the Roman Republic.

500–300 BCE The Roman Republic begins to expand its military. It becomes the leading power in an alliance of local city-states.

312 BCE The first paved Roman road, the Appian Way, is constructed.

264–218 BCE The Punic Wars see Rome battle Carthage for dominance of the western Mediterranean.

148–146 BCE Rome decisively defeats its two biggest rivals in the Mediterranean, Carthage and Macedon.

63–49 BCE The Roman military commanders Gnaeaus Pompeius and Julius Caesar begin massive campaigns of expansion.

49–31 BCE A long civil war is fought between Gnaeaus Pompeius and Julius Caesar, then subsequently between their various successors. The eventual victor was Gaius Octavius—Julius Caesar's adopted son.

27 BCE Gaius Octavius declares absolute power, styling himself Emperor Augustus Caesar. This marks the end of the republic and the start of the empire.

27 BCE–192 CE The Pax Romana (Roman peace), a long period of relative peace and prosperity. During this period the Roman Empire reaches its greatest extent.

286 CE Emperor Diocletian divides the Roman Empire into two (later four) separate administrative regions, each ruled by a co-emperor.

306 CE Constantine the Great becomes emperor of Rome. He ends the persecution of Christians and moves the capital of the empire to Byzantium (present-day Istanbul), which he renames Constantinople.

337 CE The Roman Empire goes into its final period of decline. Frequent civil wars reduce the ability of the army to respond to the growing threat from tribes to the north.

476 CE The last western emperor is forced to abdicate by the Germanic warlord Odoacer. The eastern Roman Empire survives until 1453 as the Byzantine Empire.

Inscriptions reveal that the arch was commissioned by a wealthy local merchant

Triumphal arch
This arch was erected in what is now western France to commemorate the victories of the Roman general Julius Caesar.

Romulus and Remus

According to a legend the twin brothers Romulus and Remus, who were abandoned at birth in the Tiber River in Italy, were suckled by a she-wolf and fed by a woodpecker. The story goes on to describe how Romulus later founded the city of Rome.

MILITARY POWER

The main reason the Romans were able to create such a large empire was the power of their well-disciplined and highly trained army. The army's main strength was its legions of infantrymen, recruited from Roman citizens. These were supported by auxiliaries drawn from the peoples conquered by Rome. The army used the most up-to-date military hardware, including siege towers and catapults.

Army on the march
On a march through enemy territory, the army would build a camp each night, fortified by banks and wooden fences. Soldiers on the march had to carry their own rations and digging equipment, as well as their weapons.

Soldier equipped for a march, carrying weapons and three days' rations
Unit leader, or centurion
Signifier, carrying a small unit's standard, or signum

Dacian prisoner
Soldiers build fortified camp
Emperor Trajan
Wall made from squares of turf
Timber to strengthen structure

Trajan's Column
This monument in Rome commemorates Emperor Trajan's victory in the Dacian Wars (101–106 CE). It shows many battle scenes from the campaign.

Tortoise formation
The tortoise, or *testudo*, formation of overlapping shields offered effective protection against enemy missiles.

BALLISTA

This artillery machine was like a crossbow on a stand. It fired short, iron-tipped bolts with great accuracy. Ballistae were regularly used by the Romans, especially when they were laying siege to enemy strongholds. Julius Caesar used ballistae in the invasion of Britain in 55 BCE and again, to great effect, at the siege of Alesia, a fortress in Gaul, in 52 BCE.

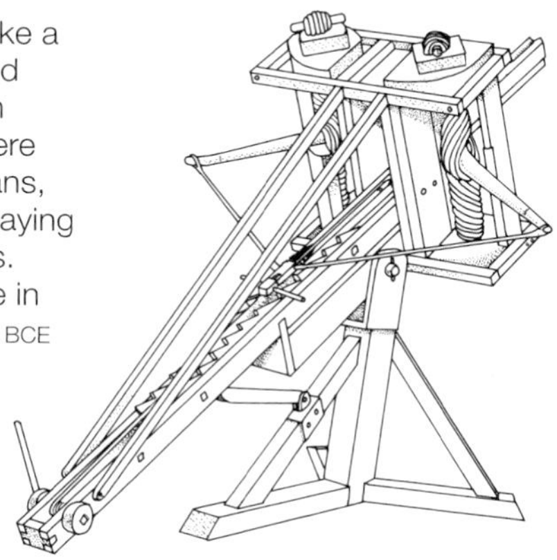

Siege warfare
This scene, which depicts the siege of Sarmizegethusa, Dacia, in 106 CE, shows both legionary soldiers and auxiliaries using ladders as they try to scale the walls. The Romans also had siege towers and battering rams.

UNIFORMS AND EQUIPMENT

The Roman army was well structured and well equipped. Senior officers included overall legion commanders, or legates. The officer rank of centurion was made up of many grades, from *primus pilus* (senior centurion) down. The army's core comprised legionaries and auxiliaries. Different ranks could be identified by their uniforms and the equipment they carried.

Auxiliaries
Whereas legionaries had to be citizens of Rome, auxiliaries did not. By the second century CE, the latter provided almost all the army's cavalry and many of its specialist troops, such as archers.

Leading from the front
Centurions (left) were responsible for the discipline of their men. Since they usually led from the front in battle, centurions often suffered particularly high casualty rates. They were paid more than the legionaries in their charge.

Full pack
A legionary carried about 66 pounds (30 kg) of kit on the march. It included tools for building camp, bags to hold a saw, pots and pans for cooking, and a leather shield cover.

Centurion
Unusully, this centurion does not have a crest on his galea, or helmet. He has shaped body armor, wears his sword on his left (a legionary's sword was on the right), and holds a *vitis*, or vine stick. The vitis was used to discipline members of his unit.

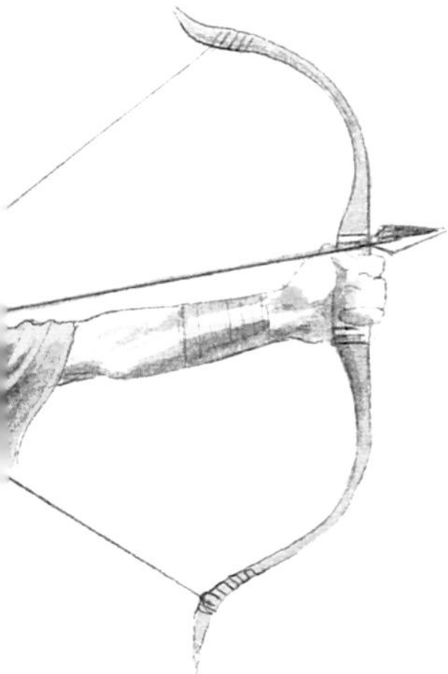

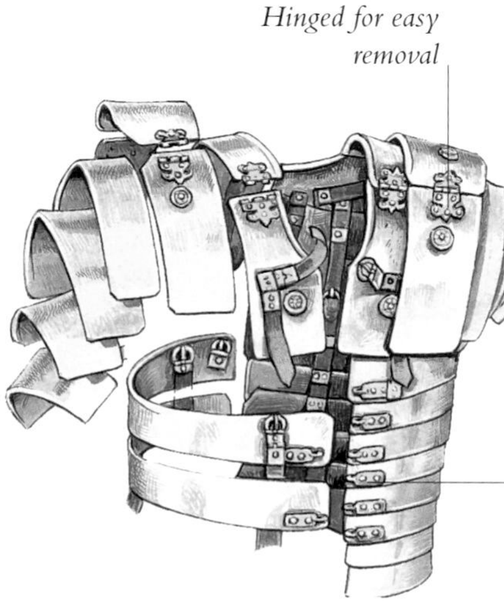

Lorica segmentata
A legionary's torso was protected by segmented armor composed of overlapping iron plates held together by leather straps.

Legionary
By the first century BCE, a legionary's standard armor and arms included segmented body armor called *lorica segmentata*, a shield, helmet, short sword, and dagger. On his feet he wore a pair of heavy sandals.

ARMY ORGANIZATION

The early Roman army was made up of part-timers: men were called upon to fight only when they were needed. Later, men volunteered to become full-time soldiers and sailors and served for 20 or 25 years. The army became extremely well disciplined. Soldiers were organized into large units, or legions, which were made up of smaller fighting groups called centuries and cohorts. Battle tactics were practised in training sessions.

Helmet
This was designed to protect the head, neck, and cheeks without interfering with hearing or vision.

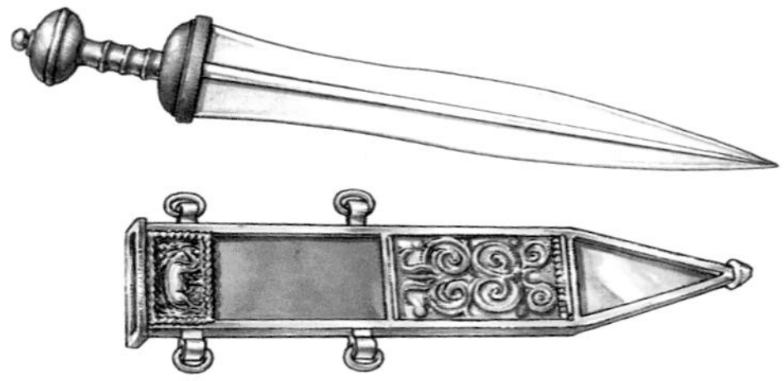

Gladius and scabbard
The legionary's main weapon was a short sword, or gladius, which was sheathed in a decorative scabbard.

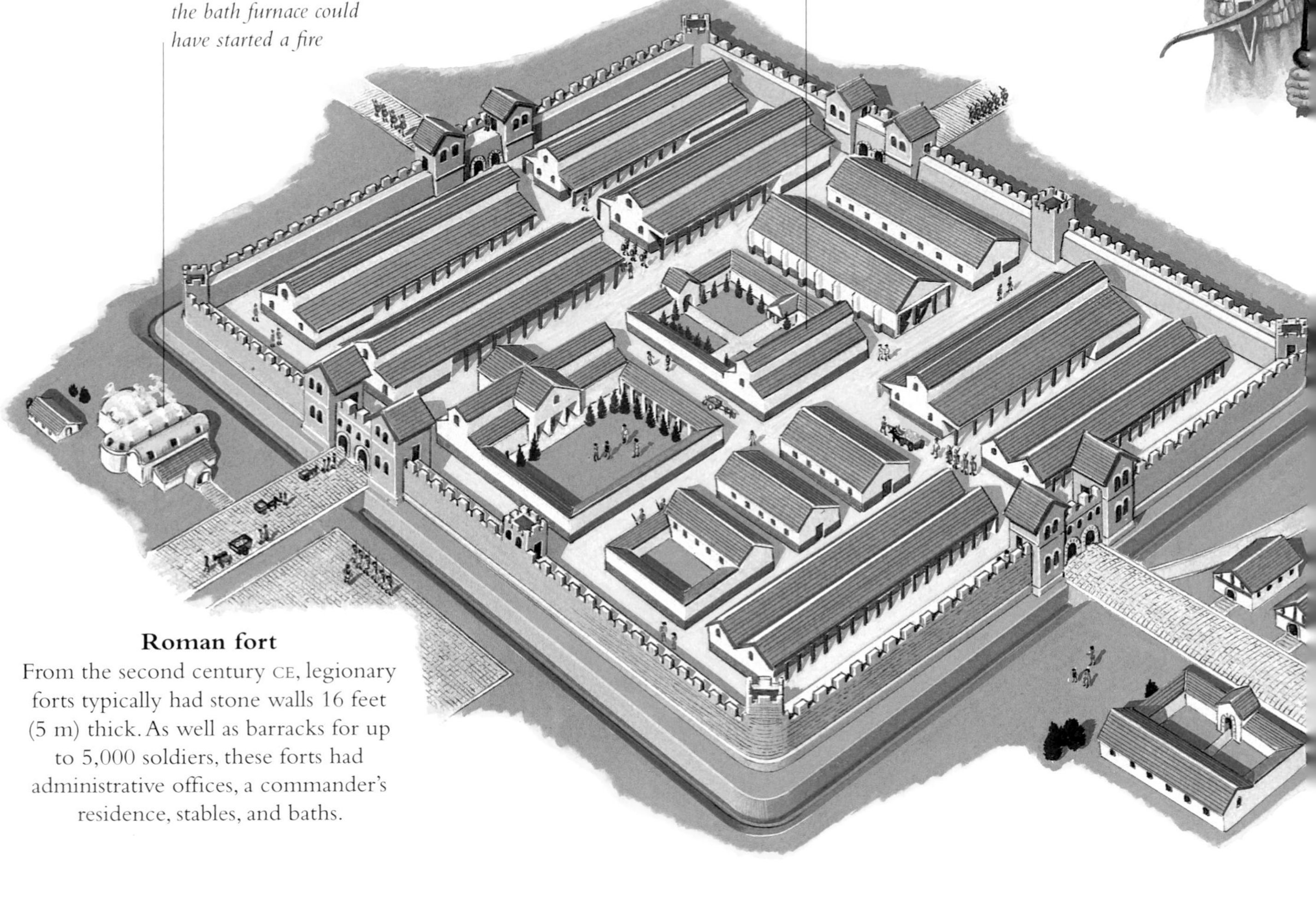

Roman fort
From the second century CE, legionary forts typically had stone walls 16 feet (5 m) thick. As well as barracks for up to 5,000 soldiers, these forts had administrative offices, a commander's residence, stables, and baths.

River crossing
Not even wide rivers proved to be obstacles to a Roman army on the march. A wooden road was laid across the decks of boats anchored to the river bed.

Legionaries carry their food rations

Centurion

Archers and cavalrymen were usually auxiliaries, who were not Roman citizens

In an emergency, soldiers rallied around their standard bearer

Houses for civilian storekeepers and innkeepers

HOW A LEGION WAS ORGANIZED

Each century had about 80 men. Six centuries joined to make a cohort. A legion was formed of 10 cohorts. The first cohort in a legion had about 800 men and would have been made up of the best soldiers.

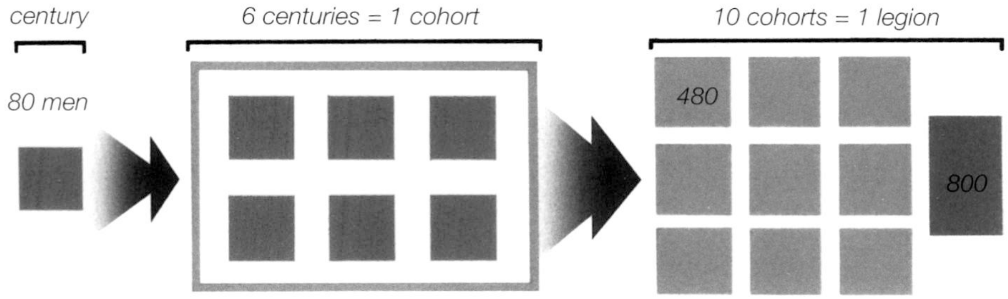

ROADS AND BRIDGES

From the fourth century BCE, the Romans built a complex network of stone roads to connect different parts of their growing empire. These roads allowed merchants, soldiers, and officials to move relatively quickly from place to place. Roman surveyors attempted to route the roads as directly as possible, so many ran in straight lines.

Bridges to last

This stone bridge in Spain was built by the Romans in around 200 CE. It carries a road 115 feet (35 m) above a river.

Surveyors

Surveyors marked out the routes of roads and the sites of bridges. They used a tool called a groma—two crossed sticks on top of a vertical staff—to work out straight lines and right angles.

Busy roads

At the height of its wealth and power, 29 paved highways radiated from the city of Rome, carrying thousands of merchants, troops, and travelers every week. Across the whole empire there were 50,000 miles (80,500 km) of paved roads.

Building a road
After surveyors had marked out the route, engineers dug parallel drainage ditches about 40 feet (12 m) apart. Construction workers—often soldiers—laid foundation stones between the ditches, with sand, gravel, or crushed stones on top. The final surface of cobbles or stone slabs was laid on top.

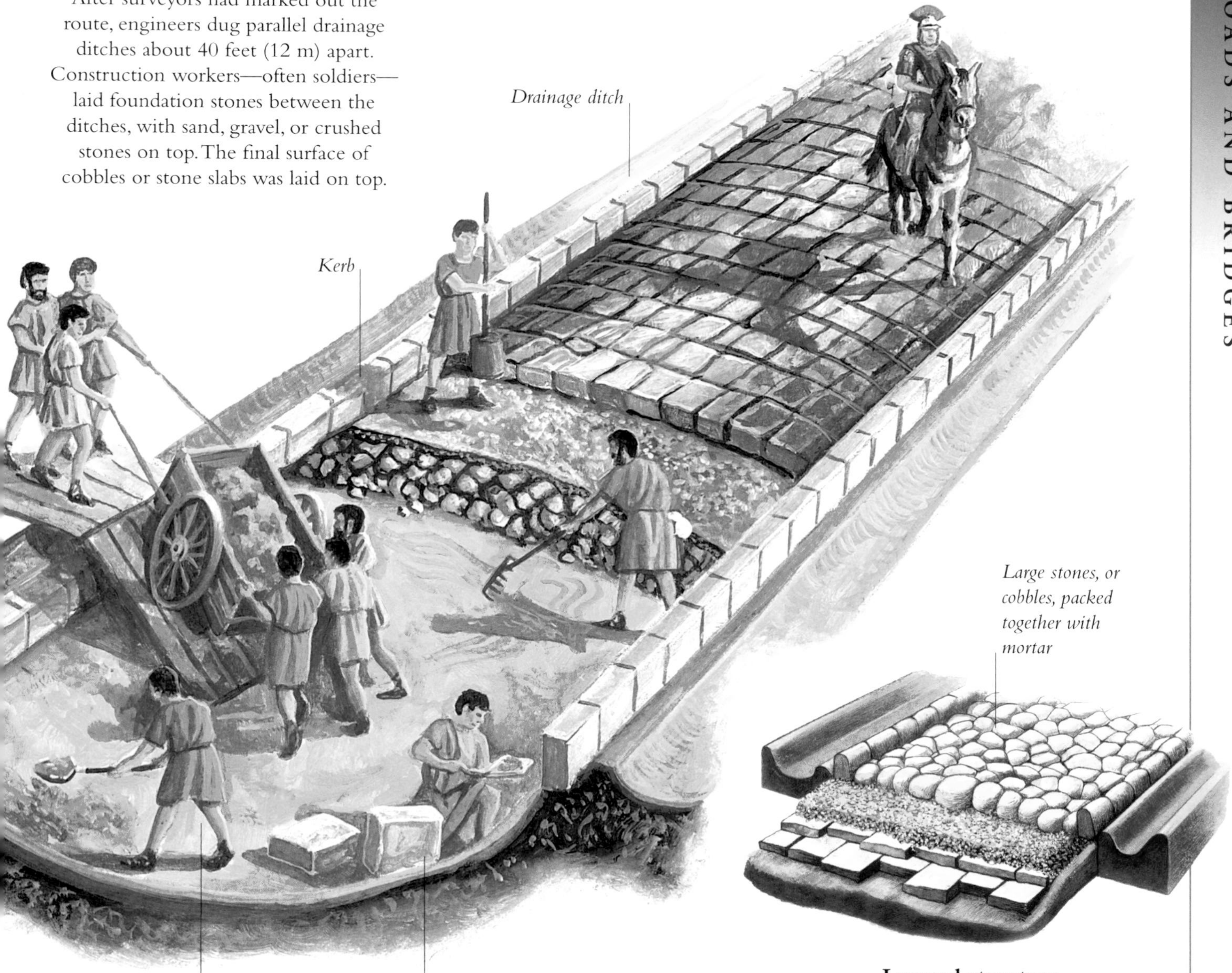

Layered structure
Foundation stones were covered in sand and gravel, with large cobbles packed together on top. Rainwater drained into ditches on either side.

BATHS AND HYGIENE

The Romans enjoyed going to the baths. They went to get clean, but there were also plenty of other attractions. The baths were good places to have a massage, go for a swim, meet friends, and play games. Some even provided food. The baths were not expensive, so everyone could afford to go. Mixed bathing was not allowed. Men and women had separate rooms. Water for steam baths was heated by furnaces, and there was also an underfloor heating system, called a hypocaust.

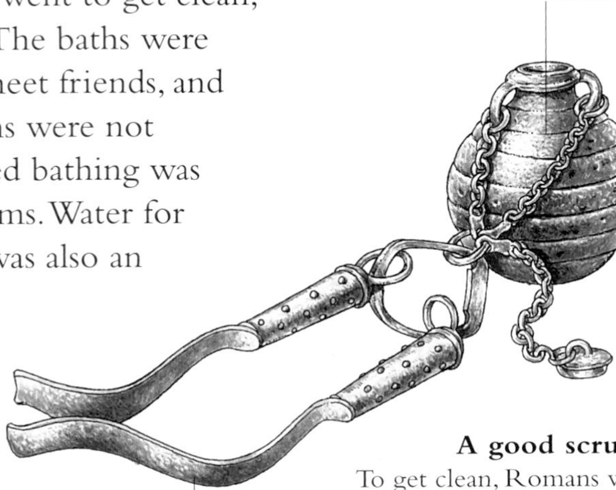

A good scrub
To get clean, Romans wiped olive oil on their skin and then scraped it off with a metal tool called a strigil.

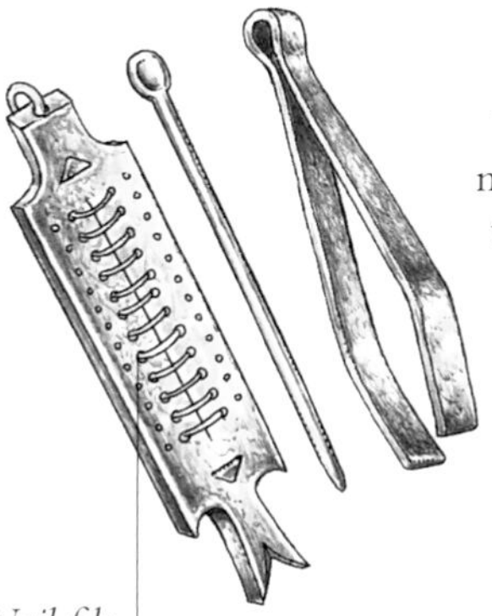

Manicure set
The Romans used nail files, tiny spoons to remove ear wax, and tweezers to remove hairs.

Stone aqueduct
Water for Rome—not least for its many baths—was carried in from the surrounding hills via large stone aqueducts. This one, below, is being constructed.

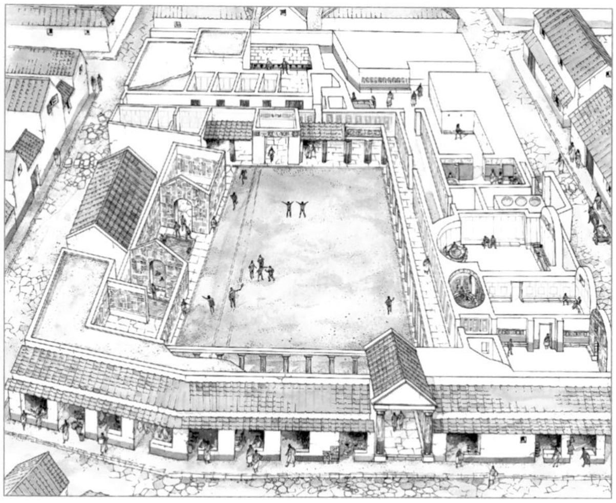

Pompeii baths
The large baths complex at the Roman city of Pompeii had changing rooms, a swimming pool, an exercise yard, and hot, warm, and cold baths.

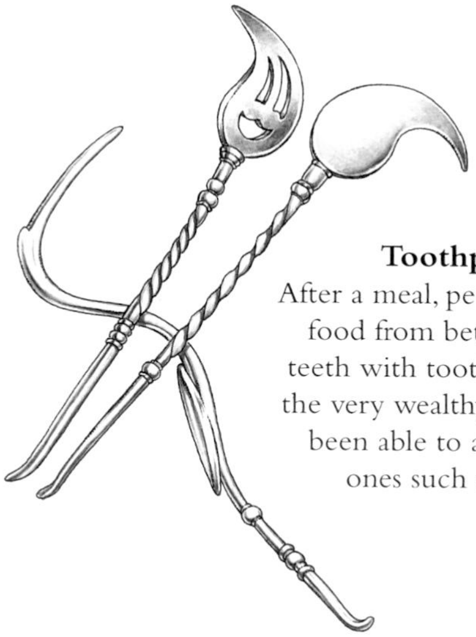

Toothpicks
After a meal, people removed food from between their teeth with toothpicks. Only the very wealthy would have been able to afford silver ones such as these!

Inside the baths
As well as baths ranging from very hot to cold, a well-equipped bath complex would also have an exercise area with weights.

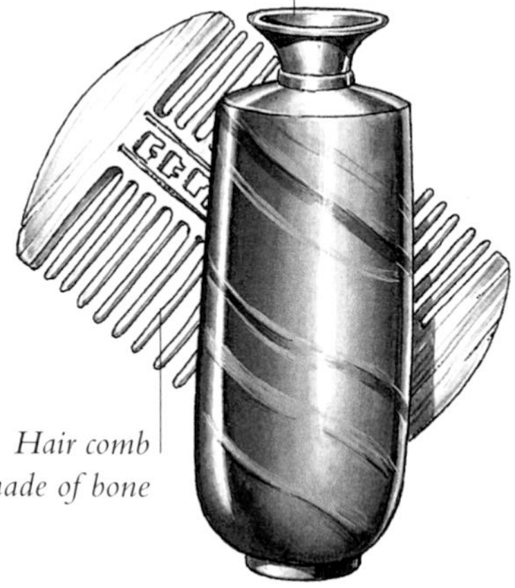

Toiletries
Women used perfumes and hair combs.

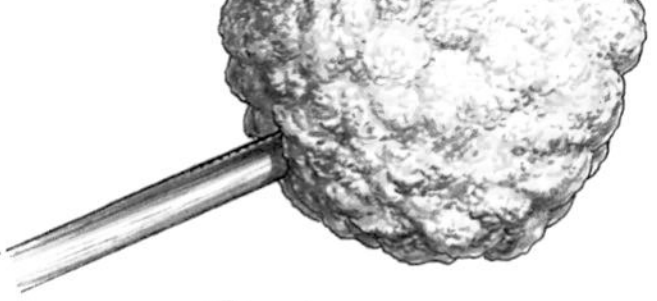

Restroom sponge
A sponge on a stick was used instead of toilet paper. The sponge was washed and dried so it could be used again.

ROMAN GAMES

Public entertainment was popular in Rome. People could see gladiatorial combat and chariot racing in large arenas called amphitheaters. Crowds of up to 50,000 attended events at the largest arenas, such as the Colosseum. Seats near the front were reserved for rich people; those at the back were for poor Romans. The winners of contests could be awarded fantastic prizes, but the losers often ended up dead! The theater was another favorite pastime. People also played games in their own homes.

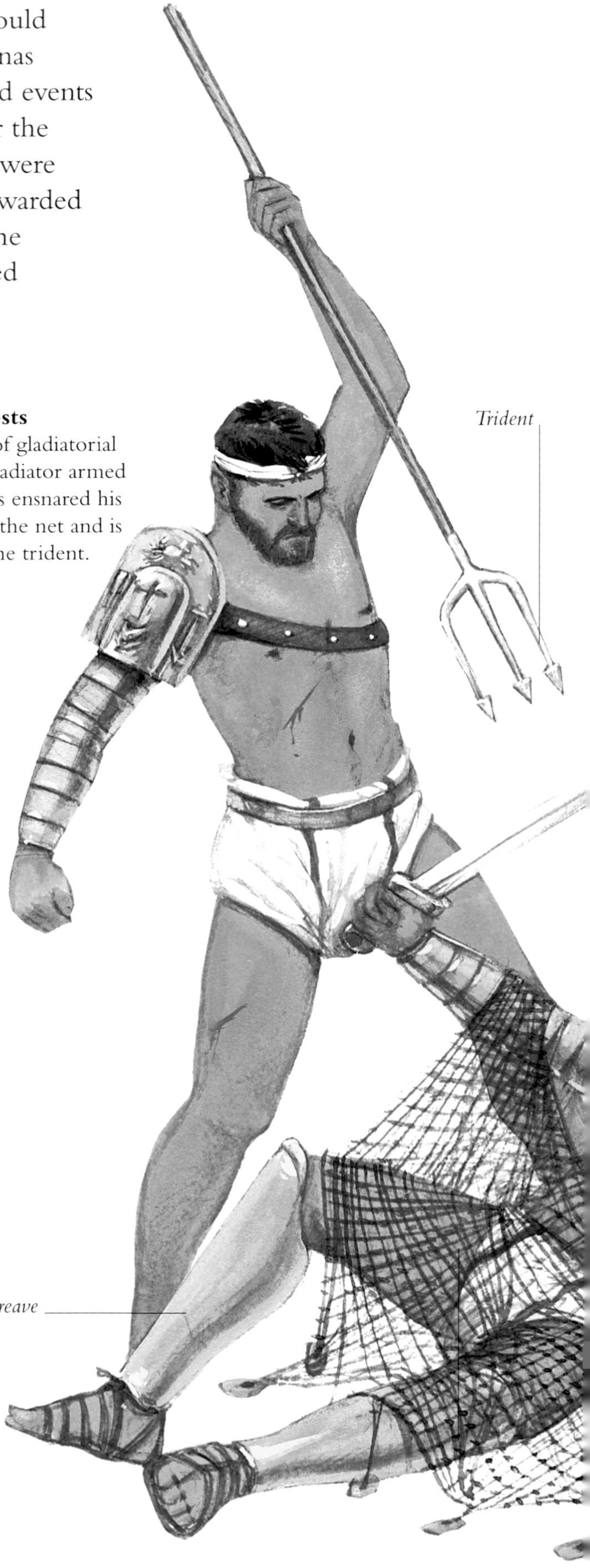

Gladiator contests
There were many varieties of gladiatorial contest. Here, a *retiarius*—a gladiator armed with a trident and a net—has ensnared his better armored opponent in the net and is about to stab him with the trident.

Trident

Bronze greave

Counters on stone tablet

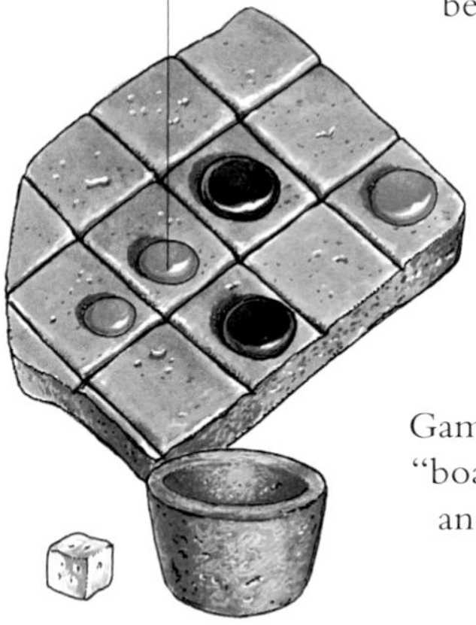

Board games
Games played with stone "boards" (*tabulae lusoriae*) and counters, or dice, were popular.

Hunting
Hunting deer and wild boar was a popular pursuit in the countryside, as shown in this Roman mosaic. Two men carry a dead deer on a pole.

Chariot races
Romans loved watching chariot racing. In one of the most popular competitions, four chariots, each pulled by four horses, raced seven laps around the arena. The charioteers did not just race—they fought to be first and people were often killed.

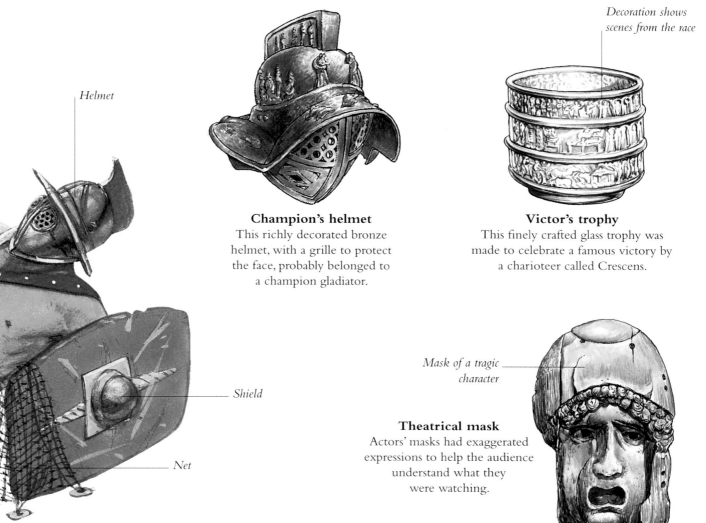

Champion's helmet
This richly decorated bronze helmet, with a grille to protect the face, probably belonged to a champion gladiator.

Victor's trophy
This finely crafted glass trophy was made to celebrate a famous victory by a charioteer called Crescens.

Theatrical mask
Actors' masks had exaggerated expressions to help the audience understand what they were watching.

THE ROMAN SHIP

Food, drink, and other goods could be moved long distances far more quickly and easily by ship than they could by land. By the second century CE many trade routes had been established across the Mediterranean Sea and even farther away. Goods arrived in Rome and other cities from places as far away as India and China.

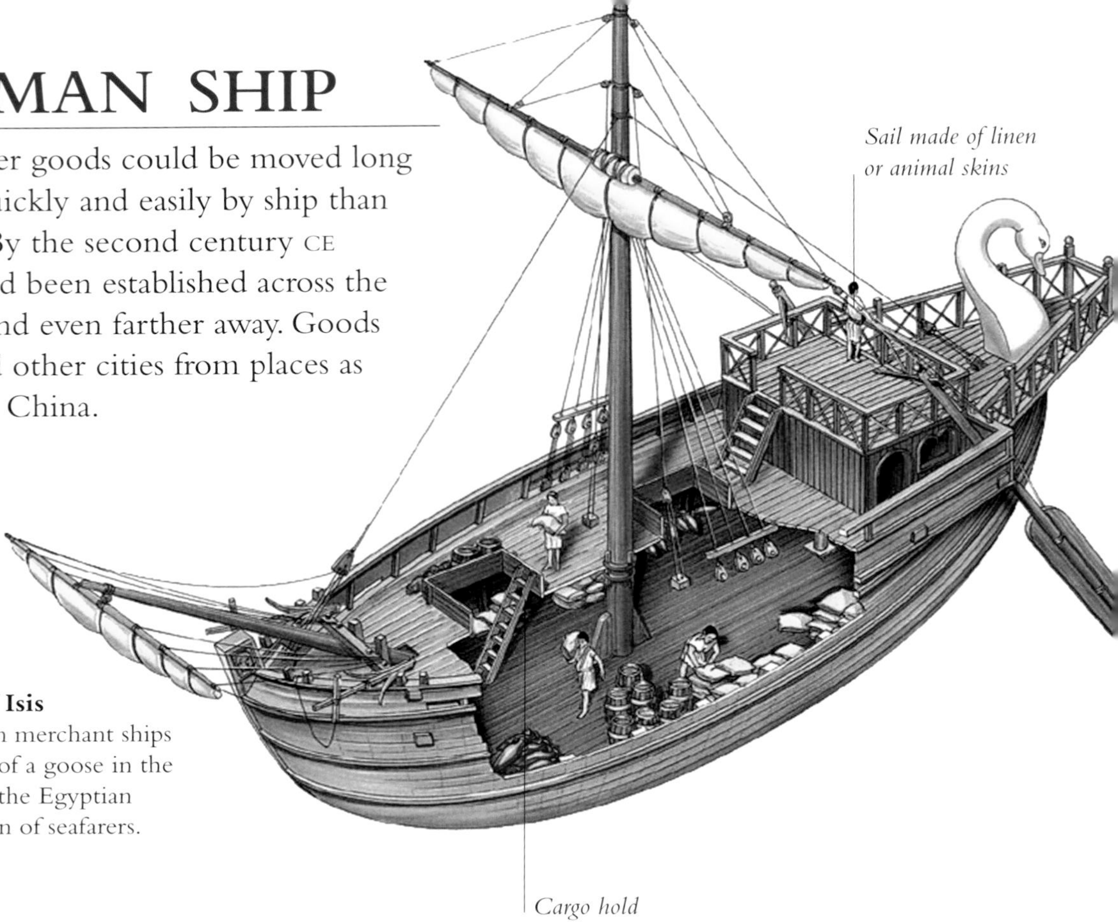

The head of Isis
It was common for Roman merchant ships to bear the head and neck of a goose in the stern. This represented the Egyptian goddess Isis, the guardian of seafarers.

Unloading cargo
Moored at the quayside, this ship is unloading its cargo of wine, olive oil, and cloth. In around 50 CE, Emperor Claudius constructed a new harbor for Rome near Ostia, the town at the mouth of the Tiber River. Fifty years later, Emperor Trajan expanded the harbor, allowing bigger ships to unload more goods for Rome.

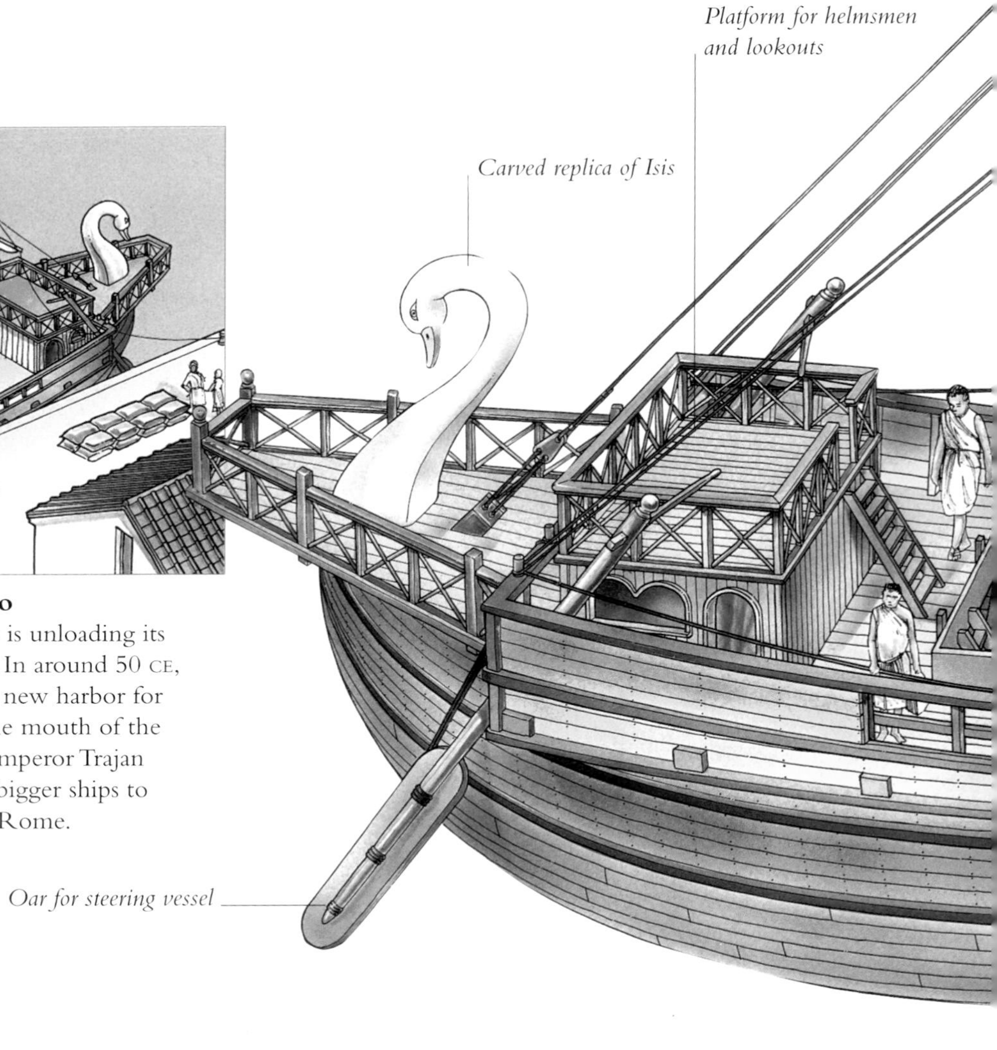

Galley
The Roman navy relied on galleys to protect the waters around the empire from pirates. As well as large sails, a galley had two banks of skilled oarsmen to drive the vessel forward.

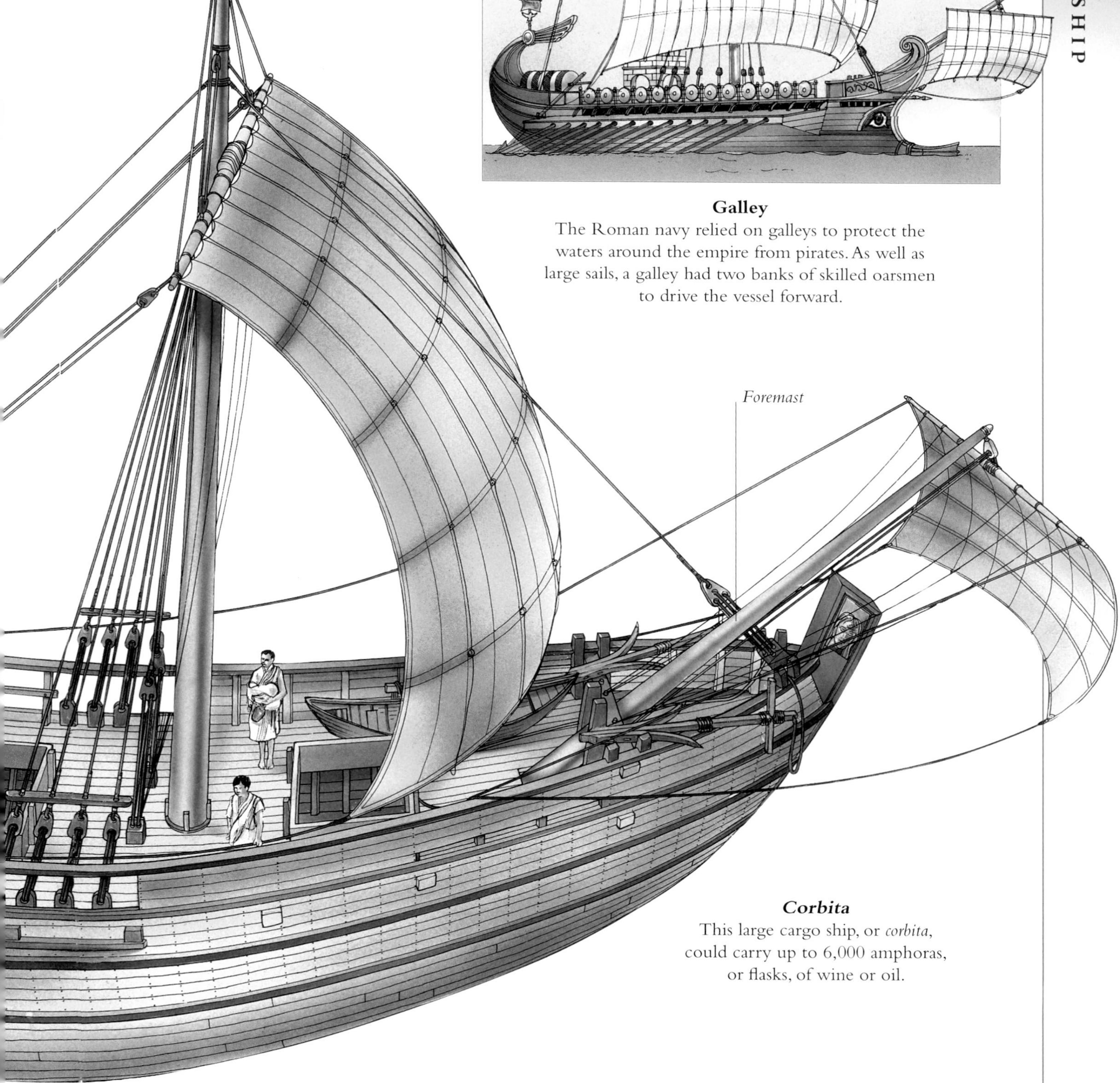

Corbita
This large cargo ship, or *corbita*, could carry up to 6,000 amphoras, or flasks, of wine or oil.

TOWN LIFE

In a typical Roman town, most buildings would be houses, shops, and workshops. The most important public area was the forum, or town square. This is where markets were held and business was conducted. Around the forum there would often be administrative offices, public halls (basilicas), and temples. No town was considered civilized if it did not have public baths. Aqueducts brought fresh water to the town, where it was distributed by underground pipes.

Herculaneum

Archeologists have excavated the town of Herculaneum, which was destroyed during the eruption of the volcano Vesuvius in 79 CE. Streets ran inland from the Bay of Naples. Some elegant villas of two and three stories had their own gardens, and many of the ordinary houses had shops or workshops on the ground floor.

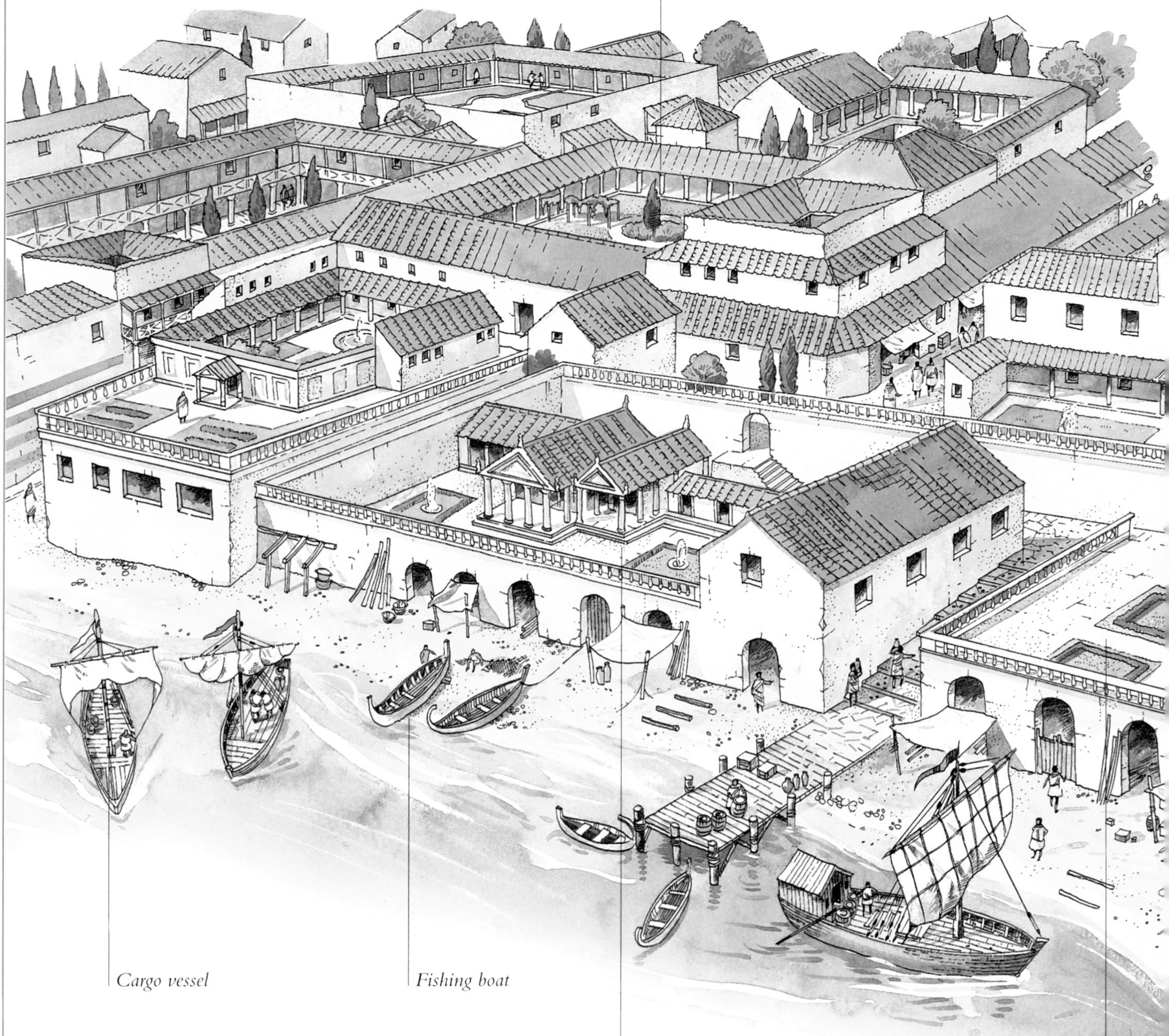

Roman coinage
Under Emperor Augustus (ruled 27 BCE–14 CE), a full range of coins was produced, from copper *quadrans* to silver *denarii* and valuable gold *aurei*.

Crowded streets
The second century CE Roman writer Juvenal described town streets as "jammed with carts and their swearing drivers, crowded with people pushing and shoving, pavements and roads filthy underfoot."

Rented shops
Many wealthy homeowners rented out the front space of their houses to shopkeepers.

VILLAS AND RURAL LIFE

Only wealthy people owned their own villas. Most city dwellers lived in multistory apartments, with the poorest people occupying the rooms near the top of the building. Unlike large villas, apartments did not have their own kitchens or bathrooms. At least in the cities there were public baths. In the countryside—where most people lived—life was even tougher for the poor.

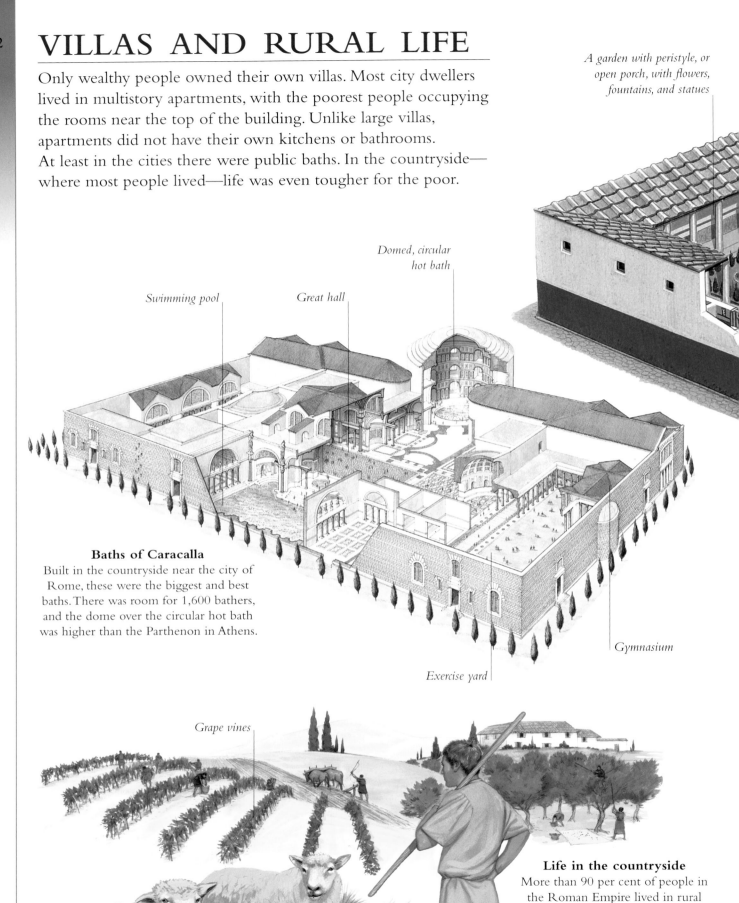

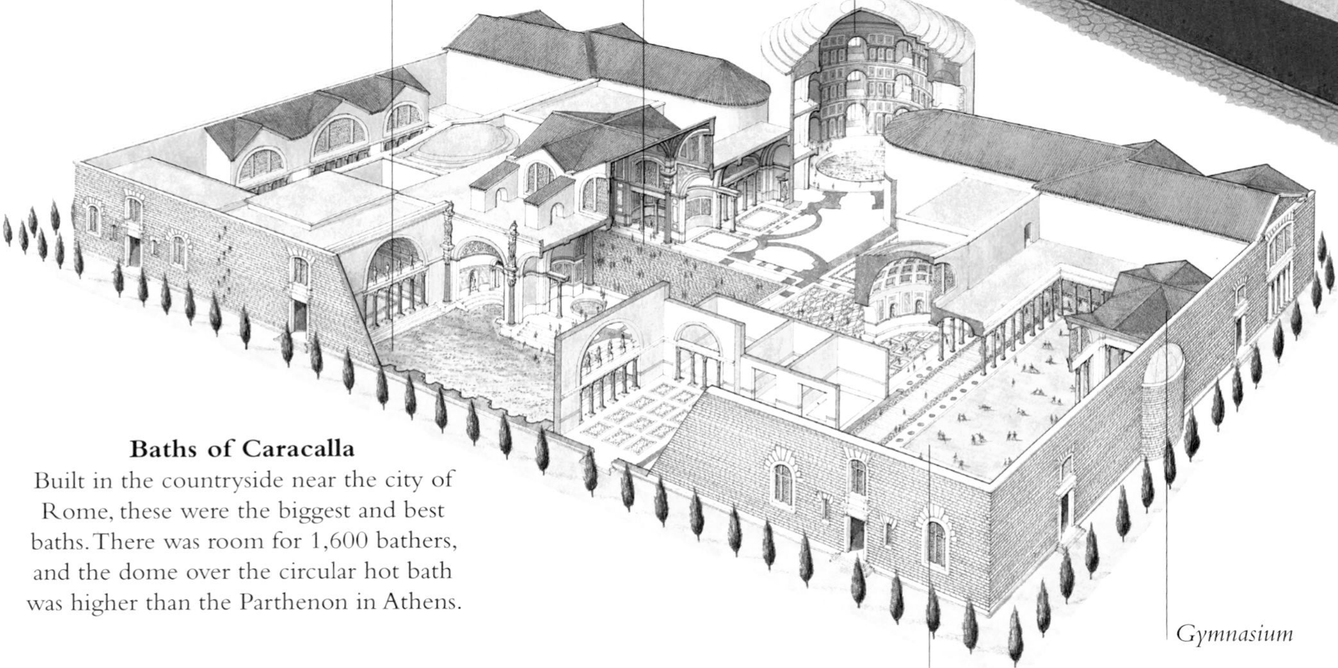

Baths of Caracalla
Built in the countryside near the city of Rome, these were the biggest and best baths. There was room for 1,600 bathers, and the dome over the circular hot bath was higher than the Parthenon in Athens.

Life in the countryside
More than 90 per cent of people in the Roman Empire lived in rural areas. Most were poor, and many were slaves. They tended sheep, picked grapes and olives, and sowed and plowed the fields.

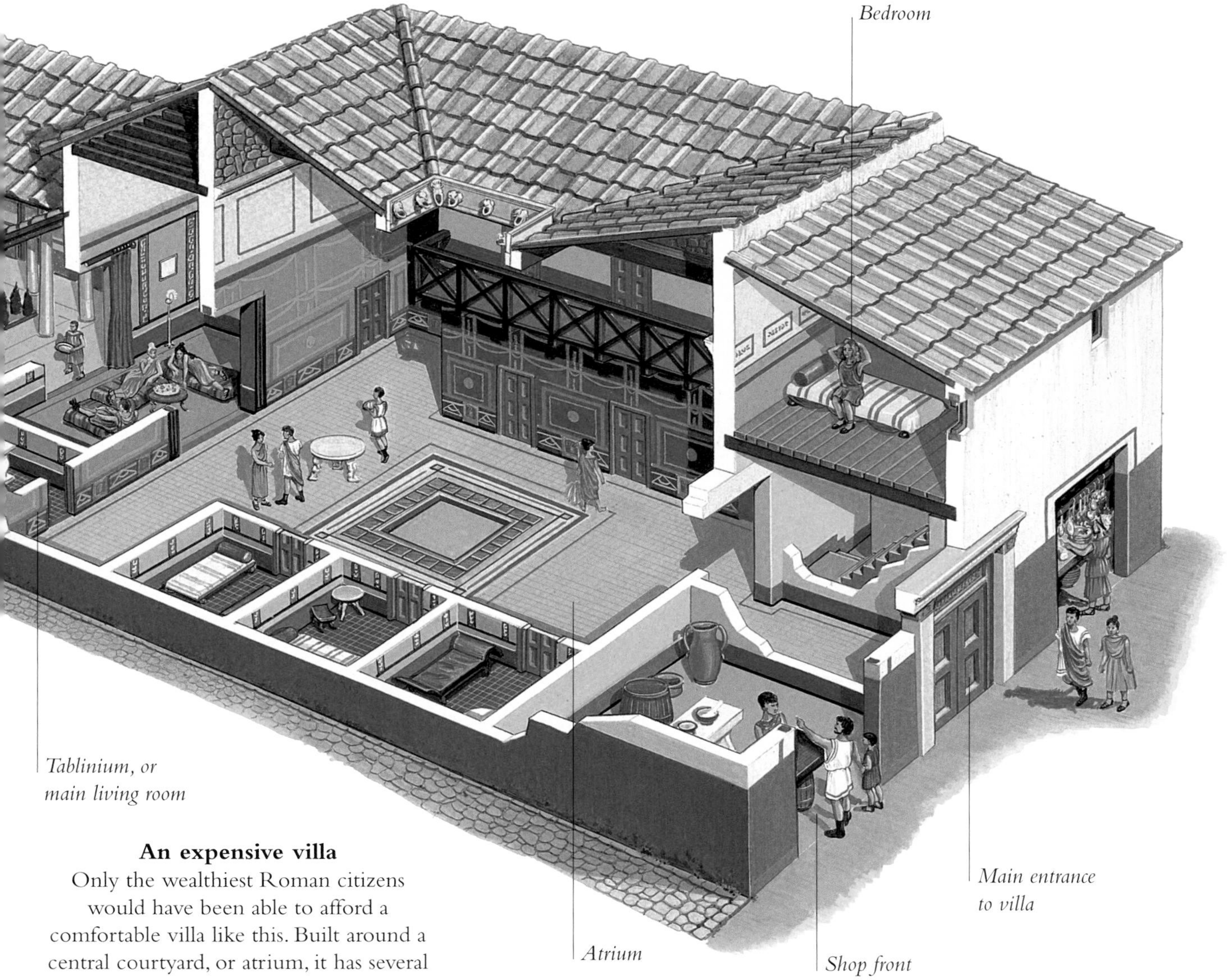

An expensive villa
Only the wealthiest Roman citizens would have been able to afford a comfortable villa like this. Built around a central courtyard, or atrium, it has several bedrooms, a living room, a kitchen, and even a flower garden.

Tools
Farm workers used iron tools like these for shearing sheep, cutting crops, and digging out weeds.

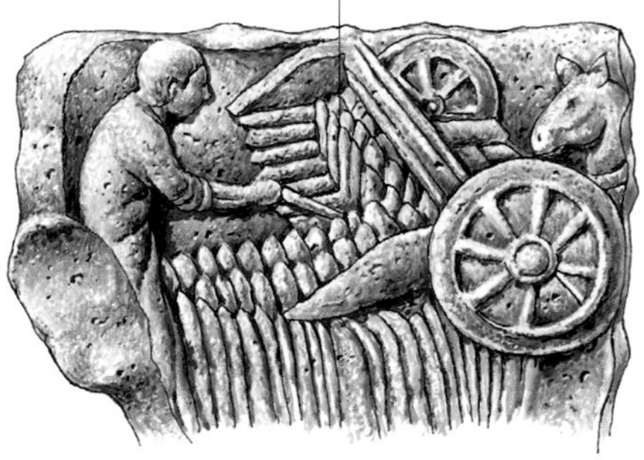

Harvesting machine
The blades of this mechanical reaper, which was powered by a walking donkey, separated ears of wheat from the stalks.

Plows
Two kinds of Roman plows. The ard was only suitable for light soils.

BUILDING TECHNOLOGY

The Romans were skilful builders. Many Roman buildings were built from bricks and concrete. Stone was expensive so it was mainly used as surface decoration. Roman builders were the first to become expert at using concrete and building arches, and they also invented the dome. Because of these techniques, buildings could be very spacious, with high roofs and big windows.

Wooden frame used to support an arched vault of brick and concrete during construction
Large timbers support structure while it is being built
Carpenter lifts wood for window frame onto scaffolding

Building a basilica
Large public buildings called basilicas were important in Roman cities. They had a large central aisle flanked by two side aisles and a high, vaulted roof.

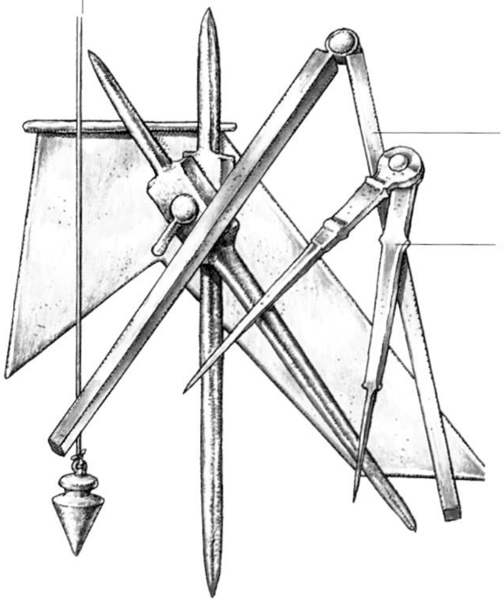
Plumb line
Folding ruler
Dividers

Architects and masons' tools
Plumb lines, dividers, right angles, and rulers were all essential tools. The folding ruler measured 1 Roman foot (29.6 cm).

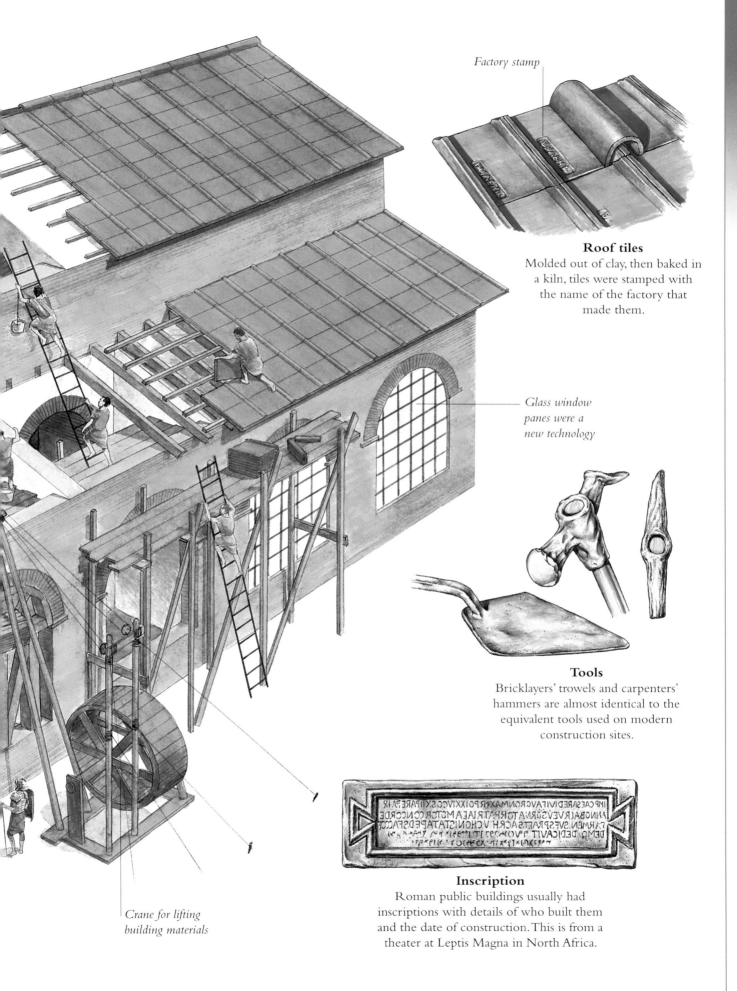

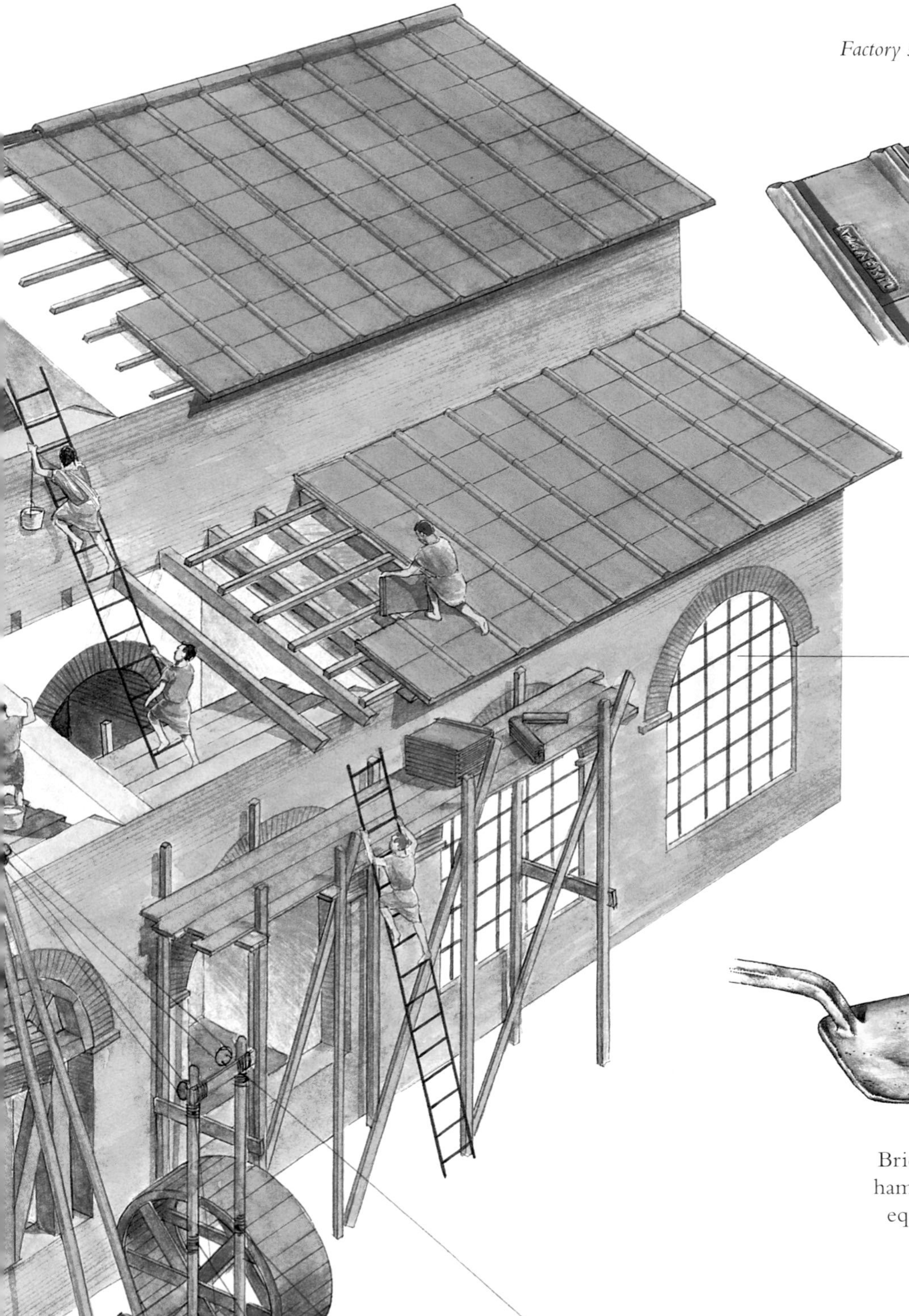
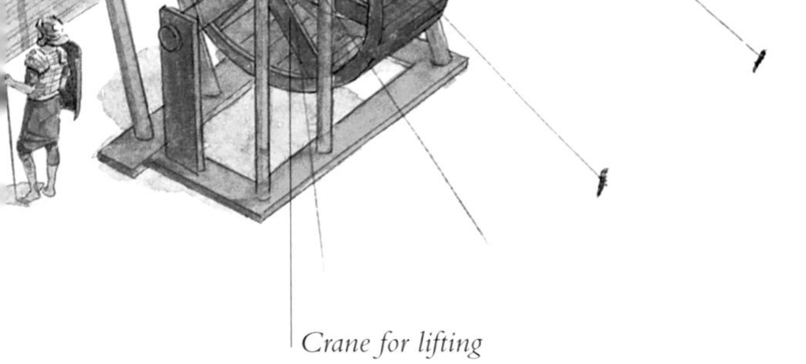
Glass window panes were a new technology
Crane for lifting building materials

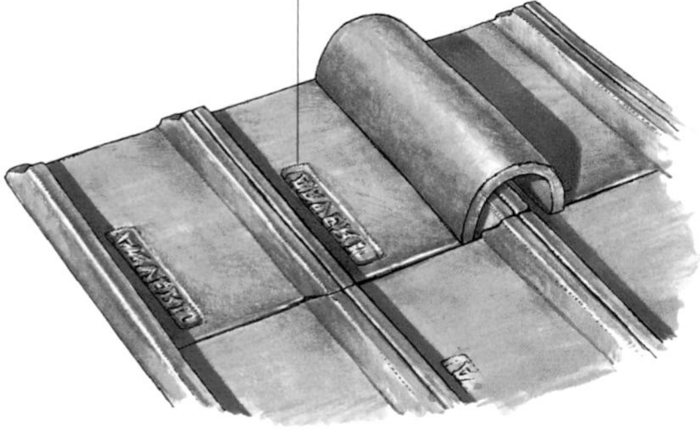
Factory stamp

Roof tiles
Molded out of clay, then baked in a kiln, tiles were stamped with the name of the factory that made them.

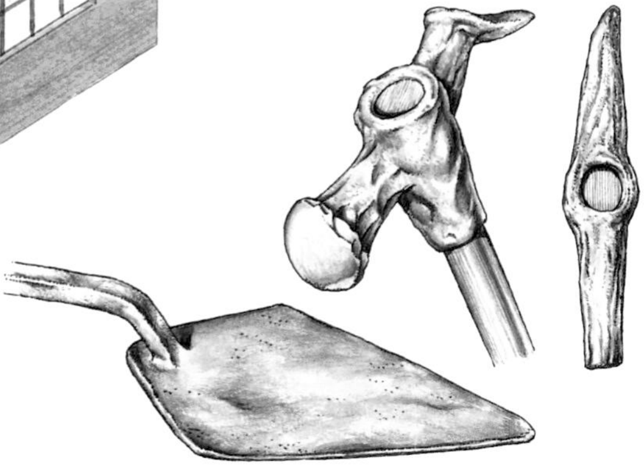

Tools
Bricklayers' trowels and carpenters' hammers are almost identical to the equivalent tools used on modern construction sites.

Inscription
Roman public buildings usually had inscriptions with details of who built them and the date of construction. This is from a theater at Leptis Magna in North Africa.

CHINA

China is the world's oldest continuous civilization. Throughout its long history—which has included invasions, famines, and numerous dramatic shifts of power—China has retained a unique artistic and cultural identity. China was largely cut off from the other civilizations of the ancient world, and new Chinese technologies matched or surpassed innovations being made in the West.

TIMELINE

2697 BCE Traditional date of the foundation of China by the semi-legendary "Yellow Emperor."

1200 BCE Earliest known examples of Chinese pictographic writing.

480–221 BCE The Warring States period. China breaks into several rival states, leading to more than two centuries of intense warfare. Some scientific and technological progress continues to be made during this period, particularly in the field of astronomy.

221 BCE King Zheng of Qin reunites China's warring states. He renames himself Emperor Shi Huangdi. An army of terracotta warriors is created for his tomb when he dies.

206 BCE Emperor Gaodi founds the Han Dynasty. This period sees the invention of paper, the compass, and the wheelbarrow, as well as advances in astronomy, the introduction of Buddhism, and the development of the Chinese civil service.

220 CE The Han Dynasty falls. China fractures into several smaller kingdoms.

589 CE China is unified once again under Emperor Sui Wendi. His short-lived dynasty is overthrown by the first Tang emperor in 618. The first major canals and the first suspension bridges are constructed during the reign of Sui Wendi.

907 CE The Tang Dynasty falls. After a few decades of instability, most of China is brought under the rule of the Song Dynasty. This is divided into two distinct periods, the Northern Song (960–1127, ruled from Kaifeng) and the Southern Song (1127–1279, ruled from Hangzhou).

Bronze horse
This small bronze figurine was made some time in the second century CE, during the late Han Dynasty.

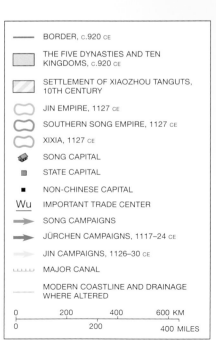

- BORDER, c.920 CE
- THE FIVE DYNASTIES AND TEN KINGDOMS, c.920 CE
- SETTLEMENT OF XIAOZHOU TANGUTS, 10TH CENTURY
- JIN EMPIRE, 1127 CE
- SOUTHERN SONG EMPIRE, 1127 CE
- XIXIA, 1127 CE
- SONG CAPITAL
- STATE CAPITAL
- NON-CHINESE CAPITAL
- Wu IMPORTANT TRADE CENTER
- SONG CAMPAIGNS
- JÜRCHEN CAMPAIGNS, 1117–24 CE
- JIN CAMPAIGNS, 1126–30 CE
- MAJOR CANAL
- MODERN COASTLINE AND DRAINAGE WHERE ALTERED

0 200 400 600 KM
0 200 400 MILES

JÜRCHEN
Linhuang
(Liao capital)
GOBI DESERT
MONGOLS
LIAO
(KHITANS)
Dading
(Jin capital)
PARHAE
Liaoyang
XIXIA
(TIBETAN-TANGUTS)
Xijin
(Beijing)
979 CE
Sanggan
Datong
Zongdu
YEN
Kaegyong
Ordos Desert
JIN
Dingzhou
Dengzhou
1115–22 CE
979 CE
Yellow River
KOREA
Ningxia
Xiaozhou
Taiyuan
Fen
Ling
Qingzhou
979 CE
Mi
Lingwu
Daming
Ji
Yellow
YELLOW SEA
Lanzhou
QIN
Ying
Kaifeng
(Northern
Song capital)
Luoyang
Qin
Lake
Hongze
Huai'an
Chang'an
QIN MTS
THE FIVE
DYNASTIES
1161 CE
Yangzhou
Nanjing
Xingyuan
Shouzou
Han
Changzhou
963 CE
Su
Lake
Tai
Xiangyang
Lu
Hu
DABA MTS
974–75 CE
Hangzhou
(Southern
Song capital)
Ningbo
HOUSHU
Kuizhou
964–65 CE
Zi
965 CE
Huanggang
Chengdu
Suizhou
Jiangling
975 CE
Qu
Yangtze
WUYUE
964–65 CE
Jiangzhou
JIANGNAN
Yangtze
Meizhou
Lizhou
963 CE
Yuezhou
Lake
Pengli
Chia
Lake
Dongting
963 CE
Longxing
Wenzhou
Tanzhou
WU
NAN CHAO
Jizhou
Fuzhou
964 CE
970 CE
CHU
Guizhou
TAIWAN
MIN
Guangzhou
SOUTHERN HAN
Nanxiang
970 CE
Qin
Yaishan
1279 CE
ANNAM
(VIETS)
SOUTH CHINA SEA
Thang Long
Qiongzhou
HAINAN

TECHNOLOGY

China was at the forefront of technological development in ancient times. For example, Chinese warriors were fighting with crossbows during the reign of the First Emperor, some 1,500 years before they were developed in the West. As well as independently inventing the wheel, agriculture, ceramics, and writing, the ancient Chinese also developed an advanced canal system and had an unparalleled knowledge of astronomy.

Hunting scenes
These scenes are from a cast bronze *hu* (storage jar) dating from around 200 BCE. The small size and delicacy of the casting suggests a high level of skill.

Bronze cauldron
This vessel is the final result of the casting process shown below.

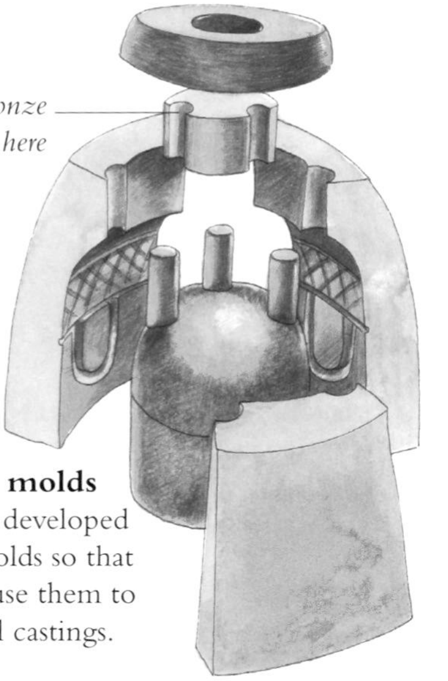
The molten bronze was poured in here

Reusable molds
The Chinese developed segmented molds so that they could reuse them to make several castings.

Laborers push open the lower gates

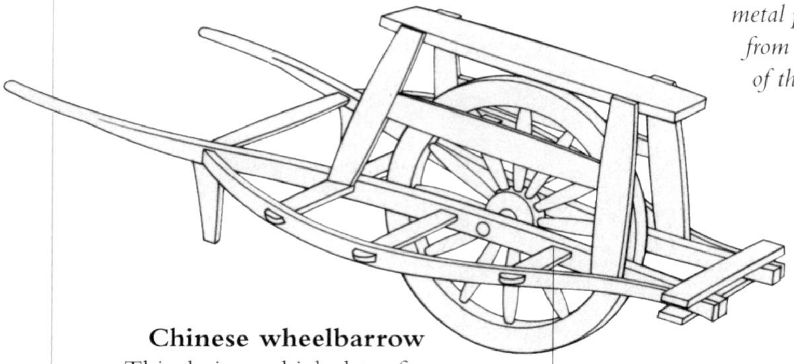
Weight is evenly distributed around the wheel

Chinese wheelbarrow
This design, which dates from the second century CE, requires far less effort to use than its western equivalent.

Vibrations shake metal pellets loose from the mouths of these dragons

Earthquake detector
The first device for measuring earthquakes was developed in China during the second century CE.

PAPERMAKING

The craft of papermaking has changed little since its invention in China in about 100 BCE. The earliest forms of paper were made from a mixture of hemp fibers and gelatin. This paper provided a poor writing surface, however, and so it was rarely used until the technique had improved.

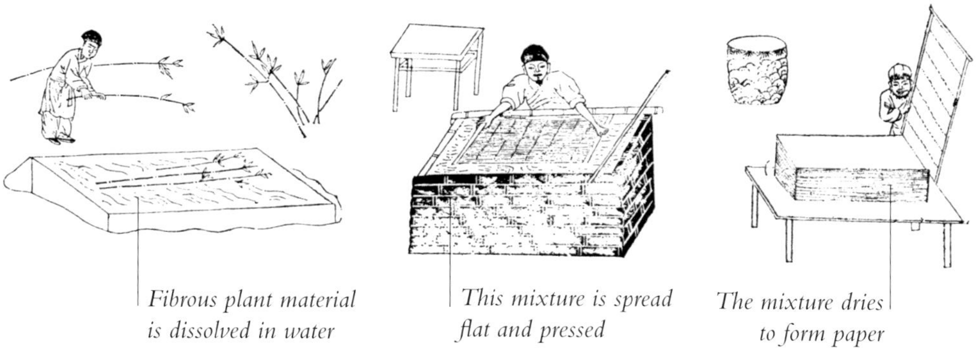

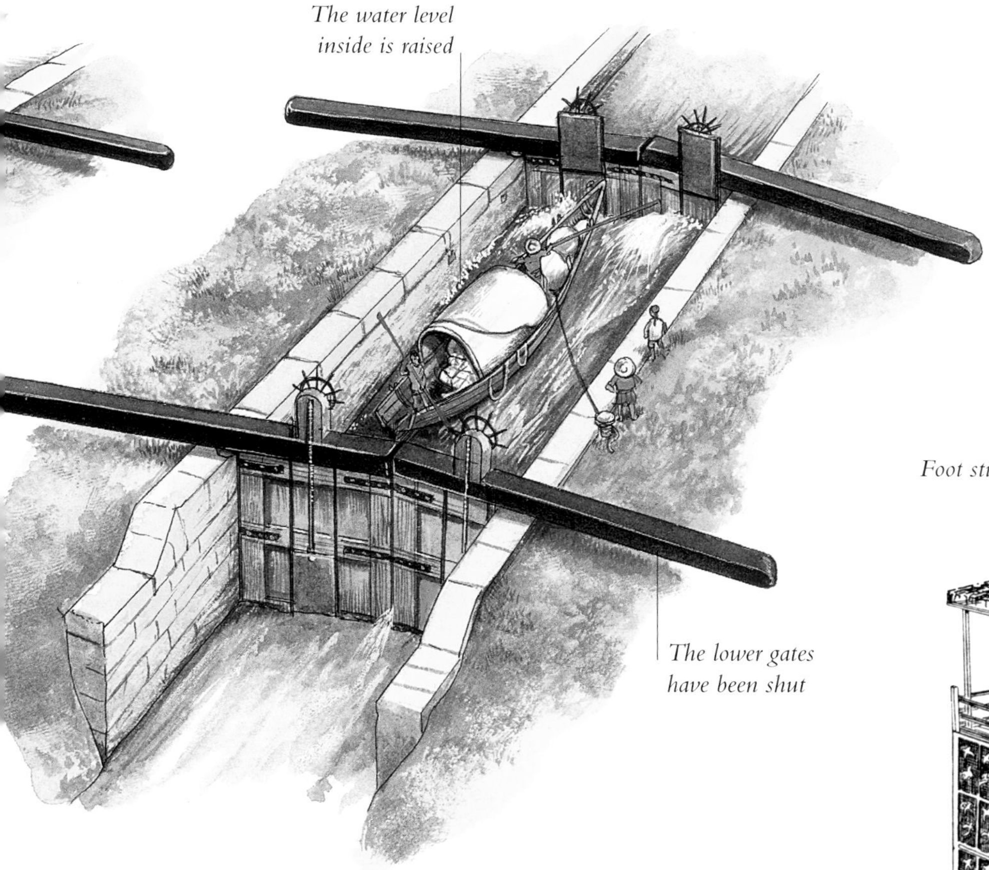

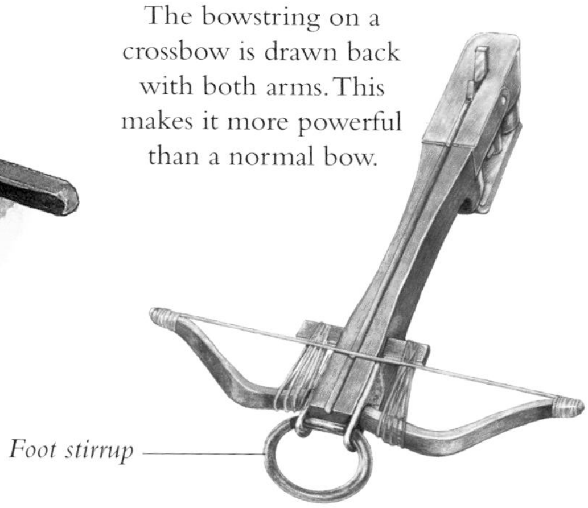

Chinese crossbow
The bowstring on a crossbow is drawn back with both arms. This makes it more powerful than a normal bow.

Canal lock
Locks allow the construction of navigable waterways that can go up as well as down. Locks of this type—called pound locks—were first built in China during the seventh century CE.

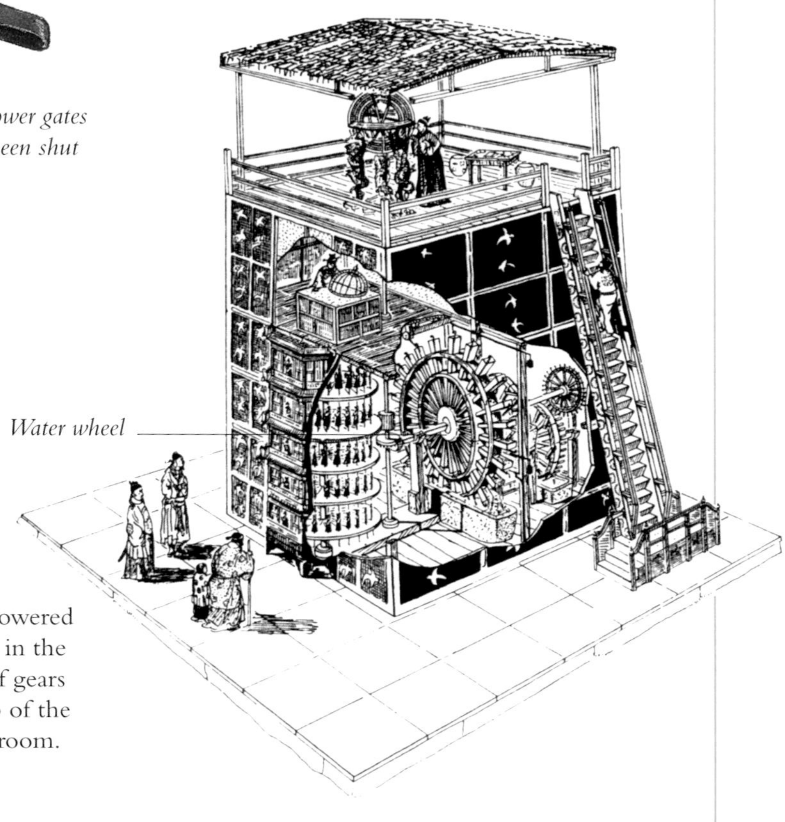

Celestial globe
This elaborate waterwheel-powered mechanism was constructed in the 11th century CE. A system of gears turned a celestial globe (map of the constellations) in an upper room.

WARFARE

Before the emergence of the first unified Chinese state under Emperor Qin Shi Huangdi, China had experienced about 300 years of almost constant warfare. This era, known as the "Warring States Period," was by no means the last major conflict on Chinese soil; the transition from one dynasty to another was rarely bloodless, and regional rebellions often required vast armies to bring them under control.

Warring States cavalry
These cavalrymen wear hardened leather and bronze armor and wield long poleaxes. Stirrups had not been invented.

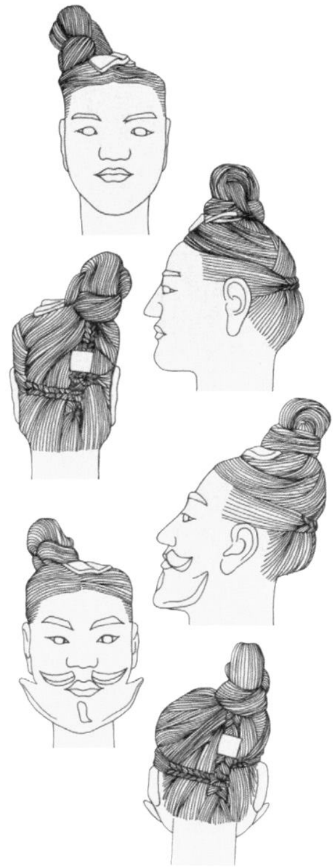

Soldiers' hairstyles
These heads of warriors from the Terracotta Army show the elaborate topknots and beards worn by soldiers.

General Zhou
This Han Dynasty warrior is wearing leather boots with metal studs, a decorative bronze breastplate, and a plumed helmet.

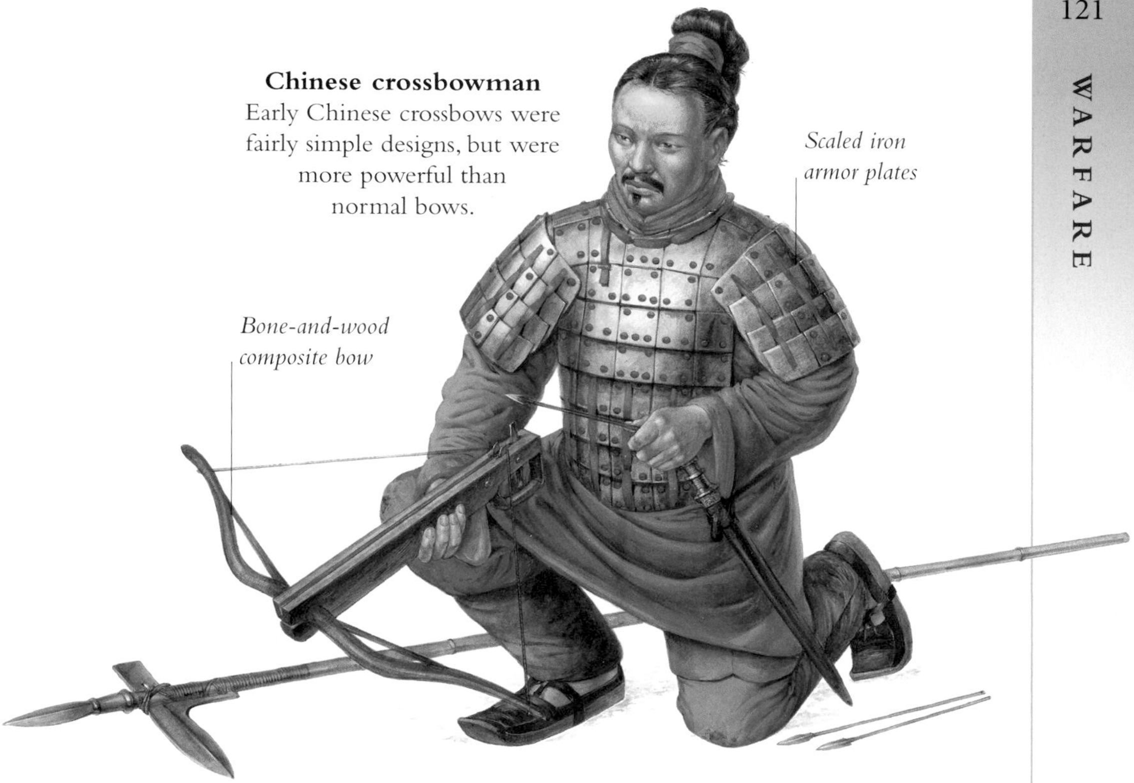

Chinese crossbowman
Early Chinese crossbows were fairly simple designs, but were more powerful than normal bows.

Emperor Song Taizu's great bridge
During the campaign against the Southern Tang (975 CE), the Song Army outmaneuvered their opponents by building a bridge of boats across the Chang Jiang.

DAILY LIFE AND WRITING

The extremely fertile soil of the Chang Jiang and Huang He valleys enabled the rapid growth of settled agricultural communities in ancient China. Cities soon emerged on these fertile plains, and with them the need for a system by which commercial and legal records could be kept. The traditional Chinese writing system developed from a number of earlier systems around 2,000 years ago and has changed relatively little since then.

Primitive Chinese writing
These partially-abstracted pictographs, shown with their traditional Chinese equivalents, were found carved into fragments of tortoise shell dating from around 1200 BCE.

Butchering an animal for a feast

Ceramic pots were made to store food

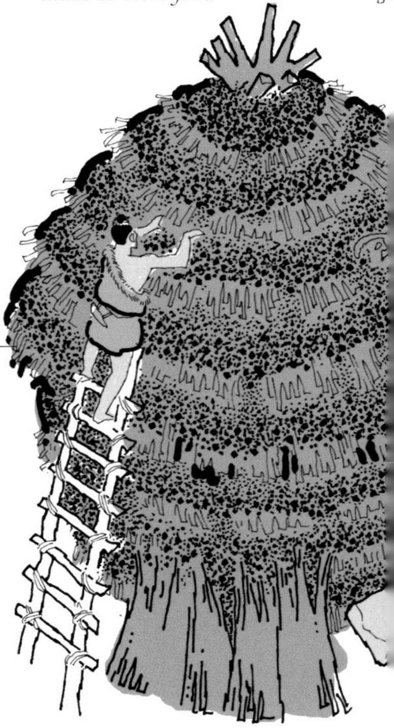

Roofs were made from matted reeds and grasses

THE CHARACTER *YONG*

The Chinese character *yong,* meaning "eternity," combines the eight basic strokes used in Chinese writing. There are several different styles of Chinese calligraphy, including some that are more loose and cursive. This type is called "regular style." It was the standard form used for official documents.

Young men prepare the timber for a new house
The head of the village was usually a woman
Domesticated dogs were used for hunting

Stone Age China
The houses of the earliest Chinese villages were made from compacted earth and woven branches. The roofs were supported by wooden posts. Most villages had fenced enclosures, where pigs were kept. Hunting was an important part of daily life.

JAPAN

Cut off from news of the innovations made in the rest of Asia, Japanese society was primarily nomadic until around 300 BCE. Once technologies such as rice cultivation and metalworking had been introduced, however, Japanese civilization progressed rapidly. Japanese culture was formed through contact with its neighbors, China and Korea, mixed with long periods of self-imposed isolation.

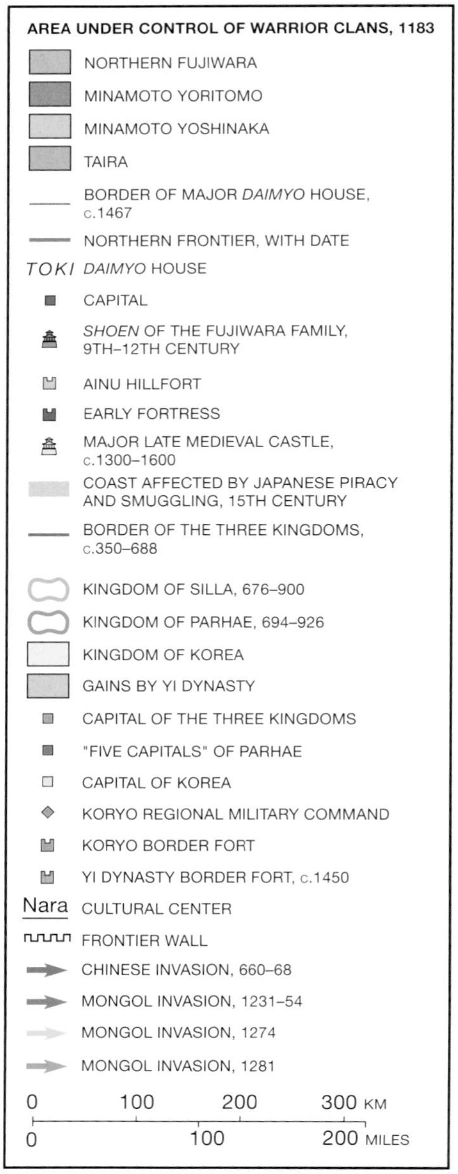

TIMELINE

300 BCE Agriculture is introduced to Japan from Korea.

300 CE Emergence of the Yamato kingdom, the first unified Japanese state.

552 CE Buddhism is introduced to Japan.

593 CE Prince Shotoku creates a centralized Japanese state, modeling its institutions and laws on those of the Chinese Han Dynasty.

850–950 CE The authority of the emperor of Japan goes into sharp decline. The country effectively breaks into numerous autonomous states ruled by samurai warlords known as *daimyo*.

1156 CE The Taira samurai clan establishes dominance over Japan. The emperor becomes a puppet for the Taira clan.

1192 CE The Minamoto clan defeats the Taira. Samurai leader Minamoto Yoritomo becomes the first shogun (military leader), who rules in the place of the emperor. The emperor becomes a purely ceremonial position.

1274 CE The Mongols attempt to invade Japan from Korea. The invasion force is contained by a Japanese army, and when the Mongols retreat to their ships a typhoon arrives and destroys them. In 1281, a second invasion fails in similar fashion.

1300–1400 CE The authority of the shogun goes into decline and Japan once again breaks into largely autonomous states ruled by samurai warlords.

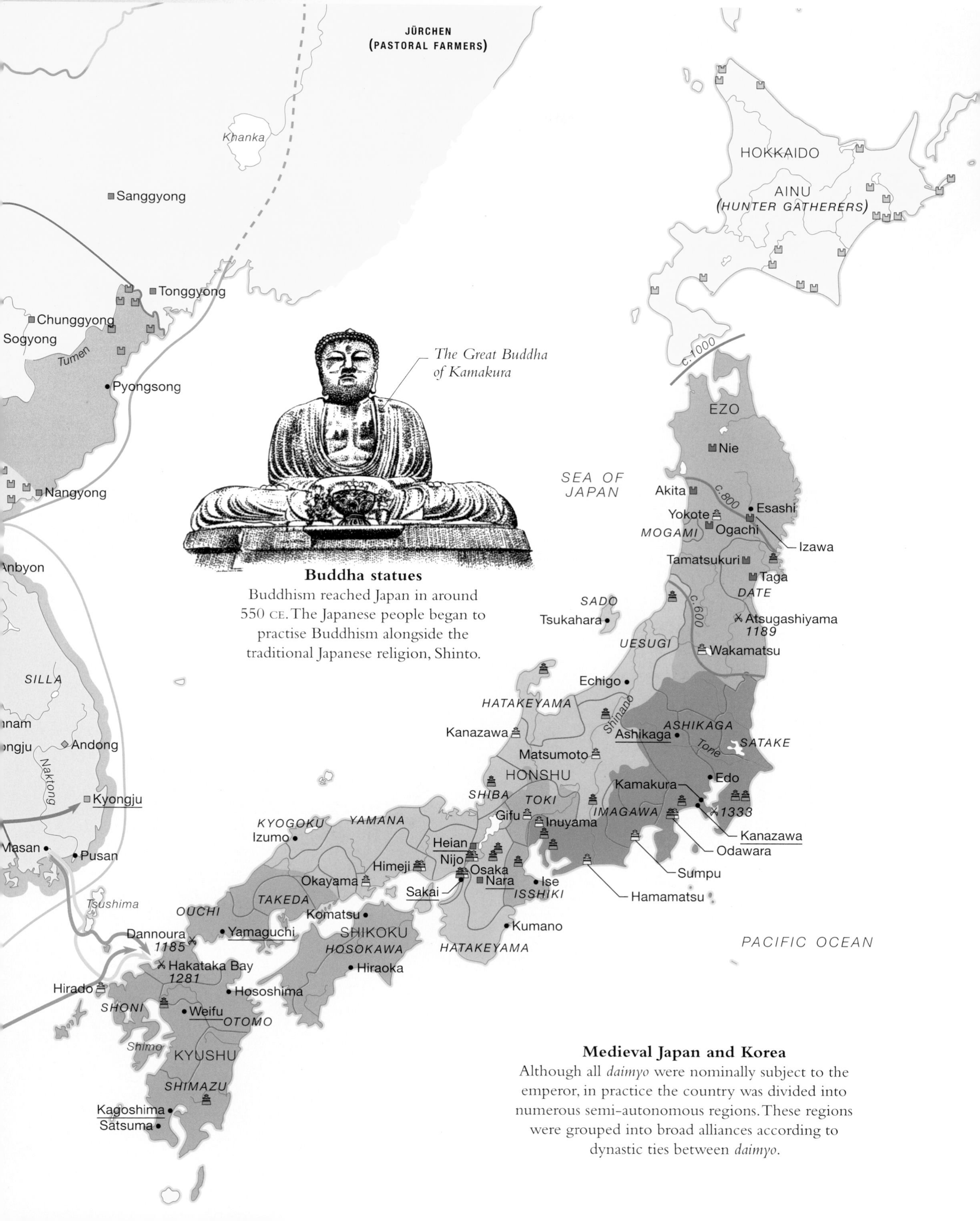

Buddha statues
Buddhism reached Japan in around 550 CE. The Japanese people began to practise Buddhism alongside the traditional Japanese religion, Shinto.

Medieval Japan and Korea
Although all *daimyo* were nominally subject to the emperor, in practice the country was divided into numerous semi-autonomous regions. These regions were grouped into broad alliances according to dynastic ties between *daimyo*.

ARCHITECTURE

Medieval Japanese buildings, with their enormous overhanging roofs and sliding wall panels, are instantly recognizable. Japanese architecture includes elements borrowed from China and Korea, as well as local inventions. Almost all buildings in medieval Japan were constructed from wood, with the use of stone limited to the foundations. This was a response to the frequent earthquakes that struck Japan: it was better to build a house that would shake and bend than one that would crack and collapse.

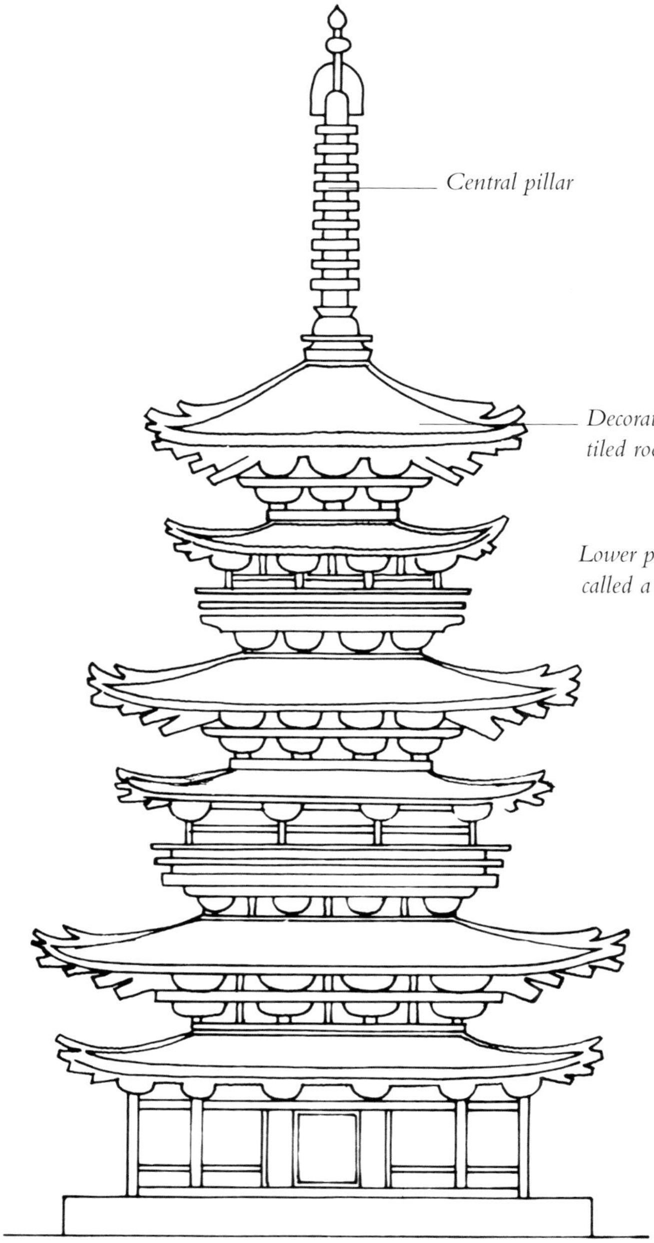

The Yakushiji Pagoda
Built in 720 CE, this 115-foot-high (35 m) pagoda is one of the finest examples of traditional Japanese architecture.

Himeji Castle
Daimyo built grand castles that served as both defensive strongholds and personal residences. This example dates from the 14th century CE. Like all Japanese buildings, it was built mostly from wood.

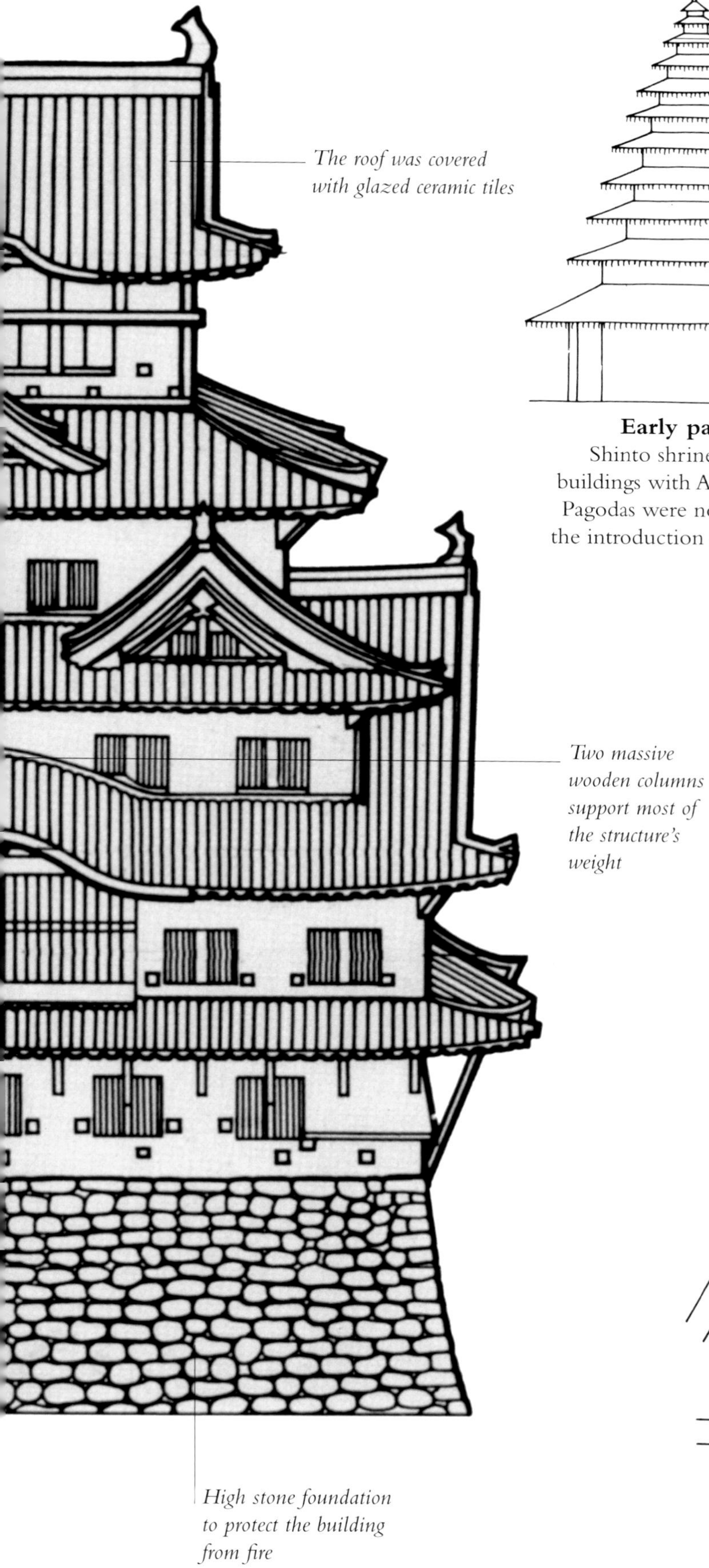

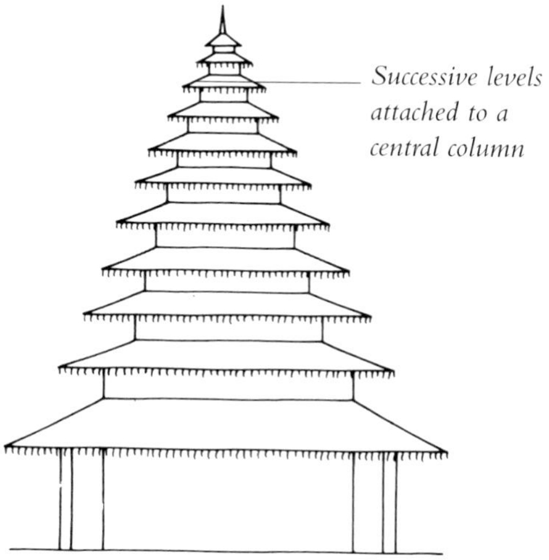

Early pagoda
Shinto shrines are low buildings with A-frame roofs. Pagodas were not built until the introduction of Buddhism.

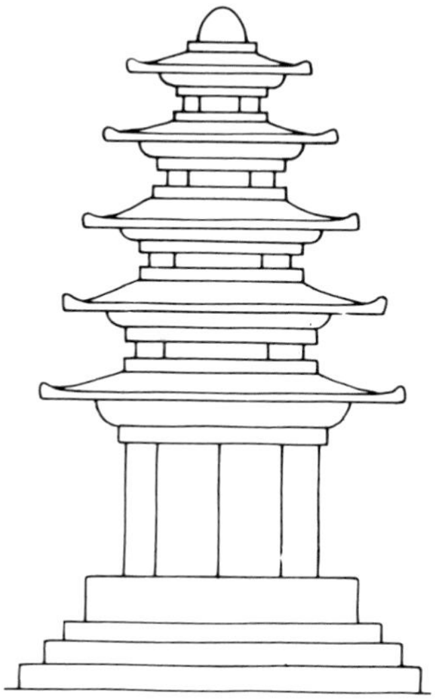

Seventh-century pagoda
The multi-leveled roofs of pagodas are ornamental. They do not normally correspond to internal floors.

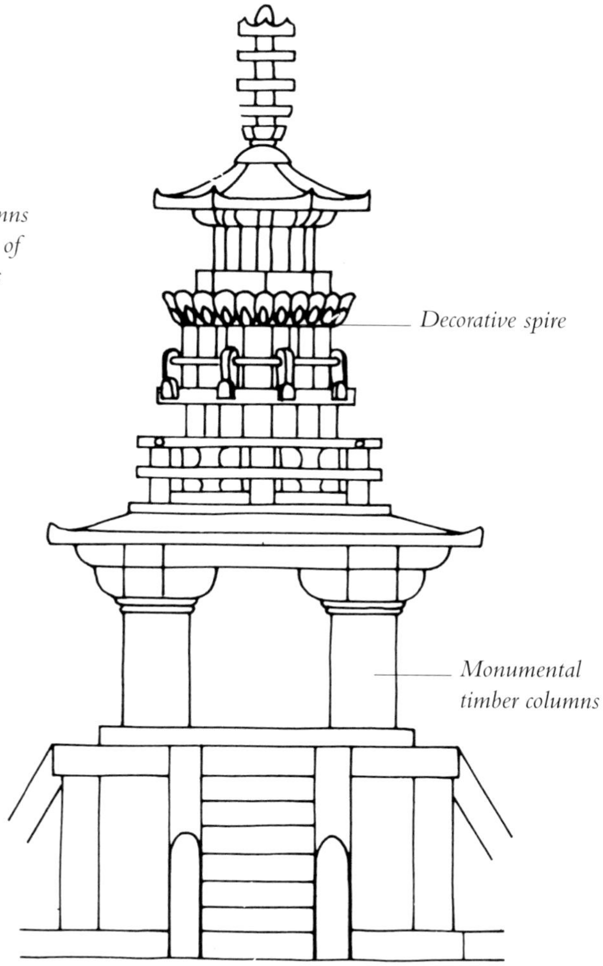

Stupa-style pagoda
The design of pagodas was descended from that of Nepalese stupas—shrines built to house Buddhist relics.

INDIA

The Indian subcontinent (present-day India, Pakistan, Sri Lanka, and Bangladesh) is a vast and populous region, home to about one in five of the world's population—a proportion that is thought to have remained stable since the Bronze Age. The many peoples of the subcontinent represent a wide variety of cultural, linguistic, and religious groups, each with its own cultural traditions.

Qutb Shahi tomb
This imposing mausoleum was built to hold the remains of one of the Muslim rulers of Golconda in central India. Islam arrived in India in the seventh century CE.

Buddhist relics
This copper casket was made in 127 CE to hold bone fragments thought to have been relics of Gautama Buddha. Buddhism was founded in India around the sixth century BCE.

Mughal pottery
This richly decorated pot, probably the base of a *hookah* (tobacco pipe), dates from the period of Mughal rule in northern India. The Muslim Mughal emperors were generous patrons who oversaw a golden age of Indian art and culture.

TIMELINE

900 BCE Unified city-states are established on the plains around the Ganges River.

500–400 BCE The epic poem *Mahabharata*, is composed by the semi-legendary poet Vyasa. This poem, which focuses on the life of Krishna, is one of the defining documents of the Hindu religion.

400-300 BCE The *Ramayana*, another epic poem, is composed by Valmiki. The poem details the life and trials of Prince Rama. The poem records many important aspects of Hindu philosophy and thought.

322–185 BCE Most of the Indian subcontinent is ruled by the Mauryan Empire, which reaches its peak under Emperor Ashoka (269–232 BCE).

230 BCE–220 CE Southern India is brought under the control of the Satavahana Empire, which originated as a vassal of the Mauryan Empire. For most of its existence it is in a state of conflict with the northern Kushan Empire.

250–550 CE Northern India is ruled by the Gupta Empire. At its greatest extent the empire's territory extends as far south as Tamil Nadu.

650–750 CE The first Muslim settlements are established on the western coast of India by Arab seafaring traders.

1000 CE
Mahmud of Ghazni, a Turkic Muslim military leader, invades what is now Pakistan and northwestern India. This is the beginning of significant Muslim settlement in northern India.

EMPIRE OF HARSHA, 606–47
CAMPAIGN OF HARSHA
GHURID EMPIRE, 1206
LINE OF DIVISION OF GHURID EMPIRE, 1206
DELHI SULTANATE UNDER QUTB-UB-DIN, 1206–10
DELHI SULTANATE UNDER ILTUTMISH, 1211–36
DELHI SULTANATE UNDER ALA-UD-DIN KHALJI, 1236–1316
DELHI SULTANATE UNDER MUHAMMAD IBN TUGHLUK, 1325–51
INDEPENDENT AREA UNDER THE KHALKI AND TUGHLUK DYNASTIES
DELHI SULTANATE UNDER SIKANDER LODI, 1489–1517
MAXIMUM EXTENT OF VIJAYANAGRA, 1485
CAMPAIGN OF ALA-UD-DIN, 1296–1311
INVASION OF TIMUR

SIGNIFICANT BUILDINGS AND PLACES OF WORSHIP
BUDDHIST TEMPLE OR STUPA
HINDU TEMPLE
JAIN TEMPLE
MOSQUE
PALACE

0 100 200 300 400 KM
0 100 200 300 MILES

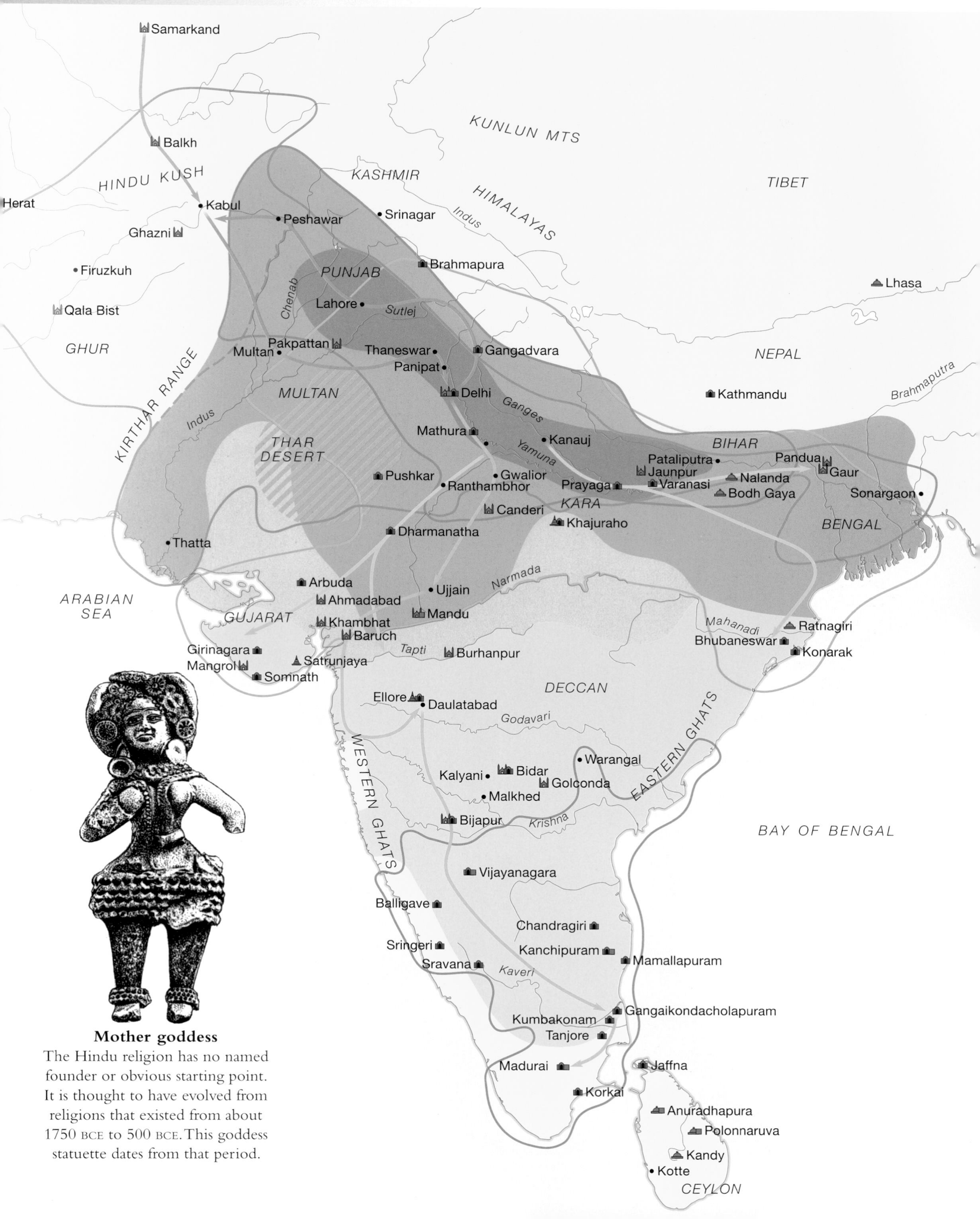

Mother goddess
The Hindu religion has no named founder or obvious starting point. It is thought to have evolved from religions that existed from about 1750 BCE to 500 BCE. This goddess statuette dates from that period.

HINDU GODS AND GODDESSSES

Three major religious traditions developed within Hinduism: Shaivism, Vaishnavism, and Shaktism—with devotions centered on the gods Shiva, Vishnu, and Devi, respectively. Although the group of major gods worshiped in each tradition is more or less the same, the powers credited to each god vary. In addition to the major gods and goddesses, the Hindu religion includes hundreds of minor gods.

Nandi
In many traditions, Shiva is carried around and attended on by a divine white bull called Nandi.

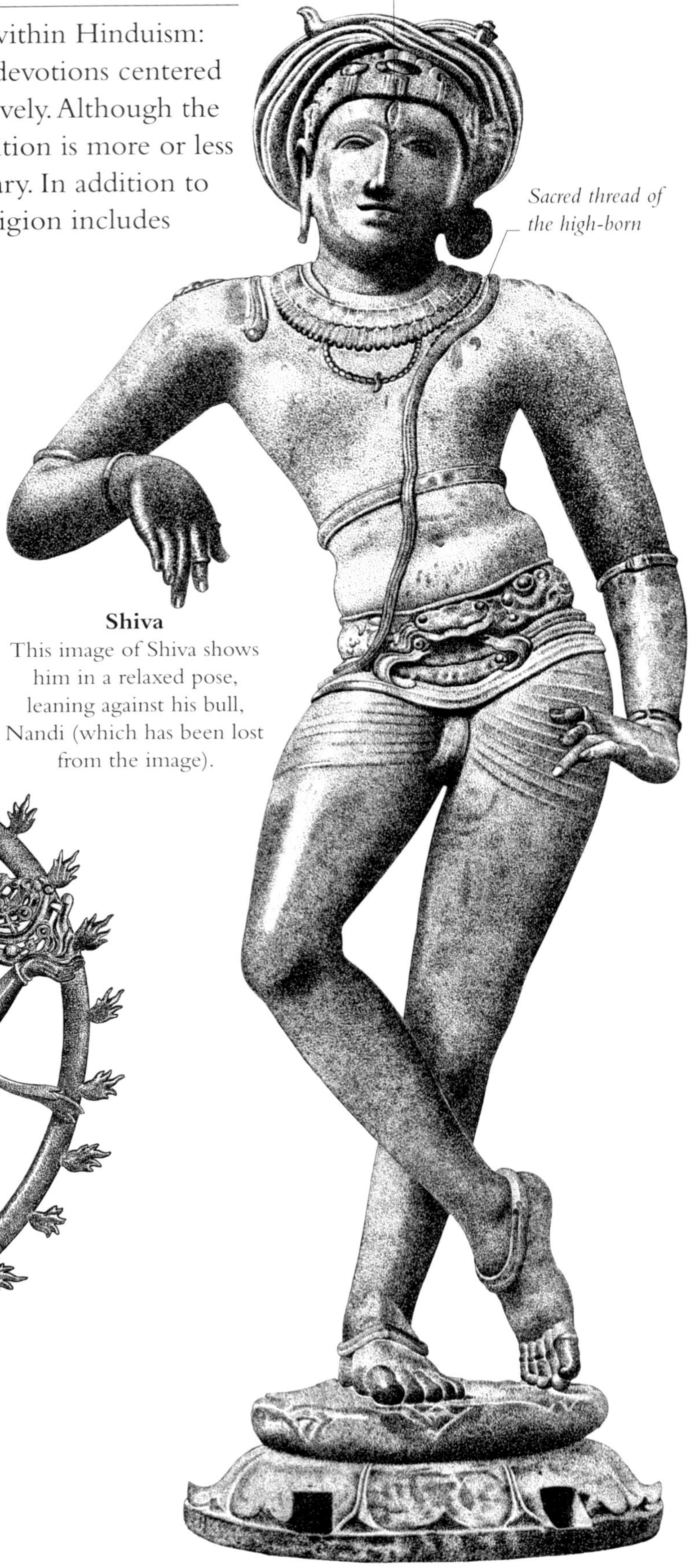
Matted hair coiled round the head like a turban
Sacred thread of the high-born

Shiva
This image of Shiva shows him in a relaxed pose, leaning against his bull, Nandi (which has been lost from the image).

The flames of the end of the world

The King of Dancers
Each Hindu god has different aspects. This is Shiva as the dancer who brings the end of a cycle of existence.

Garuda
Each Hindu god has a "vehicle" on which they ride. Vishnu's vehicle is the bird-god Garuda.

Vishnu
Depictions of the god Vishnu show him with four arms.

Rama
One of the best-known incarnations (avatars) of Vishnu is the warrior prince Rama. The legends associated with Rama and his wife Sita are told in the epic poem known as the *Ramayana*.

AFRICA

Inhabited since the dawn of human history, Africa holds an extraordinary variety of different cultures. During the ancient and medieval periods, many civilizations rose and fell across the continent. Natural divides of desert and rain forest enabled vastly different ways of life to flourish, including communities of urbanized farmers, seafaring merchants, nomadic herdsmen, and hunter-gatherers.

TIMELINE

6000–3000 BCE Wheat, barley, and millet are cultivated for the first time in the highlands of Ethiopia. These innovations spread to other parts of Africa before the Sahara Desert forms.

2150 BCE Foundation of the Nubian Kingdom of Kerma. It lasts until 1500 BCE, when it is conquered by the Egyptians.

1000 BCE The earliest-known complex agricultural societies develop in sub-Saharan Africa. The largest of these is the Nok culture of Nigeria, known for its terracotta statues.

770–712 BCE The Kingdom of Nubia, led by King Kashta and later by King Piye, conquers Egypt.

500 BCE Bantu-speaking peoples begin to spread east and south from their homeland in West Africa.

100 CE The Kingdom of Aksum is founded in what is now Ethiopia.

400 CE Urban societies develop along the Niger River in Mali. They are enriched by the trans-Saharan trade routes.

650–700 CE Arab Muslims conquer Egypt and upper Nubia. Arab traders begin to roam south down the east coast of Africa.

700 CE The Kingdom of Ghana is established in West Africa.

979 CE The mosque and madrassa of al-Azhar is founded in Cairo. It grows into one of the most respected centers of learning in the Muslim world.

1200 CE The Kingdom of Great Zimbabwe emerges in southern Africa.

1230 CE The Kingdom of Mali becomes a wealthy and powerful state, peaking in the 1260s under King Mansa Musa.

1415 CE The Portuguese capture the Moroccan port of Ceuta, marking the beginning of the European colonization of Africa.

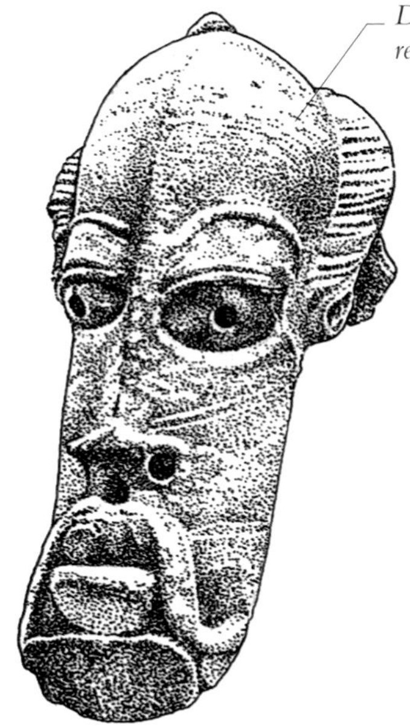

Nok sculpture
This tin sculpture was made by the Nok culture of northern Nigeria in around 200 BCE.

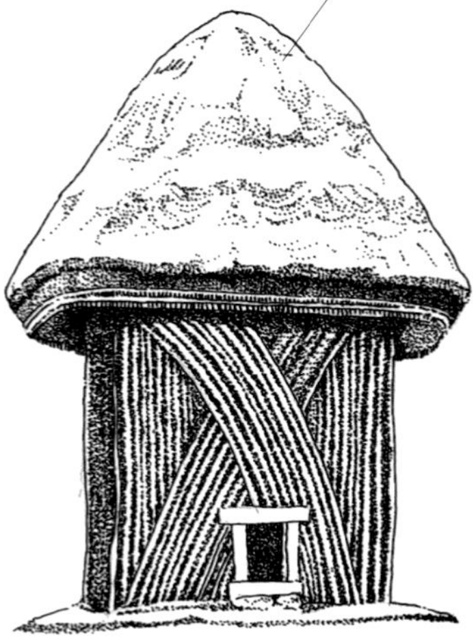

Traditional architecture
This house in Cameroon is made from packed earth and wood.

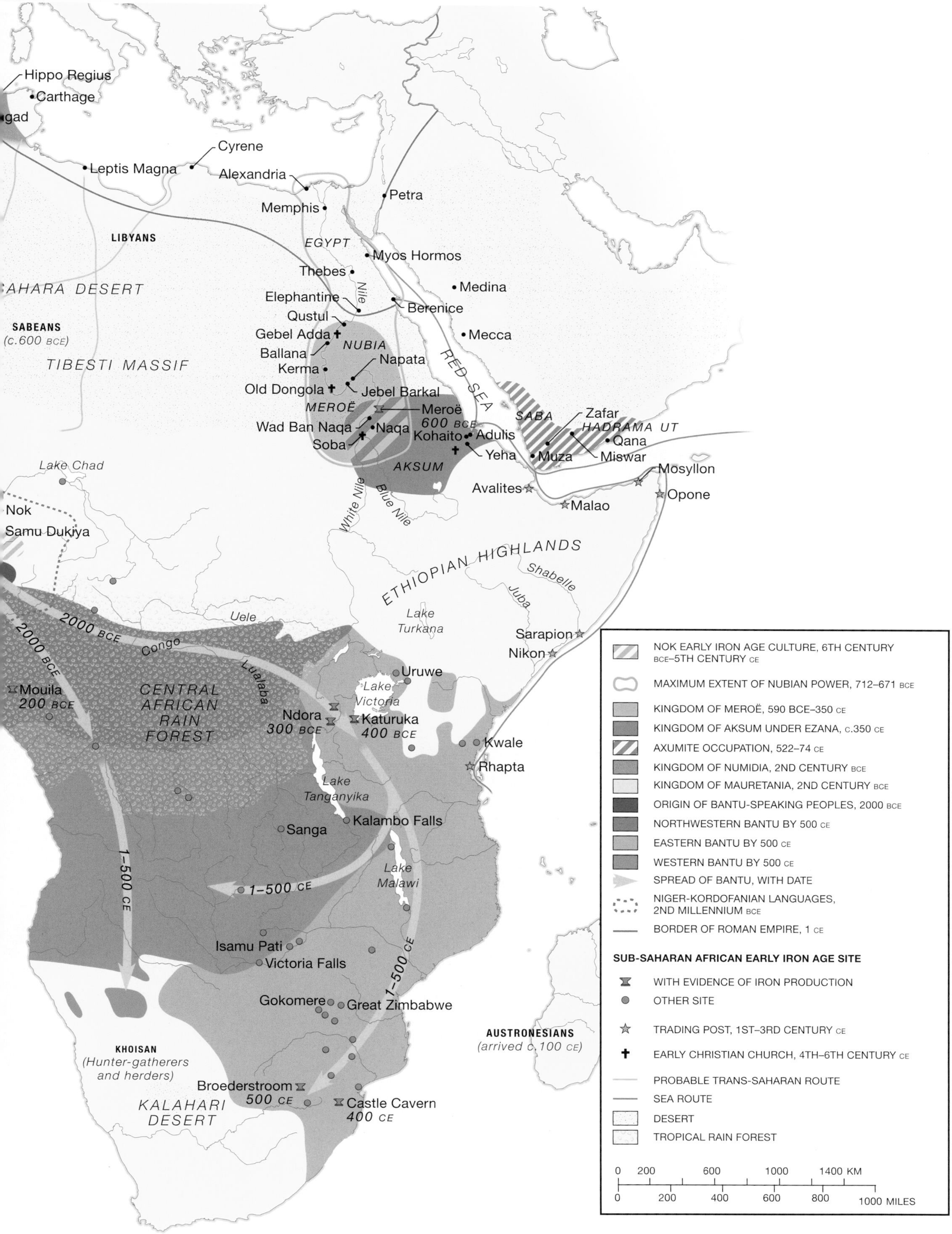

Hippo Regius
Carthage
gad
Cyrene
Leptis Magna
Alexandria
Petra
Memphis
LIBYANS
EGYPT
Myos Hormos
Thebes
Nile
AHARA DESERT
Medina
Elephantine
Berenice
Qustul
SABEANS
(c.600 BCE)
Gebel Adda
Mecca
NUBIA
Ballana
Napata
TIBESTI MASSIF
Kerma
RED SEA
Old Dongola
Jebel Barkal
MEROË
Meroë
600 BCE
SABA
Zafar
HADRAMA UT
Wad Ban Naqa
Naqa
Kohaito
Adulis
Qana
Soba
Yeha
Muza
Miswar
Lake Chad
AKSUM
Mosyllon
Avalites
Opone
Malao
Nok
White Nile
Blue Nile
Samu Dukiya
ETHIOPIAN HIGHLANDS
Shabelle
Juba
Lake Turkana
2000 BCE
Uele
Sarapion
2000 BCE
Congo
Nikon
Uruwe
Lualaba
Mouila
200 BCE
CENTRAL AFRICAN RAIN FOREST
Lake Victoria
Ndora
300 BCE
Katuruka
400 BCE
Kwale
Rhapta
Lake Tanganyika
Sanga
Kalambo Falls
1–500 CE
Lake Malawi
1–500 CE
Isamu Pati
Victoria Falls
1–500 CE
Gokomere
Great Zimbabwe
AUSTRONESIANS
(arrived c.100 CE)
KHOISAN
(Hunter-gatherers and herders)
Broederstroom
500 CE
Castle Cavern
400 CE
KALAHARI DESERT
NOK EARLY IRON AGE CULTURE, 6TH CENTURY BCE–5TH CENTURY CE
MAXIMUM EXTENT OF NUBIAN POWER, 712–671 BCE
KINGDOM OF MEROË, 590 BCE–350 CE
KINGDOM OF AKSUM UNDER EZANA, c.350 CE
AXUMITE OCCUPATION, 522–74 CE
KINGDOM OF NUMIDIA, 2ND CENTURY BCE
KINGDOM OF MAURETANIA, 2ND CENTURY BCE
ORIGIN OF BANTU-SPEAKING PEOPLES, 2000 BCE
NORTHWESTERN BANTU BY 500 CE
EASTERN BANTU BY 500 CE
WESTERN BANTU BY 500 CE
SPREAD OF BANTU, WITH DATE
NIGER-KORDOFANIAN LANGUAGES, 2ND MILLENNIUM BCE
BORDER OF ROMAN EMPIRE, 1 CE
SUB-SAHARAN AFRICAN EARLY IRON AGE SITE
WITH EVIDENCE OF IRON PRODUCTION
OTHER SITE
TRADING POST, 1ST–3RD CENTURY CE
EARLY CHRISTIAN CHURCH, 4TH–6TH CENTURY CE
PROBABLE TRANS-SAHARAN ROUTE
SEA ROUTE
DESERT
TROPICAL RAIN FOREST
0 200 600 1000 1400 KM
0 200 400 600 800 1000 MILES

TRADITIONAL HOUSES

Traditional African houses were rarely made up of one single building divided into rooms. More often, a complete homestead was a collection of separate buildings, each functioning as a "room," and the buildings would have been surrounded by a fence or a wall. The shape of these buildings varied enormously across the continent. More than 20 major styles have been identified by archeologists, as well as variations within each style. Some of these are illustrated here.

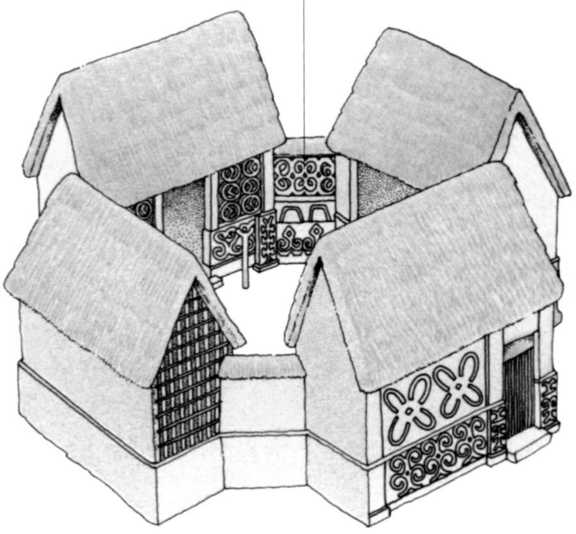

Asante, southern Ghana
A traditional Asante house was built around a courtyard, with four rooms joined at their corners by short lengths of wall. The walls of the rooms were made from mud, reinforced with a wooden framework. The walls were often decorated with patterns.

Nuba, central Sudan
Many Nuba homesteads were built on a ring pattern, with individual buildings linked by walls of red, gravelly clay. Individual buildings served as bedrooms for adults and small children, a store, and a pig house or goat house.

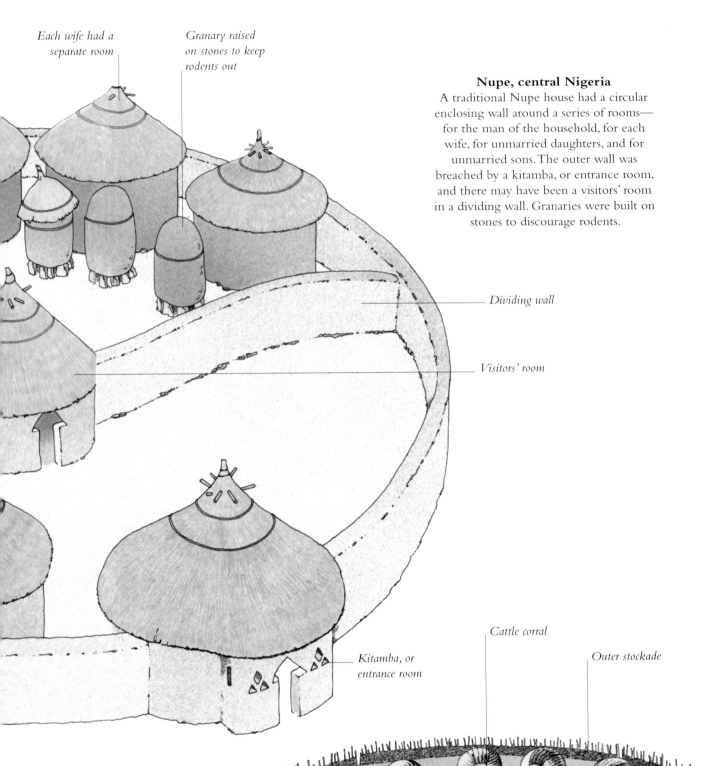

Nupe, central Nigeria
A traditional Nupe house had a circular enclosing wall around a series of rooms—for the man of the household, for each wife, for unmarried daughters, and for unmarried sons. The outer wall was breached by a kitamba, or entrance room, and there may have been a visitors' room in a dividing wall. Granaries were built on stones to discourage rodents.

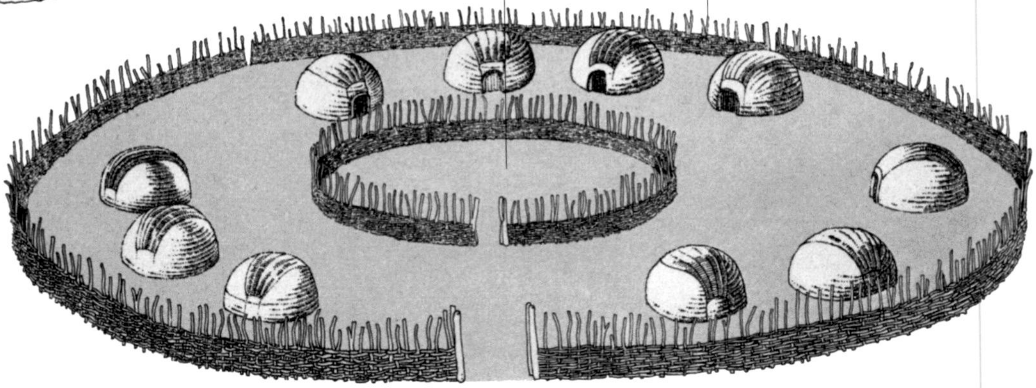

Zulu, southern Africa
The Zulus built houses in a symmetrical pattern. The rooms of different family members were enclosed within a circular stockade fence. An inner stockade ran around a cattle corral.

WAYS OF LIFE

Natural barriers such as the Sahara Desert and the Central African rain forest meant that the peoples of each region developed largely independently, adapting their ways of life to the local environment. In ancient Africa great empires ruled in the fertile river valleys of the west, hunter-gatherers foraged in the central rain forests, and nomadic herdsmen roamed the grasslands of the east.

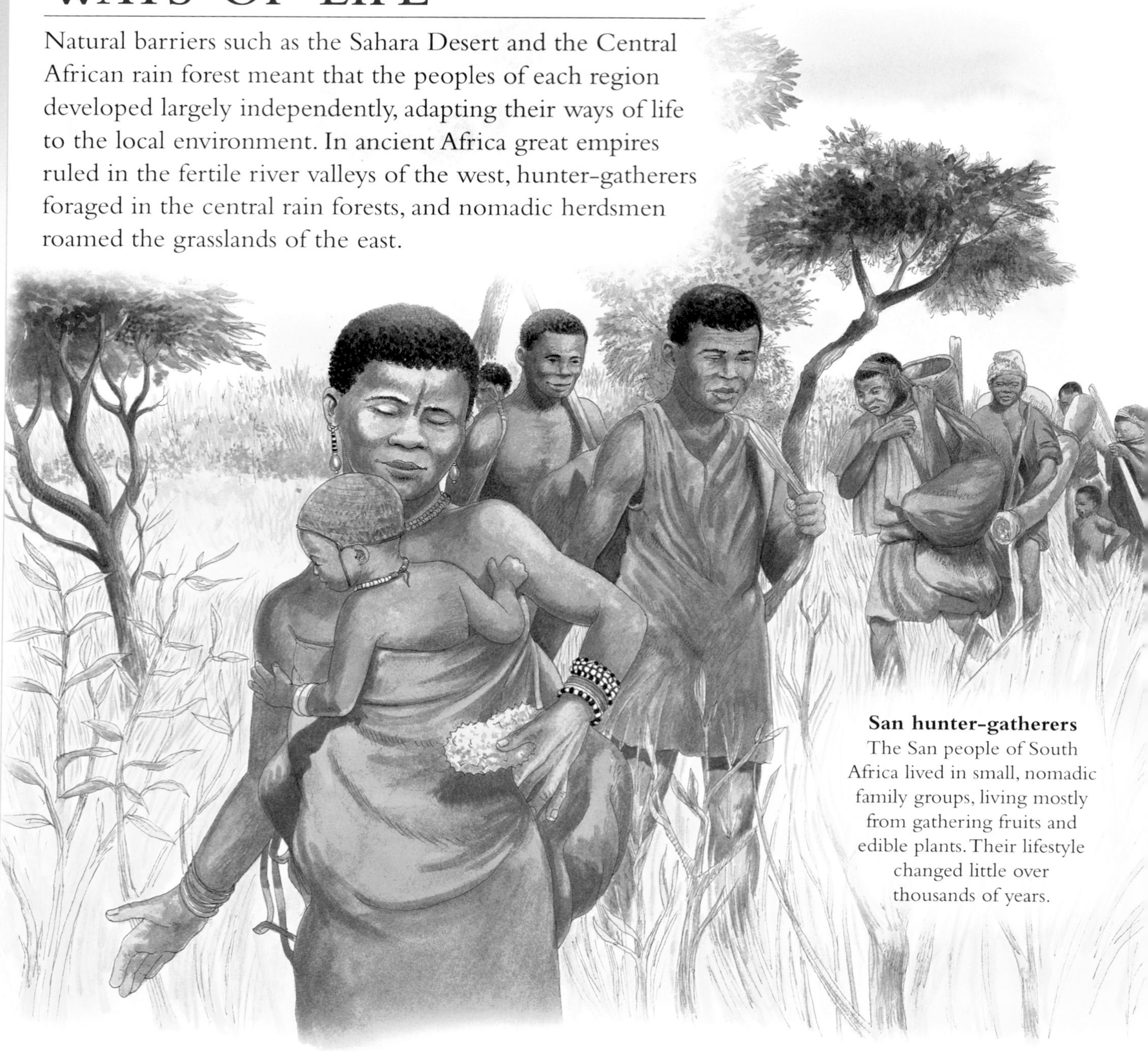

San hunter-gatherers
The San people of South Africa lived in small, nomadic family groups, living mostly from gathering fruits and edible plants. Their lifestyle changed little over thousands of years.

Mbuti
The Mbuti people are hunter-gatherers from the Congo rain forest. They are known for their diminutive stature: Mbuti men are usually no more than five feet (1.5 m) tall.

A mother decorating her child's face with charcoal patterns

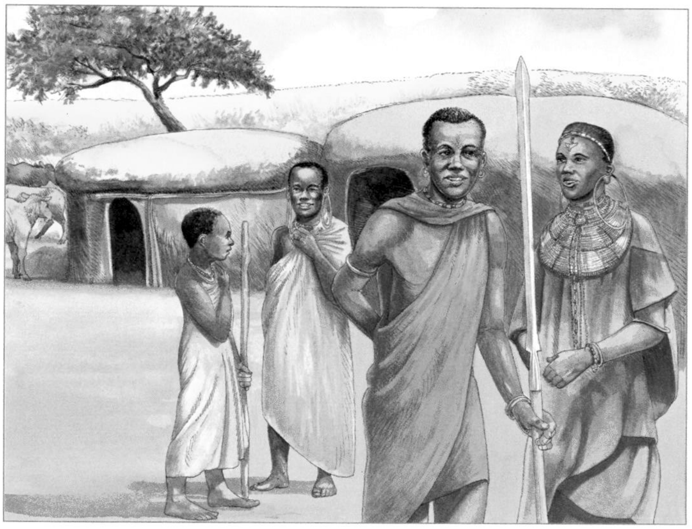

Maasai herdsmen
The Maasai live in East Africa. For centuries they have lived a seminomadic lifestyle, traveling with their animals as they migrate.

Rain forest villages
In resource-rich environments like rain forests, hunter-gatherers could live a relatively settled lifestyle.

Ibn Tulun Mosque
This mosque, located in Cairo, is a typical example of the Muslim places of worship built across North Africa in the seventh and eighth centuries CE.

URBAN CENTERS AND THE ECONOMY

Although historical records prove the existence of many great cities in ancient and medieval Africa, the perishable materials used to build these cities (mud brick and timber) mean that few traces remain. Ancient African cities were centers of art and industry, while medieval cities such as Timbuktu and Zanzibar were hubs for global trade.

The sultan's private quarters
Merchant ships would have traveled between East Africa, India, and Arabia

Great Zimbabwe
Built by the Shona people in the seventh century CE, Great Zimbabwe was the center of a powerful empire.

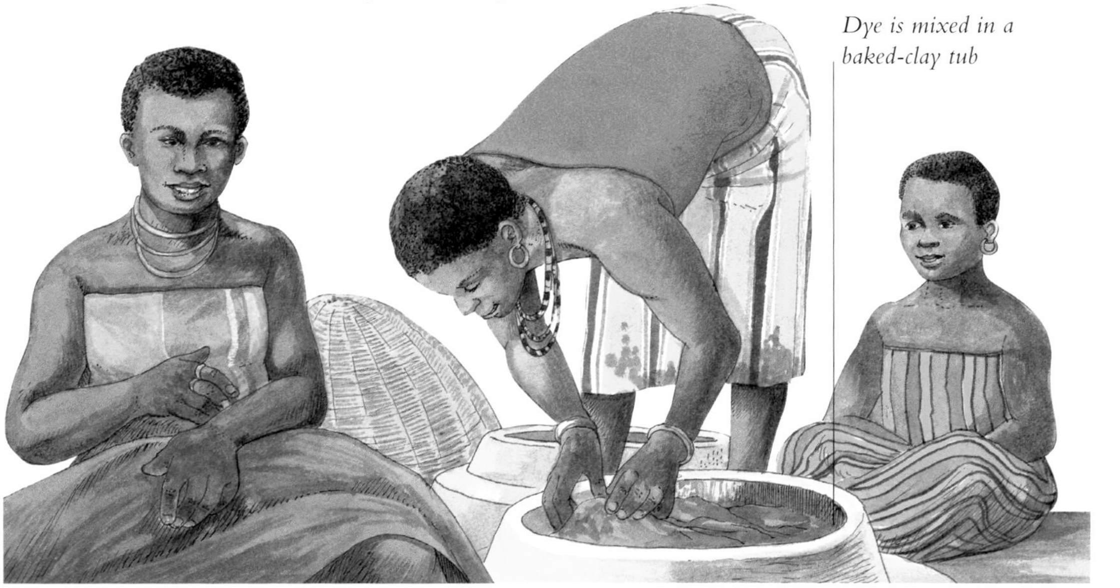
Dye is mixed in a baked-clay tub

Dyeing fabric
One of the key industries to appear in the towns of medieval Africa was the production of indigo dye and dyed cloth.

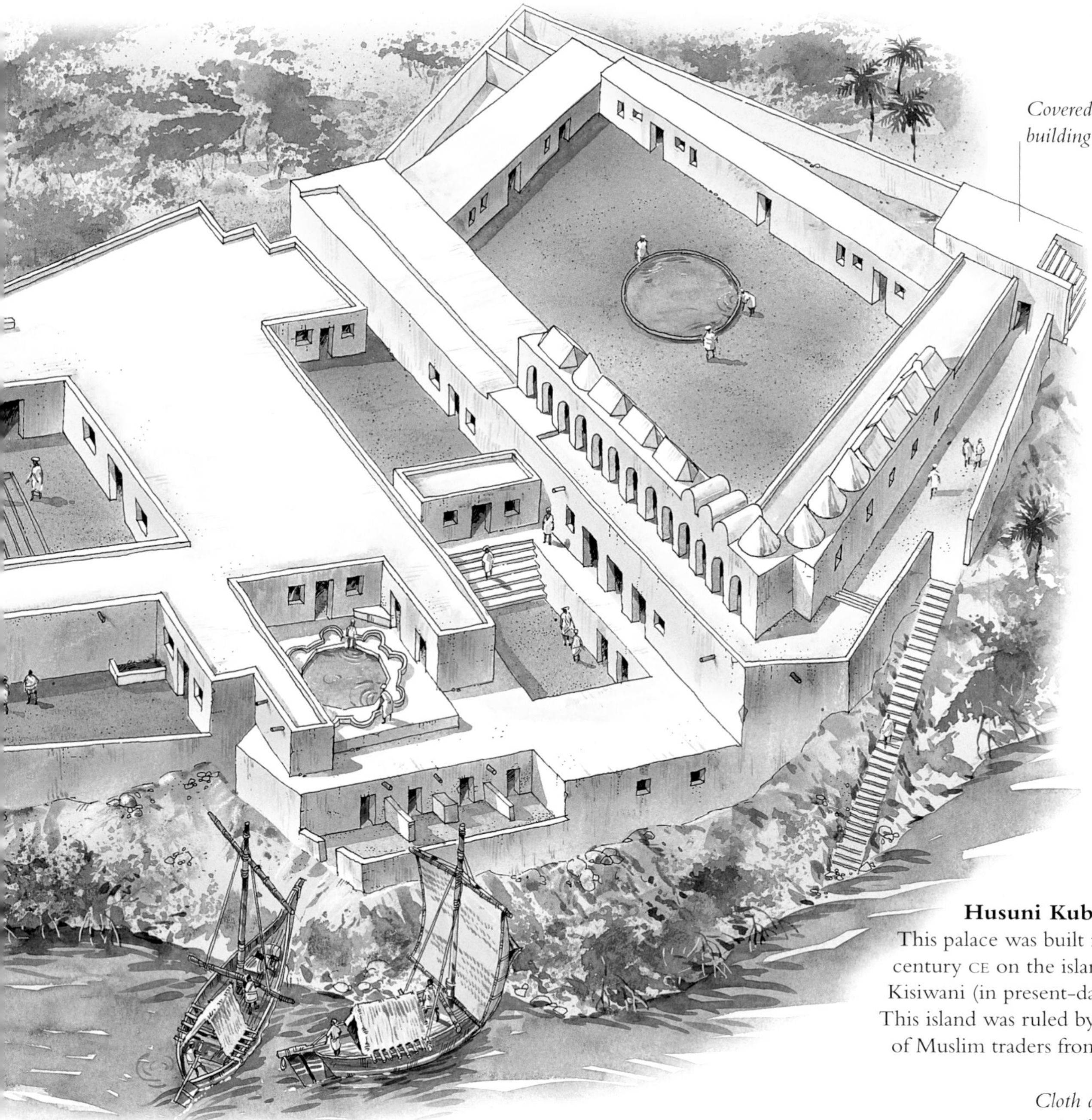

Husuni Kubwa
This palace was built in the 14th century CE on the island of Kilwa Kisiwani (in present-day Tanzania). This island was ruled by descendants of Muslim traders from the north.

The indigo trade
Natural indigo dye is made from the crushed leaves of plants from the genus *Indigofera*, which grows throughout sub-Saharan Africa. This dye provides a bright shade of blue.

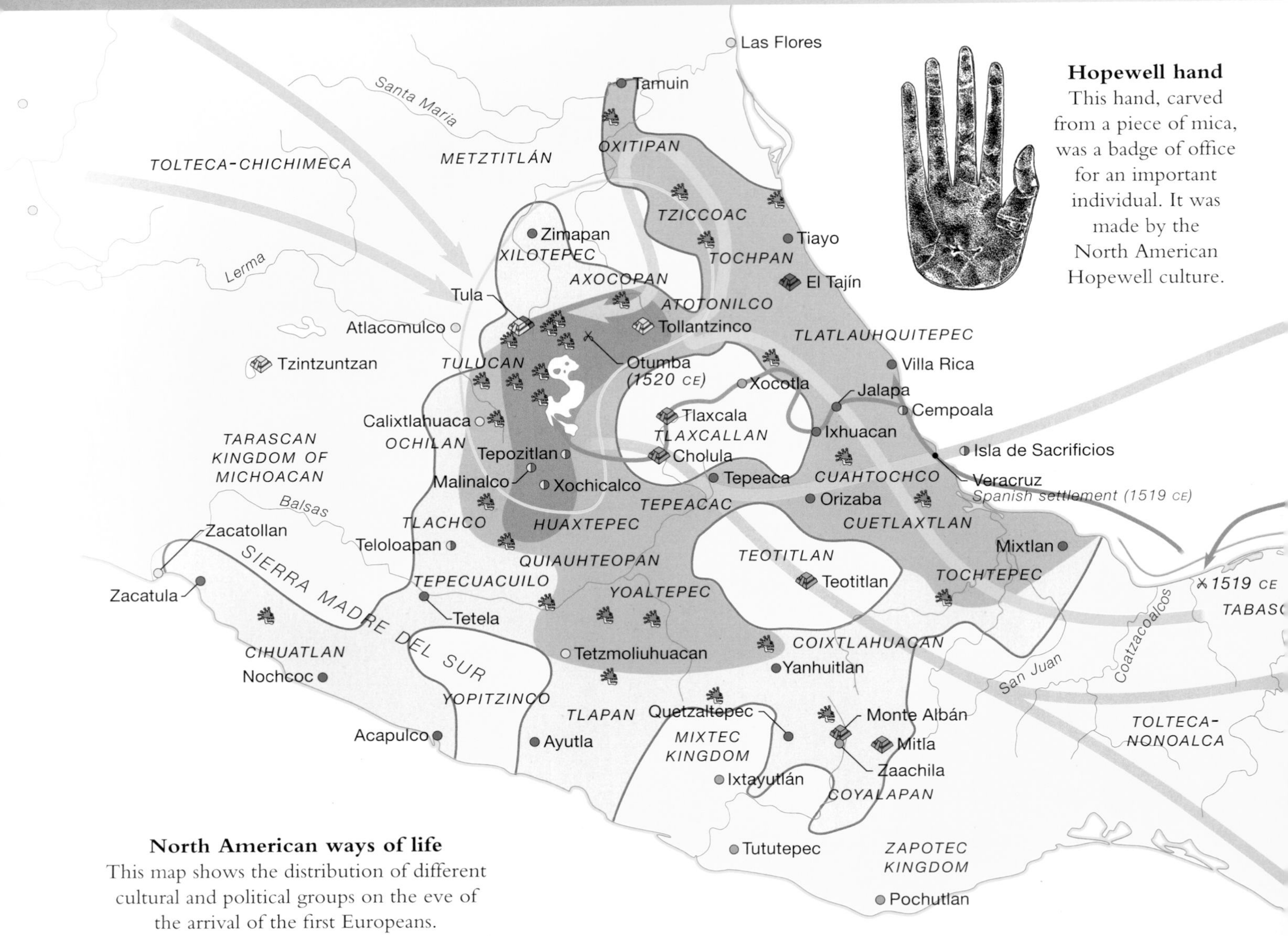

Hopewell hand
This hand, carved from a piece of mica, was a badge of office for an important individual. It was made by the North American Hopewell culture.

North American ways of life
This map shows the distribution of different cultural and political groups on the eve of the arrival of the first Europeans.

ANCIENT AMERICAS

According to archeological evidence, humans first reached the Americas around 14,000 years ago. By 1500 BCE they had colonized both North and South America. Numerous radically different cultures emerged across the Americas, from the hunter-gatherers of Arizona and New Mexico to the city-builders of Mesoamerica.

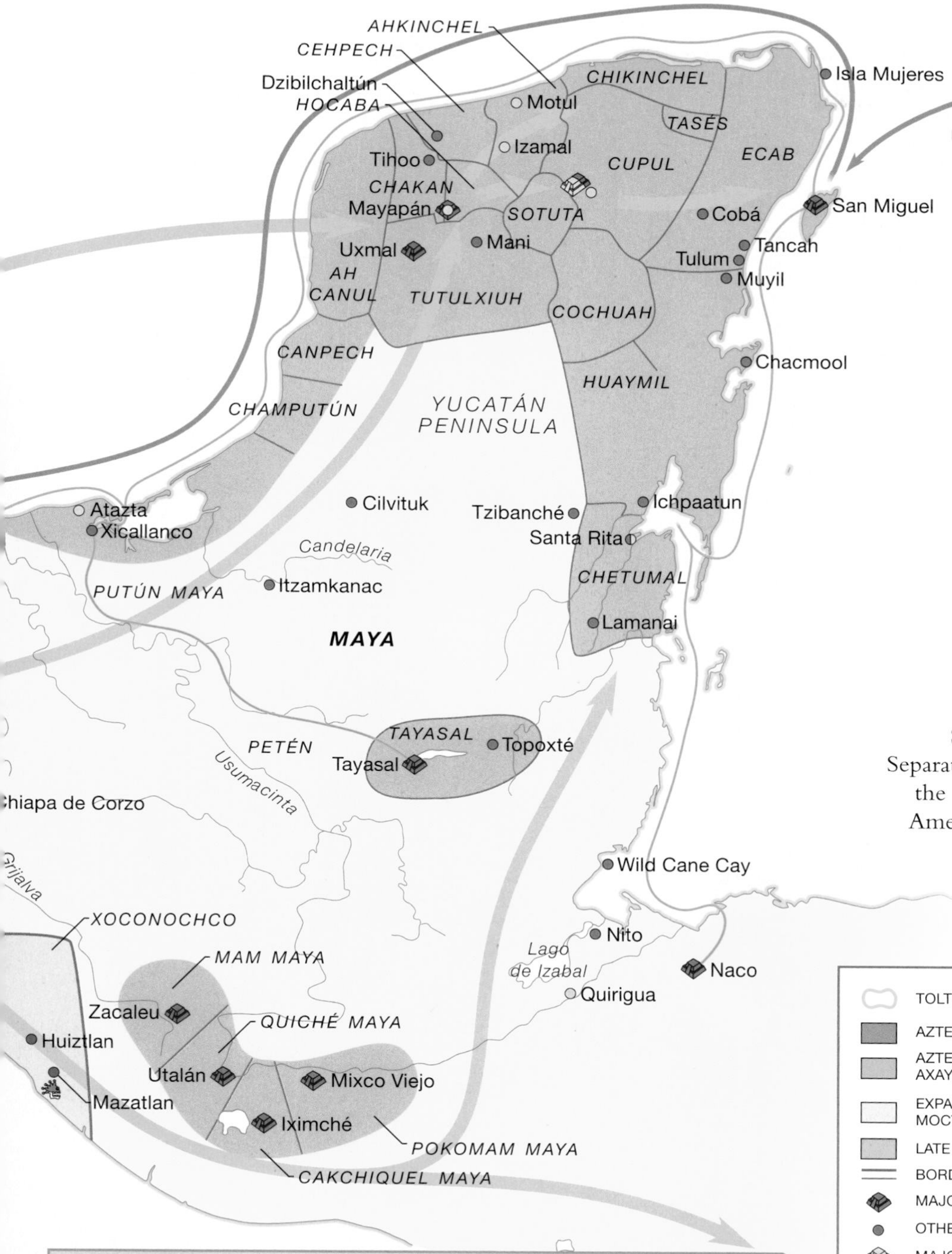

South American ways of life
Separated by the impassable Andes Mountains, the eastern and western peoples of South America developed largely independently.

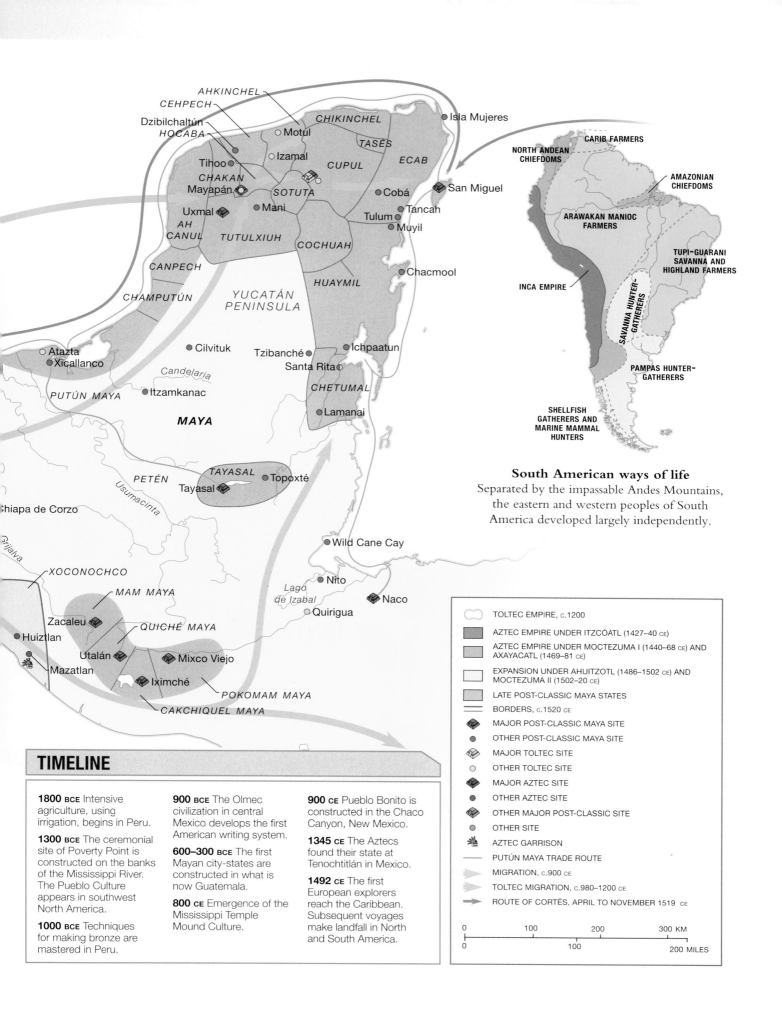

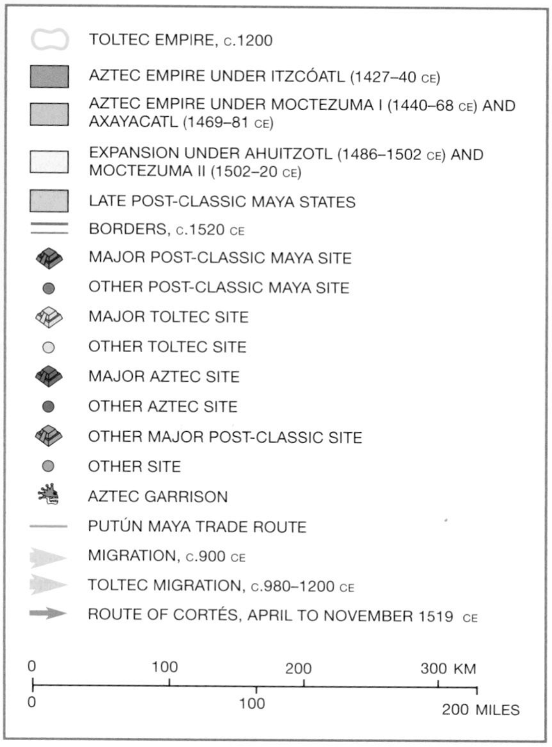

TIMELINE

1800 BCE Intensive agriculture, using irrigation, begins in Peru.

1300 BCE The ceremonial site of Poverty Point is constructed on the banks of the Mississippi River. The Pueblo Culture appears in southwest North America.

1000 BCE Techniques for making bronze are mastered in Peru.

900 BCE The Olmec civilization in central Mexico develops the first American writing system.

600–300 BCE The first Mayan city-states are constructed in what is now Guatemala.

800 CE Emergence of the Mississippi Temple Mound Culture.

900 CE Pueblo Bonito is constructed in the Chaco Canyon, New Mexico.

1345 CE The Aztecs found their state at Tenochtitlán in Mexico.

1492 CE The first European explorers reach the Caribbean. Subsequent voyages make landfall in North and South America.

MAYA AND AZTEC

The Maya and Aztec created two renowned civilizations in Mesoamerica. Both peoples built stepped pyramids, or ziggurats, where priests made sacrifices to their gods. The Maya built drainage channels to irrigate crops, carved beautiful sculptures, and produced accurate calendars. This civilization was at its height between 250–900 CE. Later, around 1300, the Aztec migrated south to Lake Texcoco, near present-day Mexico City. There, they built the extraordinary, huge city of Tenochtitlán. When Spanish explorers arrived there in 1519 they could not believe the scale of the city, nor its riches.

The Aztec capital
Aztec nobles and warriors survey the Templo Mayor in the center of their capital, Tenochtitlán, before it was destroyed by the Spanish in the 16th century.

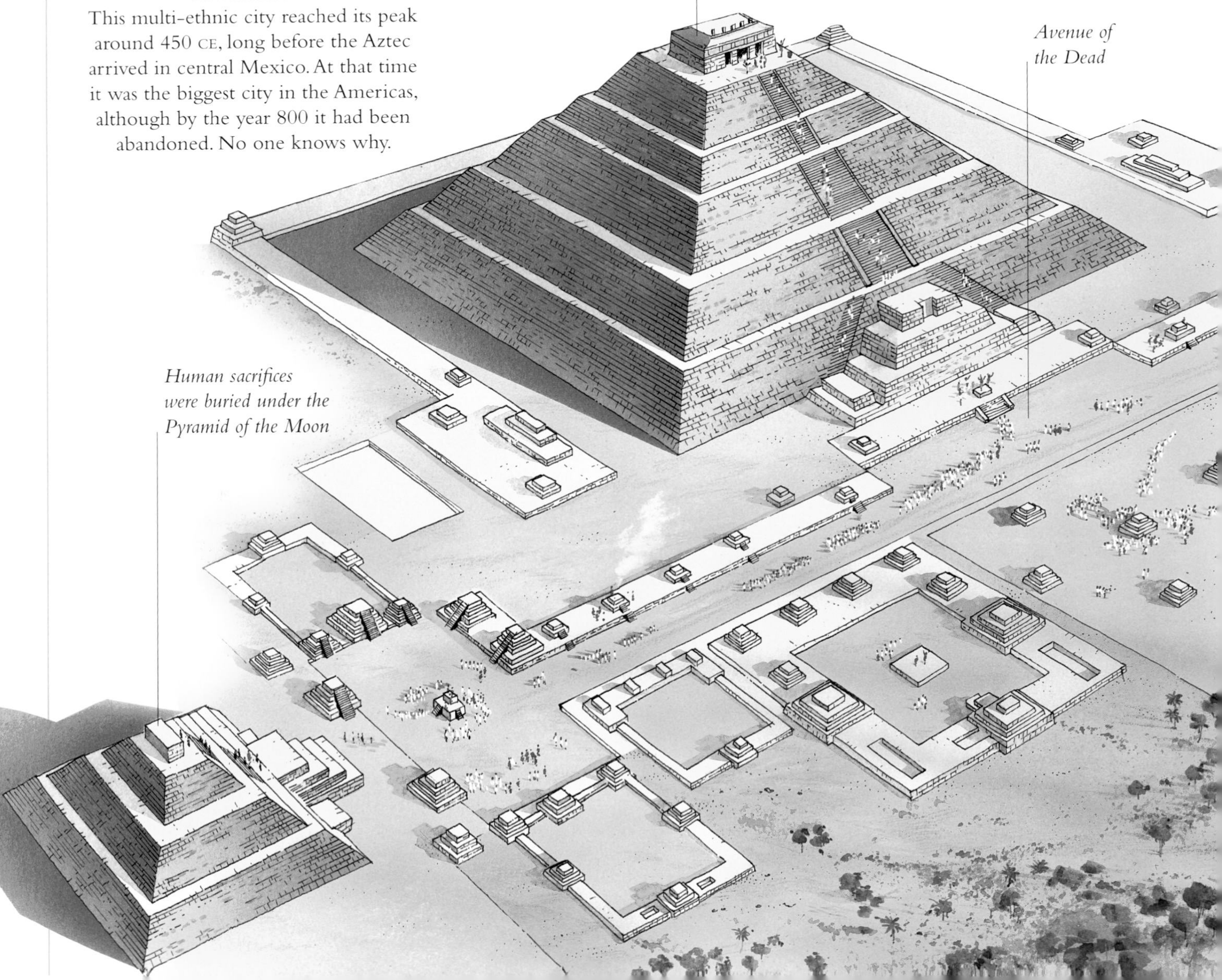
Pyramid of the Sun was 210 feet (64 m) tall and used for sacrifices
Avenue of the Dead
Human sacrifices were buried under the Pyramid of the Moon

Teotihuacán
This multi-ethnic city reached its peak around 450 CE, long before the Aztec arrived in central Mexico. At that time it was the biggest city in the Americas, although by the year 800 it had been abandoned. No one knows why.

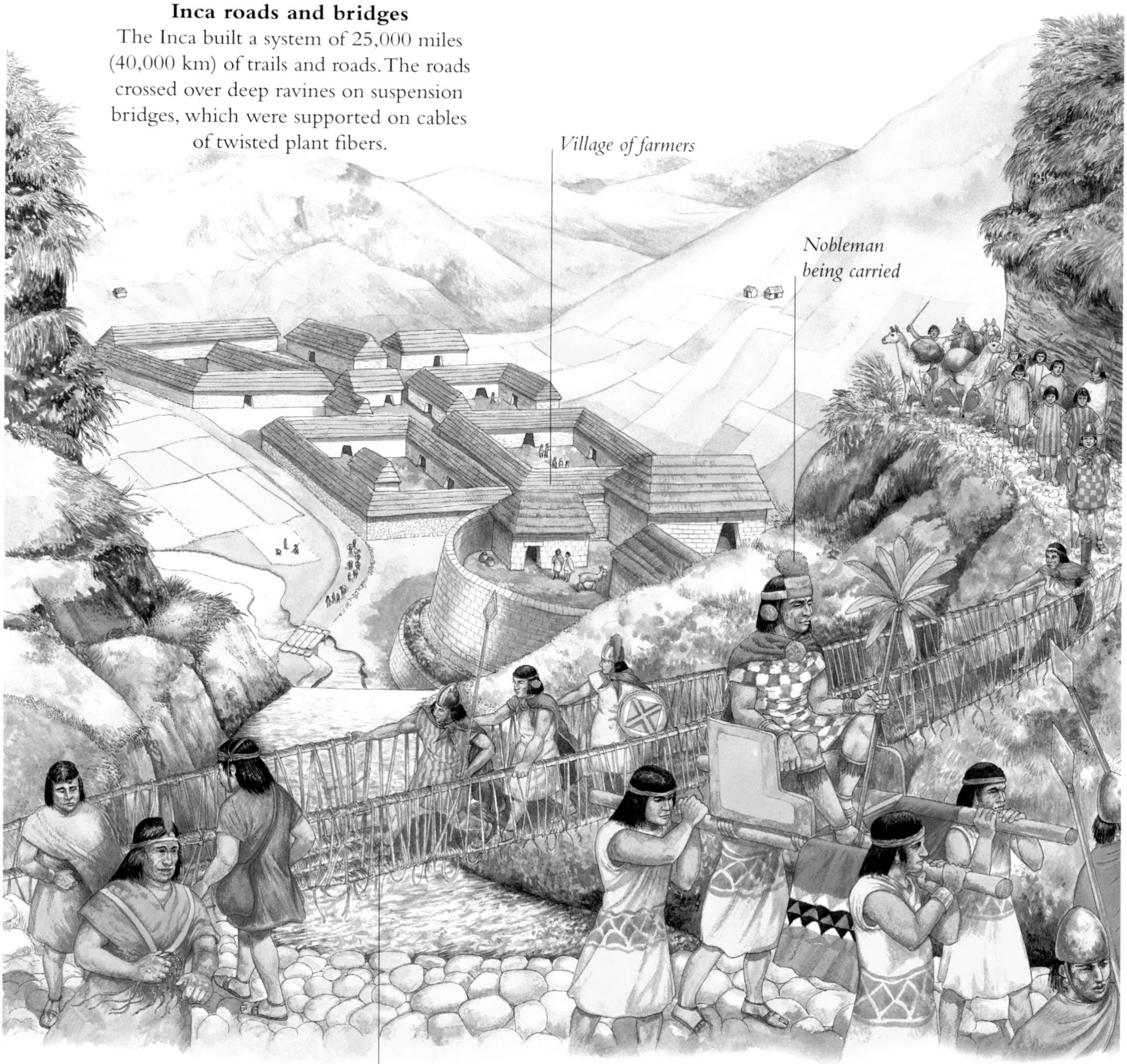

The Inca built a system of 25,000 miles (40,000 km) of trails and roads. The roads crossed over deep ravines on suspension bridges, which were supported on cables of twisted plant fibers.

Village of farmers

Nobleman being carried

Suspension bridge

INCA AND NAZCA

The Nazca and other peoples of Peru had left a cultural legacy from earlier times, including the Nazca Lines, but it was the Inca who established the greatest civilization in western South America early in the 13th century. The Inca built an extensive network of roads to connect different parts of the empire, terraced steep mountain slopes, and irrigated arid areas to grow crops. They built a capital at Cusco. The empire was conquered by the Spanish in 1572.

Nazca Lines
Between 400–650 CE, the Nazca made patterns in the desert in Peru. Formed by removing the top layer of pebbles, some line up with the setting Sun; others are shaped like animals.

NORTH AMERICA: WEST AND SOUTHWEST

A variety of Pueblo peoples are known to have lived in desert regions of the southwestern United States since at least the 12th century BCE. Their culture is best known for its stone or earth dwellings built along, or adjacent to, cliff walls. They are also known for their pottery. Farther west, in California, where more wood was available, other Native American peoples lived in timber or brushwood shelters.

Hohokan people
The Hohokan people lived in the valleys of the Salt and Gila rivers in Arizona. Their settlement of Snaketown flourished from 200–1200 CE.

Brushwood shelter
The meat of small mammals and birds provided protein
A child carries a fresh supply of acorns
Acorns pounded to pulp in a mortar

California Native Americans
The inhabitants of California in pre-Columbian times built shelters from brushwood. They hunted small animals and fished in rivers; those living near the coast were more dependent on fishing. For those living in the region's oak forests, acorns were the staple food.

Mimbres pottery

In the 11th century, the people of the Mimbres Valley, New Mexico, began to decorate their pottery.

Pueblo Bonito

This was the largest pueblo settlement in Chaco Canyon, New Mexico. This D-shaped construction could only be entered by ladder. At its height, in the 12th century, it had at least 800 connected rooms built on several levels.

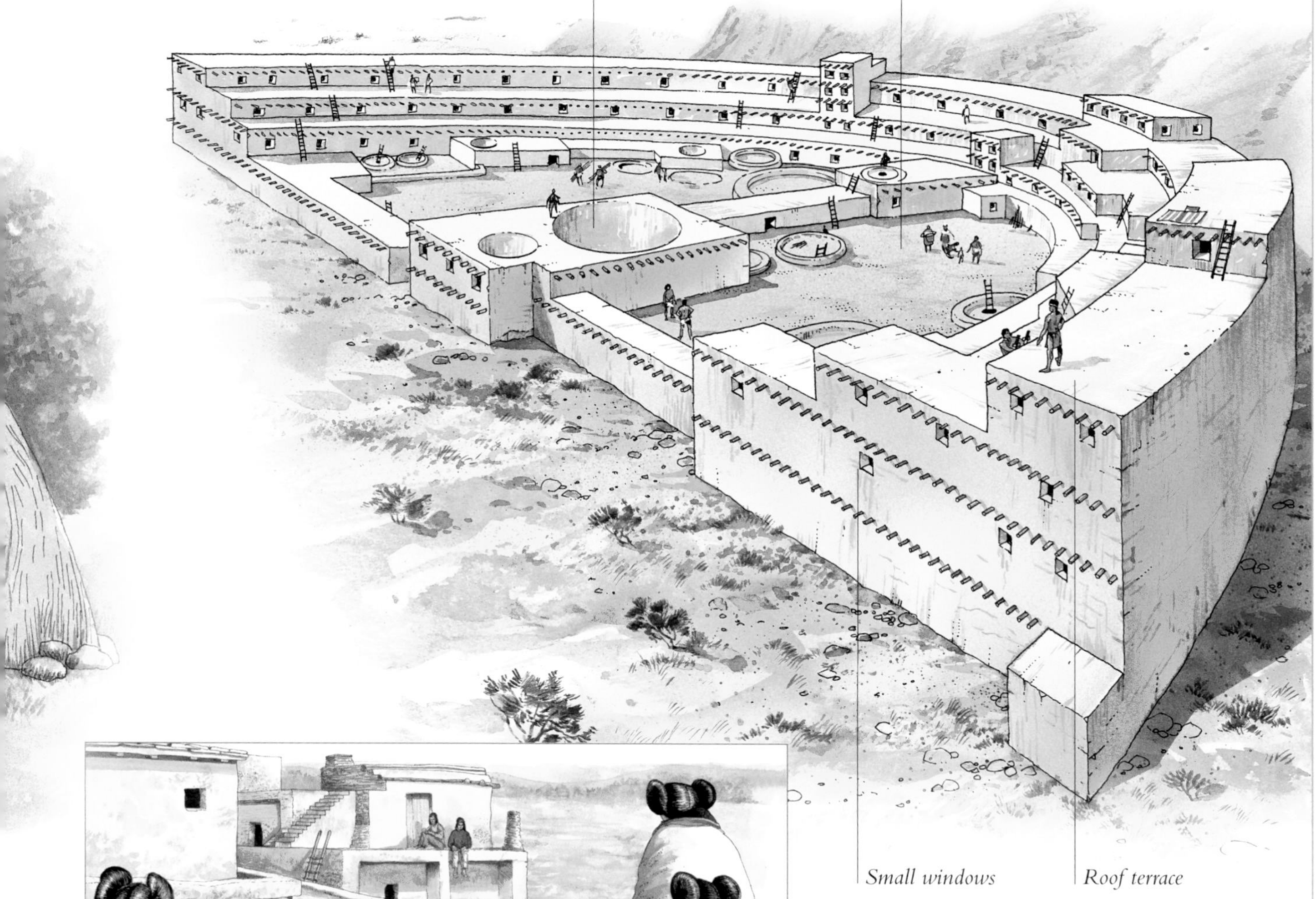

Hopi ceremony

The Hopi people are one of many Native American cultures in the southwestern United States. One Hopi village in Arizona has been inhabited since 1100. Here, women in distinctive costumes watch men perform a traditional rain dance ceremony.

THE VIKINGS

Around 1,000 years ago, the Vikings were the most powerful people in Europe. Their homeland was Scandinavia, the present-day nations of Demark, Norway, and Sweden. The Vikings are known for their raids on coastal communities—raids that earned them a reputation for brutality—but most Vikings were actually peaceful farmers or traders.

TIMELINE

793 CE The earliest recorded Viking raid takes place at Lindisfarne Abbey in England.

825 CE The first Viking settlement outside Scandinavia is established on the Faroe Islands.

864 CE The Viking warlord Rurik travels to what is now Russia, establishing (or seizing control of) settlements around Lake Ladoga and Lake Ilmen. His successors partially integrate themselves into local Slavic society, founding the state known as the Kievan Rus.

865–902 CE Viking raids on Western European towns reach their peak. The tide is turned in England when King Aflred the Great of Wessex defeats the Viking warlord Guthrum at the battle of Edington in 878.

870 CE Viking settlements are established on Iceland.

874 CE An area of Viking settlement known as the Danelaw is established in northern and eastern England.

911 CE Viking mercenaries in Constantinople fight as part of the Byzantine emperor's personal guard. Guardsmen are known to have traveled from as far away as Iceland.

965 CE King Harald Bluetooth of Denmark converts to Christianity.

986 CE Norse settlers, led by Erik the Red, establish colonies on Greenland.

995 CE King Olaf Tryggvason of Norway accelerates the process of Christianization among the Vikings, conquering his neighbors and forcing them to convert.

1000 CE Viking adventurer Leif Erikson reaches North America. His followers establish a settlement in Newfoundland (l'Anse aux Meadows) and probably ventured farther south, although the details are not known.

Viking helmets

Viking helmets did not have horns. This is a typical example of a Viking helmet, distinguished by its eye guard.

Viking trade routes

The Vikings were some of the most widely traveled people in the medieval world. Bands of young men journeyed into uncharted lands in search of treasure, or new lands to settle.

FINNS
FINNS
Trondheim
NORWAY
SVEAR (SWEDES)
Hafrsfjord
885 CE
SWEDEN
Sigtuna
Birka
Oseberg
Tune
Kaupang
Gokstad
GÖTAR
Gotland
Äskerkärr
Paviken
Roskilde
Skuldelev
Arhus
Lund
NMARK
Ladby
ibe
edeby
BALTIC SEA
Grobin
BALTS
PRUS
Elbing
Kolobrzeg
Wolin
Hamburg
POMERANIANS
ABODRITES
Gniezno
Vistula
T FRANCIA
ERMANY)
ogne
Magdeburg
POLES
Oder
Frankfurt
Mainz
FRANCONIA
Prague
Regensburg
BOHEMIANS
BAVARIA
Vienna
Salzburg
St Gall
Gran
Pest
MORAVIANS
Aquileia
Milan
Venice
Sava
Po
CROATIA
Belgrade
SERBS
Pisa
KINGDOM OF ITALY
Rome
Bari
Otranto
Sicily
Tunis
GHLABID
MIRATE
MEDITERRANEAN SEA
Crete
Staraja Ladoga
Beloozero
Novgorod
Yaroslavl
Izborsk
Pskov
Gnezdovo
VIATCHIANS
KIEVAN RUS
Chernigov
Kiev
DEREVLIANS
SEVERYANS
Don
PECHENEGS
MAGYARS
CARPATHIAN MTS
HUNGARY
Danube
Pliska
BULGAR KHANATE
BLACK SEA
GOTHS
Tmutorokan
Constantinople
860 CE
BYZANTINE EMPIRE
Bulgar
VOLGA BULGARS
KHAZAR KHANATE
Volga
Sarkel
Itil
BORDERS, c.888 CE
DANISH VIKING SETTLEMENT, 800–1000 CE
NORWEGIAN VIKING SETTLEMENT, 800–1000 CE
SWEDISH VIKING SETTLEMENT 800–1000 CE
BYZANTINE EMPIRE, c.888 CE
CAROLINGIAN KINGDOMS, c.888 CE
MUSLIM STATES, c.888 CE
BULGAR PEOPLES
SLAVIC PEOPLES
KINGDOM OF HUNGARY, 1000 CE
EMPIRE OF CNUT, 1019–35 CE
KIEVAN RUS, c.1050 CE
HOLY ROMAN EMPIRE, 1050 CE
VIKING RAIDS, TRADE AND COLONIZATION ROUTES, 793–1000 CE
VIKING-CONTROLLED TRADE CENTER
VIKING SHIP FIND
0 200 400 600 KM
0 200 400 MILES

PAGAN GODS

The pre-Christian religion of the Vikings is shrouded in mystery. They wrote almost nothing about their beliefs and practices, so distorted Christian accounts of their religion are often all we have. Our knowledge of the Norse gods comes from the myths recorded in Viking sagas. These stories describe a group of gods that included Thor, the god of thunder; Freyja, the goddess of love; and Odin, the father of the gods.

Freyr
This carving depicts Freyr (not to be confused with his sister, Freyja, the goddess of love), the Norse god of fertility.

A hollow ram's horn, used to hold mead

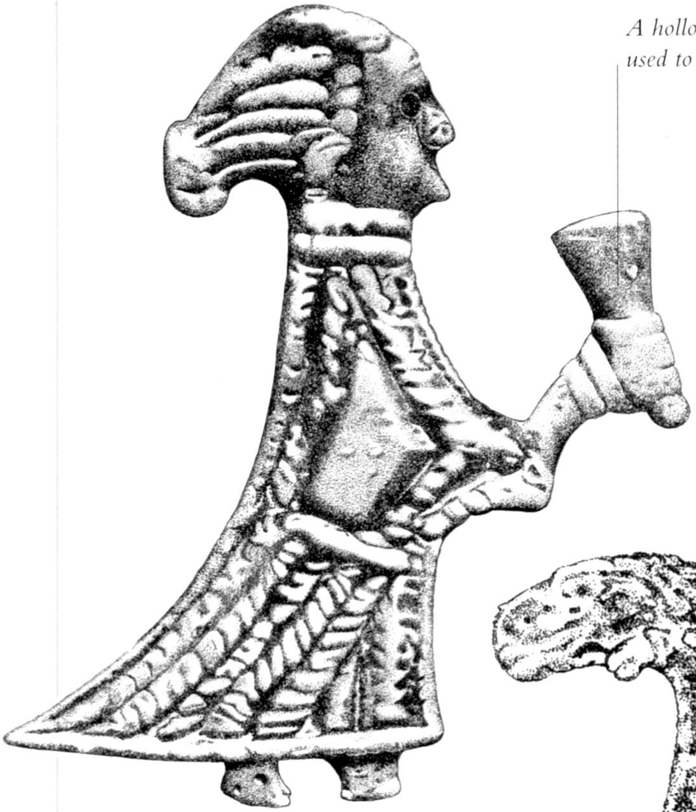

Valkyrie
This carving depicts a valkyrie, or "chooser of the slain." Valkyries selected the best fighters from among those who had fallen in battle and took them to join the gods.

Sleipnir was a demigod in Viking mythology

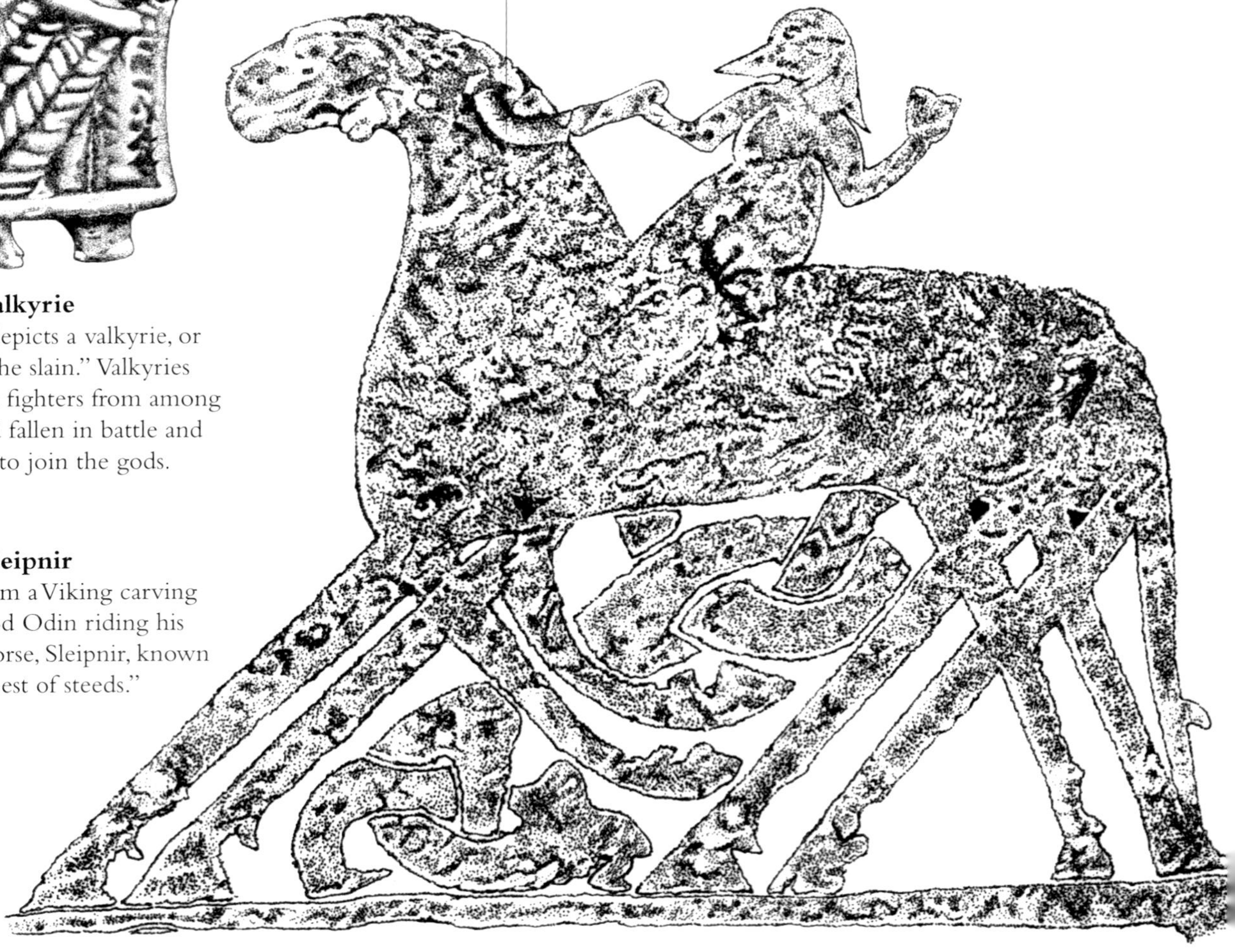

Sleipnir
This detail from a Viking carving shows the god Odin riding his eight-legged horse, Sleipnir, known as the "best of steeds."

The boar helmet indicates the wearer is under the protection of Freyr, the god of fertility

Boar helmet
The gods Freyja and Freyr were both associated with wild boars. Freyr's boar was called *Gullinbursti* ("golden bristled") while Freyja's was called *Hildisvini* ("battle boar").

Thor's hammer was called Mjölnir, which means "crusher."

Thor
This is a small stone carving of Thor, one of the most important Norse gods. Armed with his magical war hammer, Thor fought the ice giants and monsters that tried to destroy the world.

VIKING SHIPS

The Vikings were the best seafarers of their time, and their ships were the best the world had ever seen. Their narrow longships were light, flexible, and could pass through very rough seas unscathed. They were made from oak or pine, each timber carefully chosen and carved for maximum strength. Powered by a square sail and oars, longships were equally at home in shallow inland waterways and the open ocean.

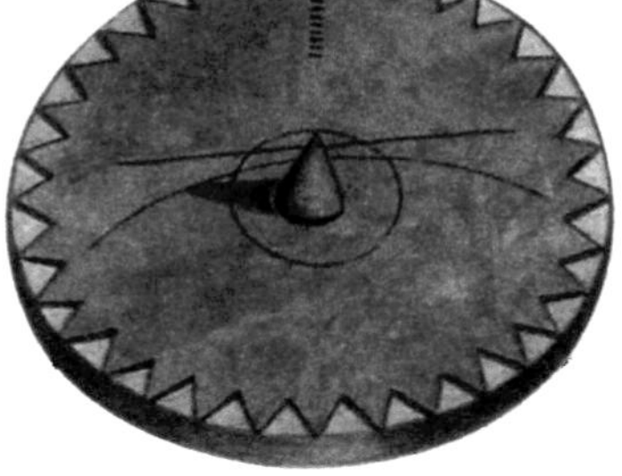

Sun compass
The Vikings had no charts, but they may have had a "Sun compass." This invention allowed crews to use the height of the Sun to roughly determine how far north or south they had traveled.

Flat-bladed axes called adzes shaped the wood
Notched drawblades were used to carve the timbers

Tools
The tools used by Viking shipbuilders were designed to work with the natural shape of the wood as much as possible. Shipbuilders avoided cutting across the grain as this weakened the timbers.

Anchor
Viking anchors were made from iron and looked much like the anchors used by small ships today.

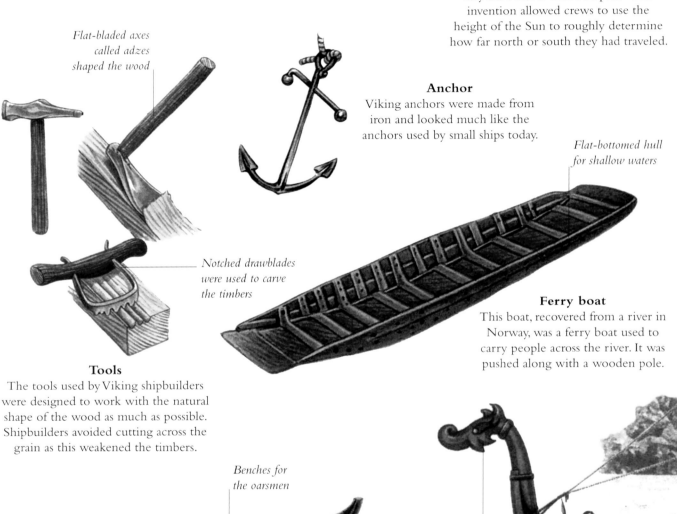

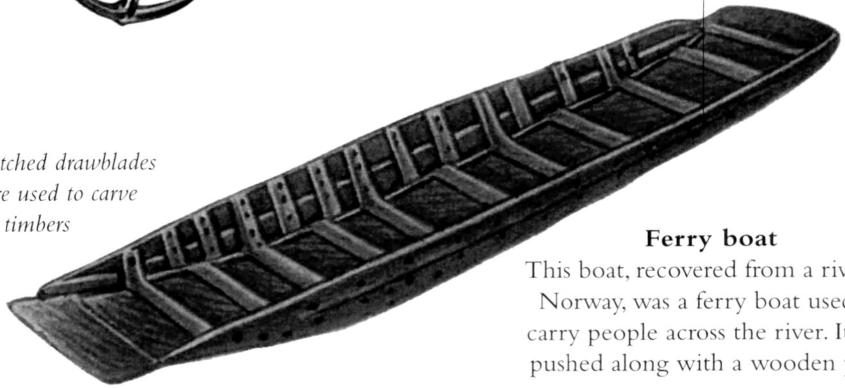
Flat-bottomed hull for shallow waters

Ferry boat
This boat, recovered from a river in Norway, was a ferry boat used to carry people across the river. It was pushed along with a wooden pole.

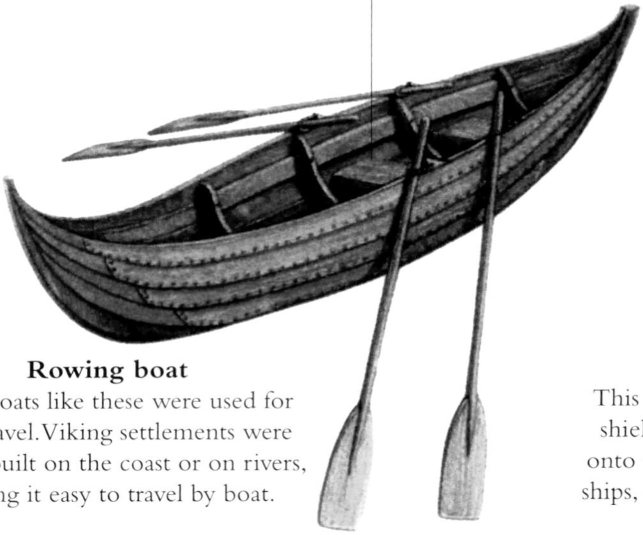
Benches for the oarsmen

Rowing boat
Small boats like these were used for local travel. Viking settlements were usually built on the coast or on rivers, making it easy to travel by boat.

The raised prow of a longship was usually decorated with a carved dragon's head

Viking longship
This longship is equiped for a raid. The shields of its warrior crew are hooked onto the sides of the hull. Viking trading ships, called *knarrs*, were wider and larger.

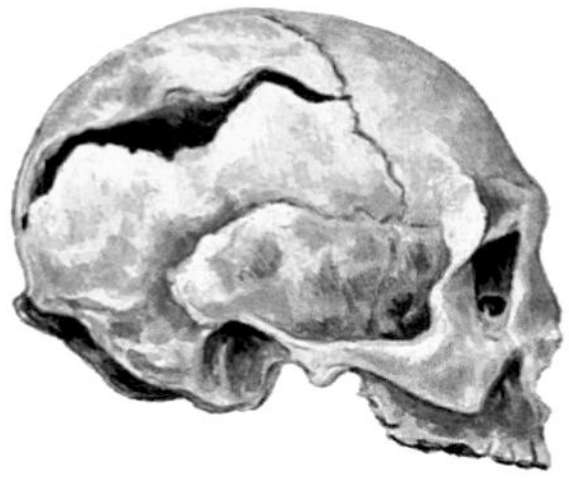

Viking raiders
Raiding parties were feared for their brutality. This skull, found at a site in England, has been almost split in two by a blow from an ax.

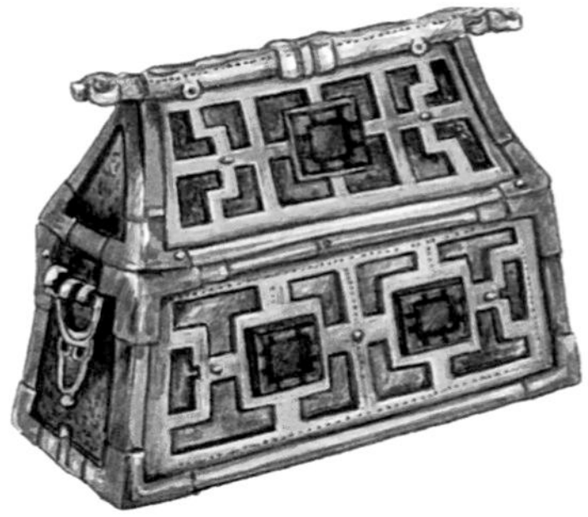

Casket
A jeweled casket, which once held the relics of a saint, was found in Denmark. It was probably stolen from a monastery in Ireland.

Gold brooch
This brooch, found in Sweden, was originally a gold clasp from an illuminated bible. It was treasure from a raid on a monastery.

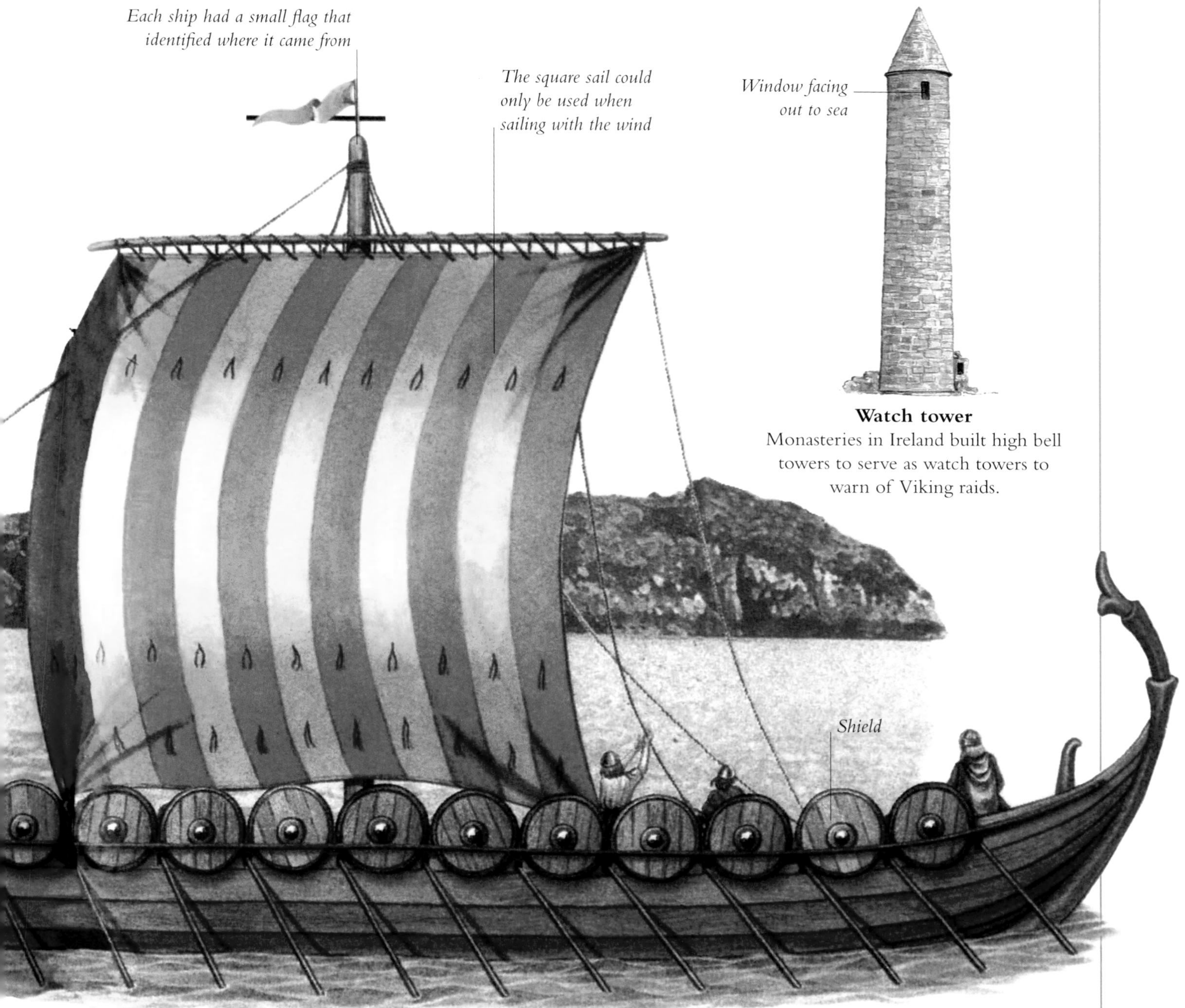
Window facing out to sea
Each ship had a small flag that identified where it came from
The square sail could only be used when sailing with the wind
Shield

Watch tower
Monasteries in Ireland built high bell towers to serve as watch towers to warn of Viking raids.

DAILY LIFE

Although they are best known as a seafaring people, most Vikings were settled farmers. Scandinavia was a harsh, difficult place for agriculture, with long, freezing winters and unpredictable spring frosts. Farms were often isolated. Farming communities had to be almost entirely self-sufficient, making not only their own food, but also their own clothes, furniture, buildings, and tools.

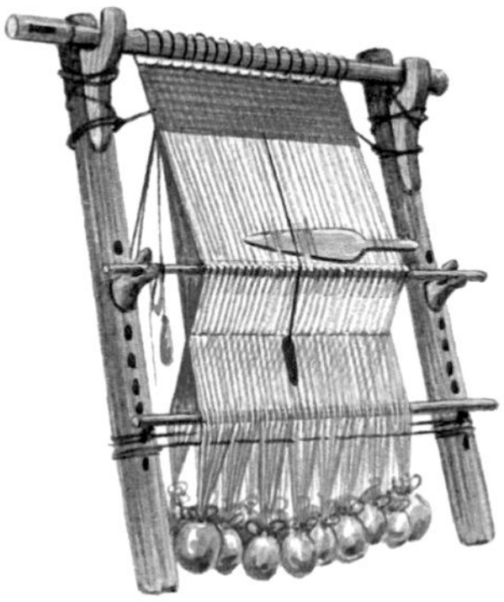

Loom
All woolen fabric, including clothes and ship's sails, had to be woven by hand on looms.

Woven seat

High chair
Most people sat on rugs or stools in their homes. Chairs were only for the head of the household.

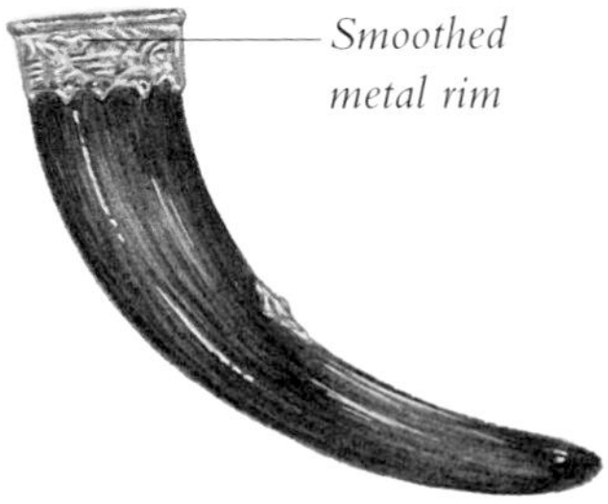
Smoothed metal rim

Drinking horn
Animal horns were used as drinking cups by the Vikings.

Smokehouse for preserving fish and meat

Home life
Designed primarily for warmth in the bitter Scandinavian winter, Viking homes were dark and smoky, with no windows and a large central hearth.

This woman is spinning yarn to use on the loom shown behind her
Food was cooked in iron pots and served on wooden plates

This farmstead's only connection with the outside world would have been by boat
Farmers grew cereals such as oats, barley, and rye
Straw had to be carefully gathered and stored to feed animals in the winter

A Viking farmstead
A large farm like this one would have been owned by a local chieftain. Besides his family it would have been home to his *thralls* (slaves) and *karls* (tenant farmers), who worked the land.

Iron ore
Iron ore could be found close to the surface in Scandinavia. It was smelted in a charcoal furnace, a costly operation as fuel was often scarce.

Quern stones

Grain milling
On most farms, grain was ground into flour with a quern, or hand mill. This consisted of two heavy circular stones mounted on a spindle.

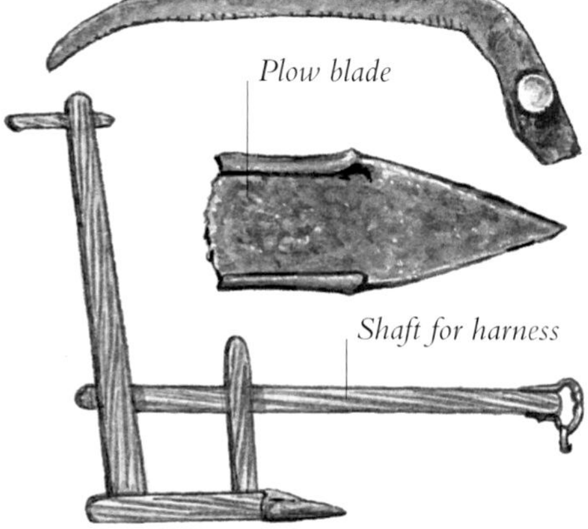
Sickle blade
Plow blade
Shaft for harness

Farm tools
Farmers used iron tools. Sickles were used for harvesting and have been found in many graves. Plows had an iron plowshare, or cutting blade.

BUILDINGS

The Vikings built many different kinds of houses, depending on what materials were available and what the local climate was like. Their houses were not built to last very long. After some years, villages and farms were often abandoned and rebuilt nearby. Because they had open fires and no chimney (smoke escaped through a hole in the roof), houses often burned down.

Thatchers were highly skilled

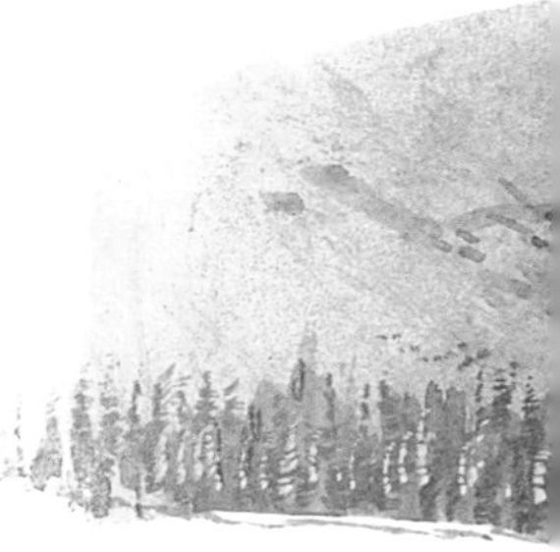

Thatched roofs

Most Viking houses had thatched roofs, made from dried marsh reeds. In places where these materials were not available builders used wood shingles or turf.

Willow branches were woven like thread on a loom

Wattle

Simple walls were made from wattle—woven willow branches. Wattle could be waterproofed by coating it with daub, a mixture of mud, straw, and clay.

Dry stone wall

Stone was sometimes used for the lower part of a building's walls, especially when timber was scarce. The Vikings did not use mortar. Each stone was selected so it was a tight fit with the others.

Roads

Vikings did not do much long-distance overland travel. Wooden roads were used in towns were traffic was heavy.

Buttresses prevented the weight of the roof from pushing the walls over

Denmark
Danish houses had thatched roofs and lean-to buttress timbers to support the roof.

Russia
In Russia, the Vikings built houses from whole pine logs with a few vertical timbers to support the roof.

Ireland
In Ireland, Viking houses were built with timber frames. The walls were made from wattle and daub.

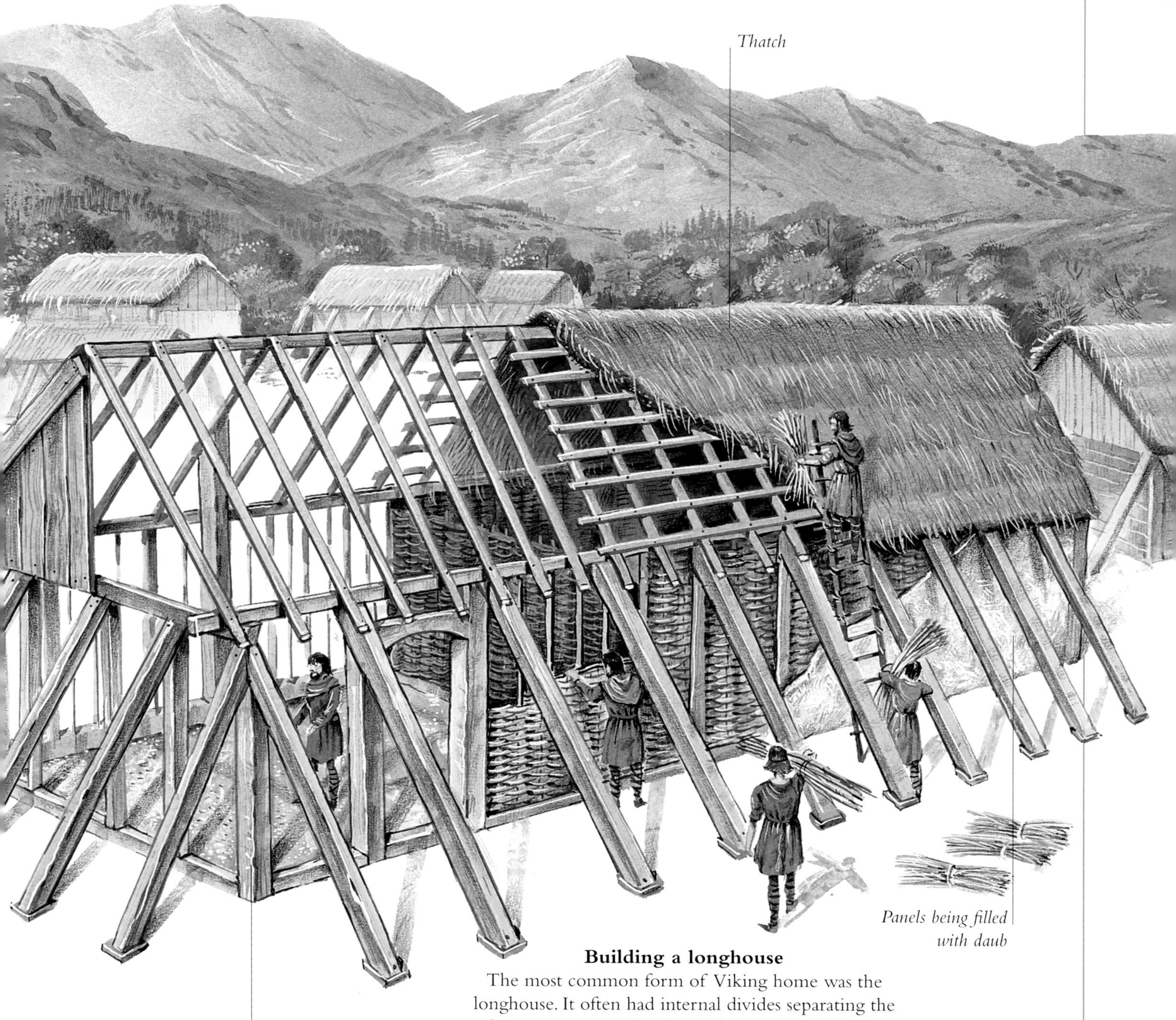

Building a longhouse
The most common form of Viking home was the longhouse. It often had internal divides separating the sleeping quarters of different familes or, sometimes, separating people from their animals' winter quarters.

ARTS AND CRAFTS

Viking craftsmen worked primarily with wood and iron. This meant that much of their finest work rusted or rotted away centuries ago. Similarly, their literature was not written down until centuries after it was composed, if it was recorded at all. What survives of Viking art and culture—in the form of carved stones, jewelry, and copies of the sagas written in the 12th century CE—is still impressive, however.

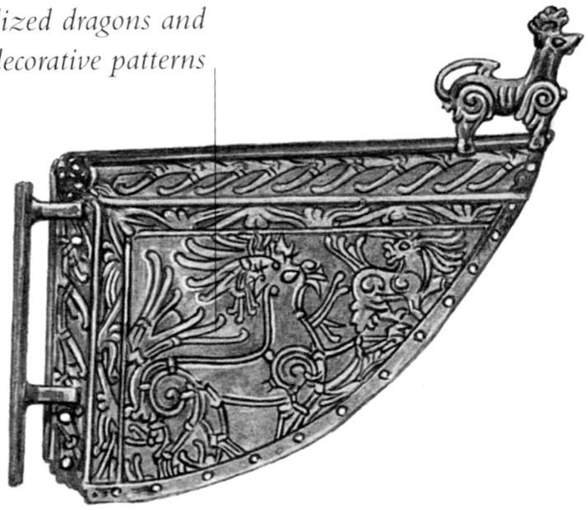
Stylized dragons and decorative patterns

Bronze weathervane
This ornate weathervane—which was once attached to the mast of a longship—was cast in bronze and gilded with a thin layer of gold.

Modern analysis suggests that runestones were originally painted

Runestones
These were stone memorials commemorating the lives of local warriors or marking specific events. They usually had inscriptions written in runes (the script used to write old Norse).

Brooch
The most common forms of jewelry were large, round brooches. These were used to fasten clothing.

Blacksmithing
The Vikings were expert swordsmiths. They made their blades from folded and welded iron rods.

Carpentry
Viking carpenters were capable of both efficient and practical design and fancy decorative carving.

Storytellers
The myths and legends of Viking culture were preserved in long poems called sagas. These would originally have been memorized by storytellers and recited at feasts.

Knot patterns were common

Picture stones
Not all carved stones had runic inscriptions; some were carved with complex abstract patterns and pictures. It is not clear whether these were decorative or if they had ritual significance.

Runic insciptions were usually carved around the edge of the stone

Carving a runestone
Some runestones are clearly the work of local amateurs, but others appear to have been made by skilled craftsmen. The designs followed established patterns but changed over time.

Woodcarving
Viking furniture and the internal timbers of their homes were often decorated with carvings like this one.

MAKING A COMB

The Vikings took great care of personal grooming. They made combs using carefully carved reindeer antlers. First they would saw the antler into thin strips, then cut it roughly to shape (1). Next they would use a fine-toothed saw to cut out the teeth of the comb. Finally the comb would be attached to two thicker pieces of carved antler to create a comfortable handle (2). The handle was usually covered with decorative carvings.

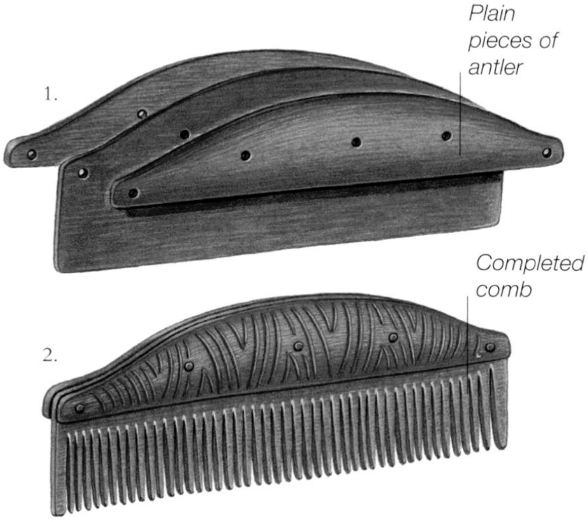
1.
Plain pieces of antler
2.
Completed comb

FIGHTING AND RAIDING

The Vikings first appeared in other parts of northern Europe as violent raiders. They attacked undefended ports, coastal villages, and monasteries. They killed unarmed people without mercy, carried young men and women away to be slaves, and seized anything valuable they could find. At first their raids lasted a few weeks in the summer, but soon armies began to arrive and stay all winter, eventually establishing settlements all over Europe.

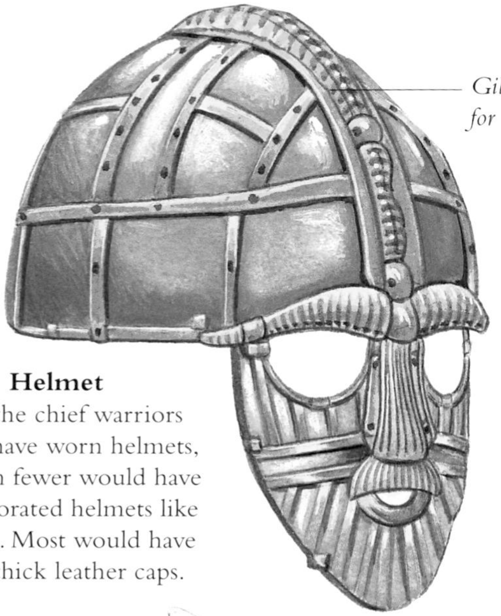
Gilded ridge, added for strength

Helmet
Only the chief warriors would have worn helmets, and even fewer would have had decorated helmets like this one. Most would have worn thick leather caps.

The double-edged sword was the most common Viking weapon
Most Viking warriors wore thick leather overshirts as their only armor

A Viking raid

The first major Viking raids were conducted on monastic communities in northeast England. These monasteries were inviting targets, as they were usually undefended and extremely wealthy.

Each Viking raider had a sea chest that doubled as his seat on the boat

A chain mail shirt called a hauberk

Chainmail

A full suit of chainmail, made from interlocking iron rings, took a long time to make and was very expensive.

Shield

Vikings carried round shields roughly 3 feet (1 m) across with an iron boss in the center for pushing opponents.

The Vikings in battle

Viking raiders tried to avoid confrontations with enemy militias, but could not always escape in time. The clashes that followed were desperate and brutal, usually with every man fighting for himself.

Ax

Axes were useful both as tools and weapons. Viking war axes, known as "bearded" axes, usually had a broader cutting blade.

VIKING TRADE

Some Vikings became very wealthy, not through raiding parties but through trade. In the early years, most trade took the form of barter—exchanging one kind of goods for another. But as time went on and the Vikings grew richer, more and more goods were bought and sold for silver or gold coins. The most valuable Viking exports were slaves and furs, while the most valued imports were foodstuffs, wine, and manufactured goods.

Bronze Buddha
This Indian statue of Buddha was found in Scandinavia. It probably changed hands several times before it reached the Vikings.

Scales
Scales made from bronze were used with small lead weights for weighing silver. A merchant carried his scale, folded up in a small wooden box.

To make less valuable coins, the Vikings cut large ones in half

Coins
The Vikings valued coins as standard weights of valuable metals, rather than as currency. They rarely made their own coins.

Carving of Freyr, the Viking god of fertility

Ivory
Walrus ivory (tusks) was imported from Greenland, Norway, and Iceland. Ivory was a dense material that could be carved with tiny details.

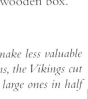

The Vikings could not grow grapes because the climate in Scandinavia was too cold. They imported large quantities of wine from southern Europe.

Viking trading vessels
Viking trading ships, known as *knarrs,* were broader and deeper than longships but could still sail up rivers and be dragged across land for short distances. This enabled the creation of trade routes that stretched as far as Iran and Greenland.

Vikings traded slaves all over the world

Merchants from all over the world visited Viking trading centers on the Volga and Don rivers in Russia.

ICELAND AND GREENLAND

Vikings from Norway began to settle in Iceland during the 870s. The first settlers were led by chiefs who wanted more land or hoped to escape the growing power of the king in Norway. Viking Iceland was a kind of republic, ruled by a national assembly called the Althing. The best land in Iceland was soon occupied, however, and in 985 CE a chief called Erik the Red led settlers from Iceland to Greenland, looking for new lands to settle.

Barley
Although the climate of Iceland was warmer than it is now, it was still too cold to grow wheat. Only barley could be grown on Iceland. It was used to make bread and beer.

Stone edges made it easier to get in and out for bathing

Hot spring
Iceland has many hot springs. People who built houses close to springs enjoyed hot water year-round.

Stone walls packed with earth

Farmhouse
The upper walls and roof of an Icelandic farmhouse were made of turf. Turf was a better insulator than wood.

Illuminated manuscript

Saga
Iceland is the home of many Viking sagas, which were stories written down centuries after they were first composed.

The large egg of a Great Auk

Birds' eggs
Huge flocks of sea birds visit the coastal cliffs of Iceland. Their eggs provided a welcome change of diet.

The "Lawspeaker"
The chairman of meetings of the Althing was the "Lawspeaker"—a judge who had to memorize all the laws of the land. He addressed his fellow chiefs from the Law Rock, a natural pulpit where the Althing met.

Local meetings
Only chiefs attended the Althing. Ordinary people attended a *thing,* or assembly, chaired by the local chief.

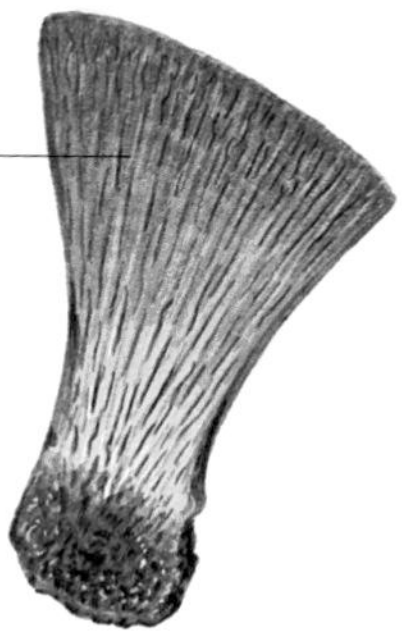

Whalebone ax head

Whale bone
Hunting whales was an important activity in Viking Greenland.

Traders from Iceland

Fish were gutted, skinned, and dried

Life in Greenland
The hunting and fishing in Greenland were good, with plentiful stocks of reindeer and salmon. Furs were traded with merchants from Iceland.

Reindeer pelts were traded for food

INTO RUSSIA

Viking merchants traveled across the Baltic Sea to Russia in the ninth century CE and traded with Slavic peoples. They sailed down the great Russian rivers, carrying their ships past rapids and between river basins, to reach the Black Sea and the Caspian Sea. Some Vikings, led by a chief called Rurik, settled in northern Russia, where they came to be known as the Rus. Rurik's descendants ruled Russia for centuries.

Silver amulet
This amulet, or lucky charm, was found in Scandinavia. It is thought to have been made in Baghdad.

The long journey south
The voyage from the Baltic Sea to the Black Sea often took months. The men had to cross three river basins—carrying their ships between each—as well as numerous rapids. They frequently came under attack during the journey and many men died.

Gilded horse collar
Viking merchants were able to make vast sums of money, as shown by their possessions.

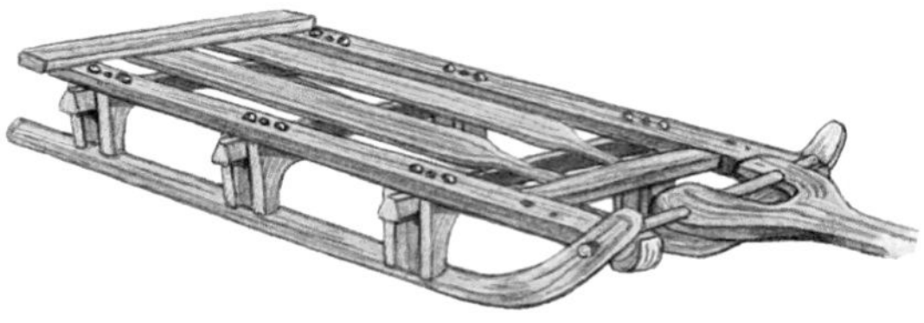

Wooden sled
This sled was used to transport goods during the winter months. In deep snow it was more useful than a cart.

Runestone
Runestones have been found as far away as the Black Sea coast, left there by Viking travelers.

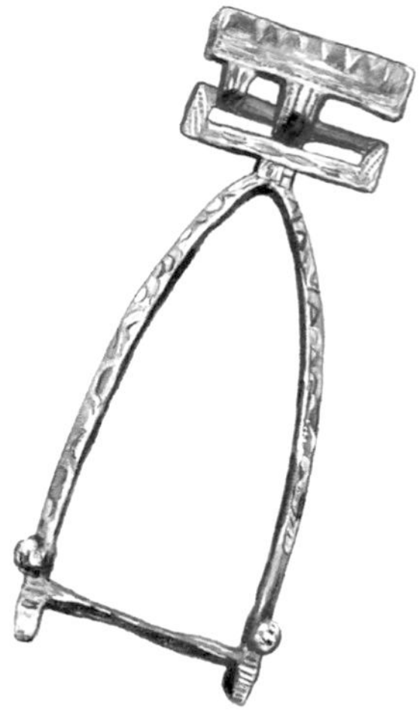

Stirrup
The Vikings in Russia were more dependent on overland transport than their western contemporaries.

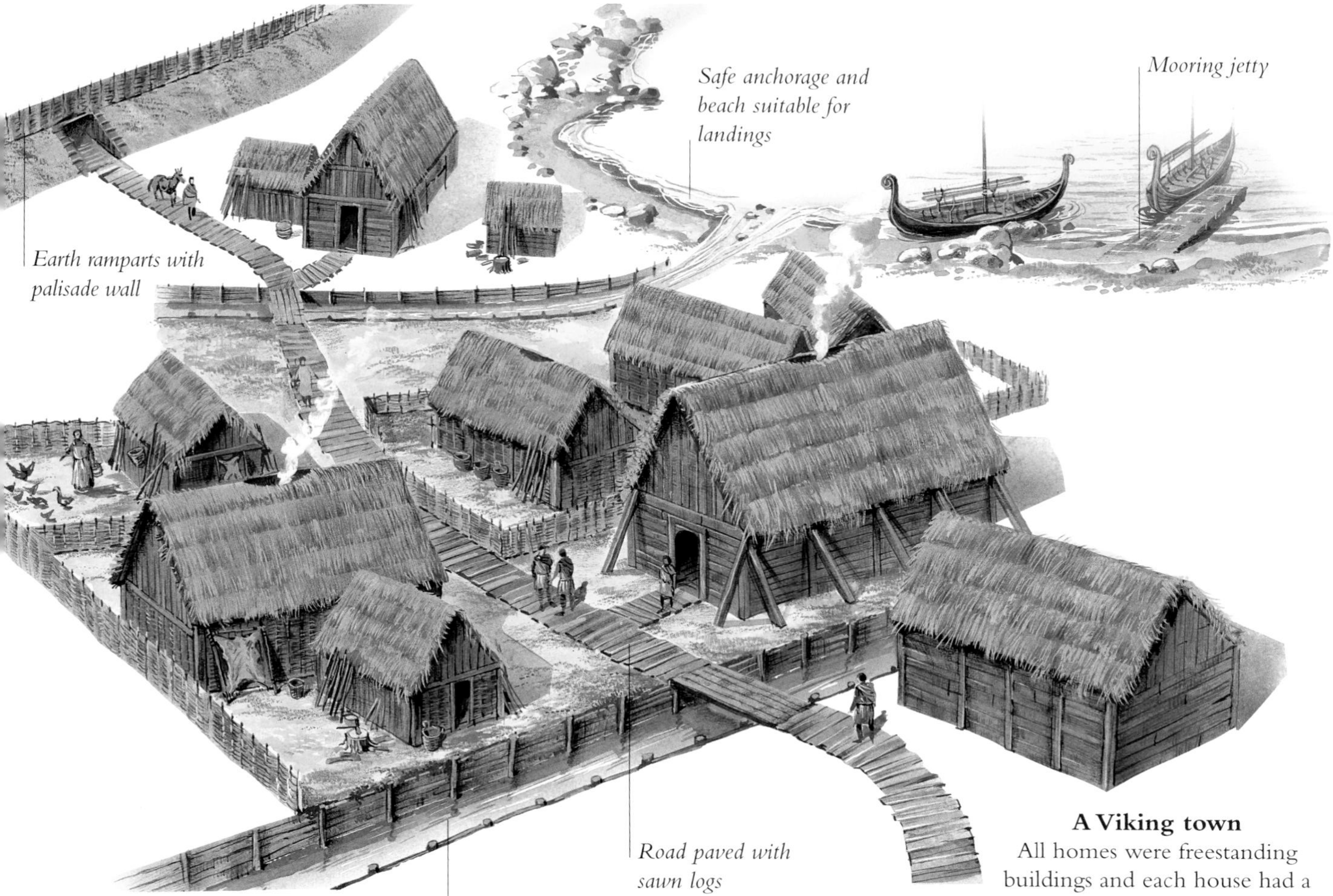

A Viking town
All homes were freestanding buildings and each house had a fenced yard with outbuildings, animal pens, and vegetable plots.

Honey
Honey was highly valued by the Vikings, who had few other sources of sugar.

Rushes
Dried rushes—grasslike plants—were often spread on the floor of Viking homes.

Well
River water was brackish (salty) on the coast where Viking towns were built, so water came from wells.

TOWNS

The Vikings were not townspeople by preference, but towns always grow up where merchants gather. Viking towns were typically built on the coast, often at the mouths of navigable rivers. This was because seas and inland waterways were the primary trade routes of the Viking Age. Towns were protected on their landward side by high earth ramparts, topped with wooden palisade walls.

CHRISTIANITY

The Vikings were among the last peoples in Europe to convert to Chrstianity. Although they had been in contact with the religion for centuries, it was not until the mid-10th century CE that there were any mass conversions. Even after converting, Vikings often retained many pre-Christian beliefs, a fact that annoyed missionaries. By the 11th century, however, the Vikings appear to have embraced the religion fully, building elaborate wooden churches throughout Scandinvia.

DRAGON CARVINGS

The church at Borgund has many small details that show the influence of pre-Christian culture. The roof, for example, is decorated with carved dragons as well as Christian crosses. The Vikings believed the dragons scared away demons.

Stone cross
This stone cross shows the image of a Viking warrior buried with his weapons in the old Viking way.

Wooden churches
Scandinavian Christians built magnificent wooden churches, such as this one at Borgund, Norway, which dates from around 1180 CE.

Borgund floor plan
This diagram shows how the walls of the upper floor (in pink) sat on the core timbers of the floor below.

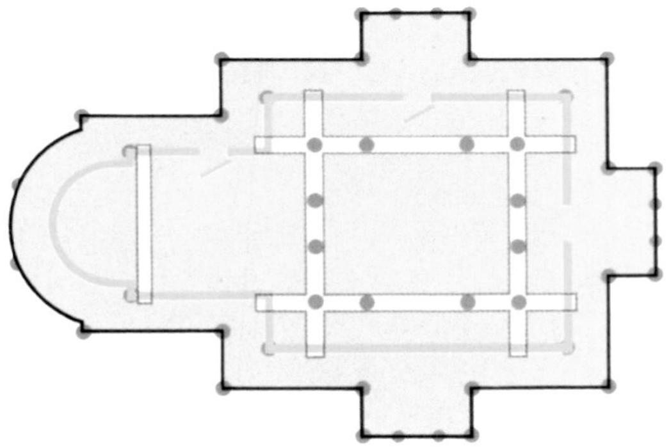

Church design
Early churches had timber walls sunk into the earth. This caused problems with rot.

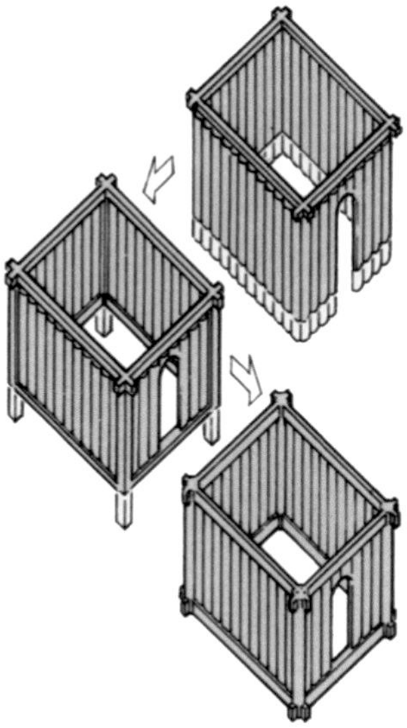

Stave construction
Viking churches were built using a technique that did not require vertical timbers to be anchored in the earth. This protected them from rot. It used a system of cross-braces to strengthen the walls.

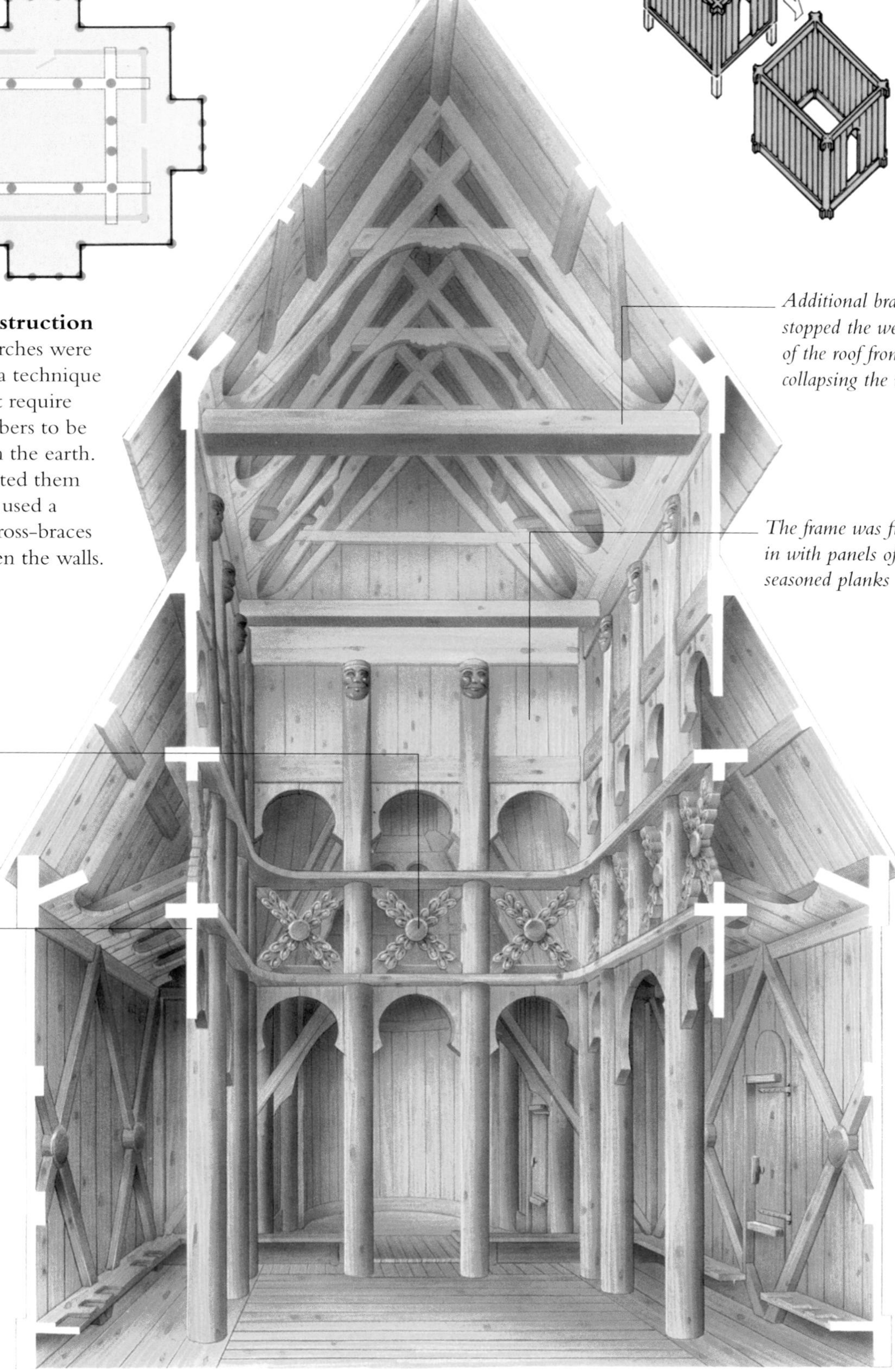

Additional bracing stopped the weight of the roof from collapsing the walls

The frame was filled in with panels of seasoned planks

The structural timbers were heavily carved

The horizantal beams, called "staves" held in the walls like the staves on a barrel

MIDDLE AGES

The collapse of the Western Roman Empire in 476 CE plunged Europe into a "dark age"—a period of social and political turmoil from which few records survive. From this chaos emerged medieval Europe, which was made up of many small, warring kingdoms. As time passed, these kingdoms grew and merged, creating most of the countries of present-day Europe.

TIMELINE

476 CE The last Western Roman Emperor is deposed.

800 CE Charlemagne, king of the Franks, is allowed to take the title of "Roman Emperor" by the pope.

889 CE The Frankish kingdom breaks up into France, Germany, Italy, Provence, and Burgundy.

900 CE Waves of migrants from the steppes of Central Asia reach eastern Europe.

950–1000 CE The first stone castles are built in Europe.

988 CE Vladimir, the Grand Prince of Kiev, converts to Christianity.

1008–31 CE The Umayyad Caliphate breaks into smaller kingdoms.

1030–91 CE The Normans conquer southern Italy, Sicily, and England.

1096–99 CE The First Crusade against the Muslim rulers of the Holy Land.

1237–41 CE The Mongols, under Genghis Khan, invade Russia and eastern Europe.

1227 CE The Teutonic Knights establish colonies among the pagan peoples of the southern Baltic.

1327 CE Earliest evidence of gunpowder weapons being used in Europe.

1381 CE The Peasant's Revolt—a massive popular uprising—begins the decline of feudal serfdom in England.

Emperor Charlemagne
The Middle Ages saw the re-emergence of strong states ruled by powerful military elites.

DUCHY OF NORMANDY, 1066 CE
NORMAN GAINS, 1066–1154 CE
HOLY ROMAN EMPIRE, c.1175 CE
AREAS OF GERMAN SETTLEMENT
ANGEVIN CONTROL, c.1175 CE
NOMINAL ANGEVIN CONTROL, c.1175 CE
FRENCH ROYAL DEMESNE
ANGEVIN FIEFS IN FRANCE AFTER 1214 CE
BYZANTINE EMPIRE, c.1175 CE
NORWEGIAN EMPIRE, c.1175 CE
SWEDISH TERRITORY, c.1175 CE
CONTROLLED BY TEUTONIC KNIGHTS
RUSSIAN PRINCIPALITIES
PAGAN AREA

SPANISH STATES, c.1300 CE
ARAGON
CASTILLE
EMIRATE OF GRANADA
PORTUGAL

0 200 400 600 KM
0 200 400 MILES

Byzantium
In southeast Europe, the Byzantine Empire held on to the achievements of Greco-Roman civilization.

Diocletian and Maximian
Co-emperors Maximian and Diocletian were the last rulers of a unified Roman Empire.

The fall of the Romans
Under pressure from the "barbarian" tribes to the north and east in the late third century CE, Emperor Diocletian split the Roman Empire. The empire's decline continued, however, and by the late fifth century CE the western half of the empire had collapsed.

THE AGE OF INVASIONS

The final years of the Roman Empire were marked by constant invasions by "barbarian" peoples from the north and east. The Vandals invaded Spain and North Africa; the Jutes, Angles, and Saxons invaded England; the Goths and Lombards invaded Italy and Gaul (France). In time these peoples established their own states, which, in turn, came under attack by a new wave of invaders, including the Vikings, Arabs, and Hungarians.

Building a longship
A longship could cross oceans, sail up rivers, and be dragged easily across land. Longships made it possible to travel from Iceland to Kiev, or from England to Constantinople.

Oath of allegiance
This scene from a medieval tapestry shows a nobleman swearing an oath of loyalty to his lord.

A feudal lord's court
Under the feudal system, conquering kings gave land to their supporters. The peasants who worked this land were essentially the property of their lord.

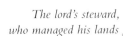

The lord's steward, who managed his lands

The lord himself

Disputes between peasants were taken to the lord's court

Peasant tenant farmer

The lord's advisor and scribe

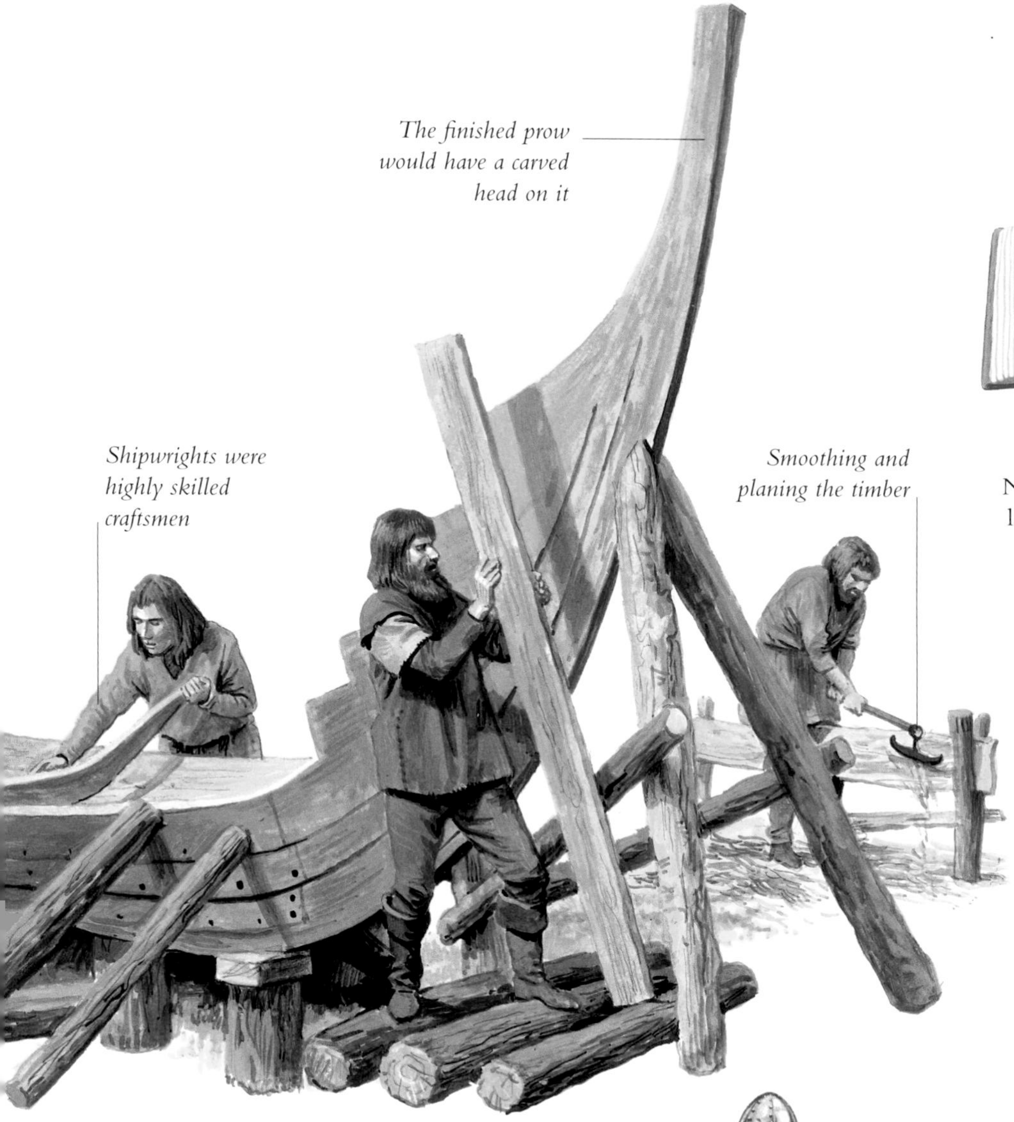
The finished prow would have a carved head on it
Shipwrights were highly skilled craftsmen
Smoothing and planing the timber

Domesday Book
After conquering the country, the Normans made a list of all England's landowners so they could tax them.

Treasure
This gold buckle is part of a treasure hoard buried in the fourth century CE.

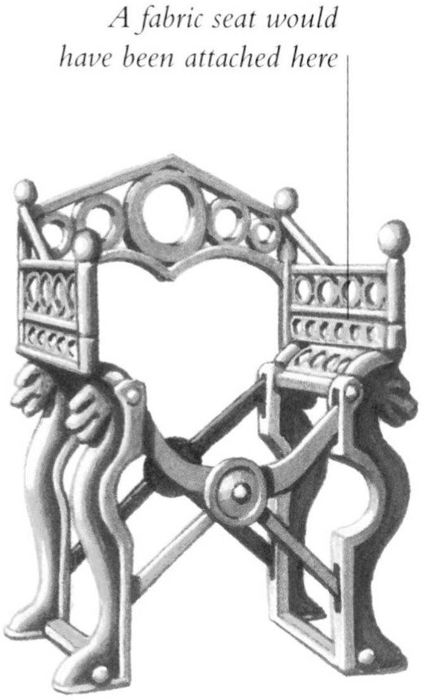
A fabric seat would have been attached here

Wooden throne
This folding wooden throne would have been carried with the king's belongings as he moved from town to town.

Anglo-Saxon warrior
This well-armed and armored soldier is an English "housecarl," part of the elite bodyguard of an Anglo-Saxon king.

A medieval king
This bronze statue depicts the Frankish Emperor Charlemagne with his crown and orb of office.

THE NORMANS

The Normans were descendants of the Vikings who conquered northern France during the ninth century CE. They rose to prominence in the 11th century, having adopted French as their language and converted to Christianity. They were renowned for their military prowess, which included a Viking-influenced seafaring tradition. Their most famous conquest was England in 1066, but at their height they held territory throughout Europe.

Pennon
Important commanders had their own pennons (flags) to help their men find them in the heat of battle.

The Battle of Hastings
Fought in the autumn of 1066, the Battle of Hastings saw King Harold of England defeated by the Norman King William. It opened the way for the Norman conquest of England.

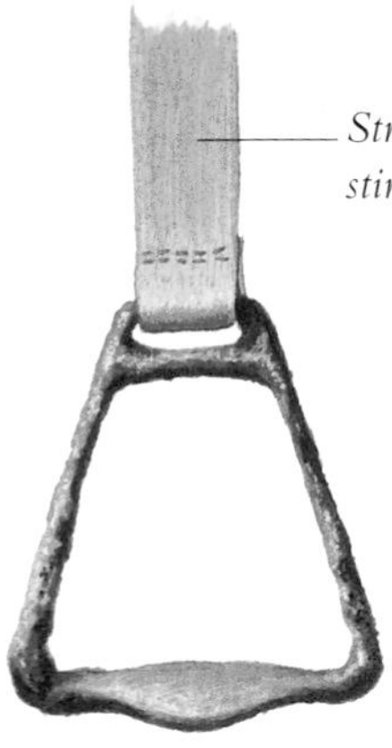

The stirrup
This seemingly simple invention revolutionized warfare. It enabled cavalrymen to lean down and fight enemy infantry without falling from their horses.

Baggage train
Norman armies had large wagon trains that carried their armor, weapons, food, and even temporary fortifications.

Looting
Military equipment was extremely valuable, so conquering armies always looted (stole) weapons and clothes from the bodies of their defeated enemies.

Each man had to hold his position for the formation to work

Anglo-Saxon shield-wall
The shield-wall was a cornerstone of early medieval military tactics. It involved an infantry force standing in close formation with their shields locked together.

The Anglo-Saxons were defeated when their formation was broken

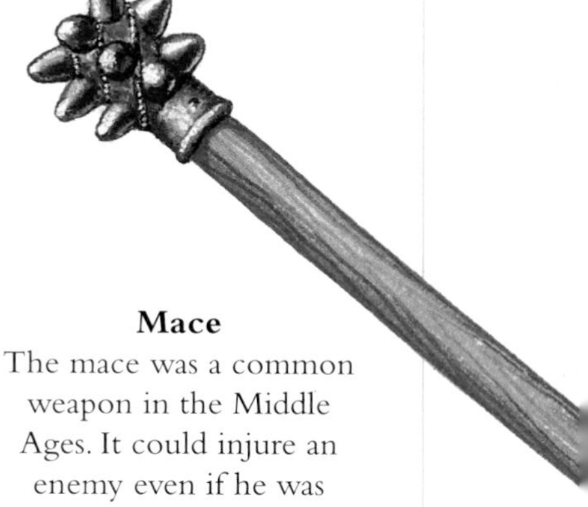

These spikes could crush helmets

Mace
The mace was a common weapon in the Middle Ages. It could injure an enemy even if he was wearing armor.

THE CRUSADES

In 1076 a dramatic shift in power took place in the Muslim world. The Arab Abbasid Caliphate was displaced by the Seljuk Turks, who closed Jerusalem to Christian pilgrims and began seriously to threaten the Christian Byzantine Empire. In response, Pope Urban II authorized a holy war, or "crusade," to retake the Holy Land from the Muslims. This marked the beginning of a centuries-long conflict.

Crusaders on the attack
During the First Crusade the Christian armies, experienced in siege warfare, were able to capture many Muslim castles and fortified cities.

Lamellar armor
Armorers in the east had different ways of making armor from those who worked in Europe. They developed lamellar, or "scaled," armor.

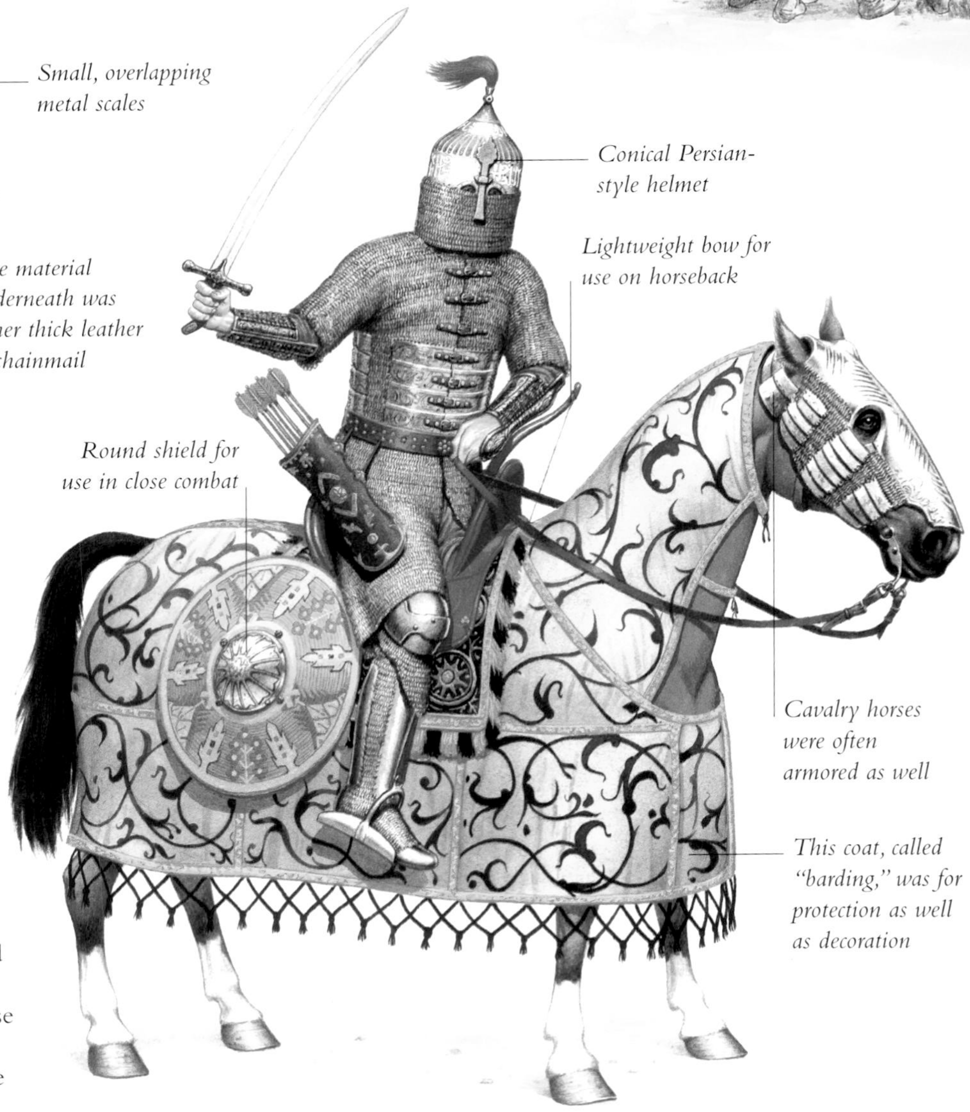

Seljuk cavalry
The First Crusade (1096–1099) pitted European knights against the *ghulam* cavalry of the Seljuk Turks (right). These soldiers wore heavy armor, but were much faster and more mobile than the crusader knights.

Crusading knights wore white overshirts with red crosses painted on them
Stone-throwing catapults called mangonels

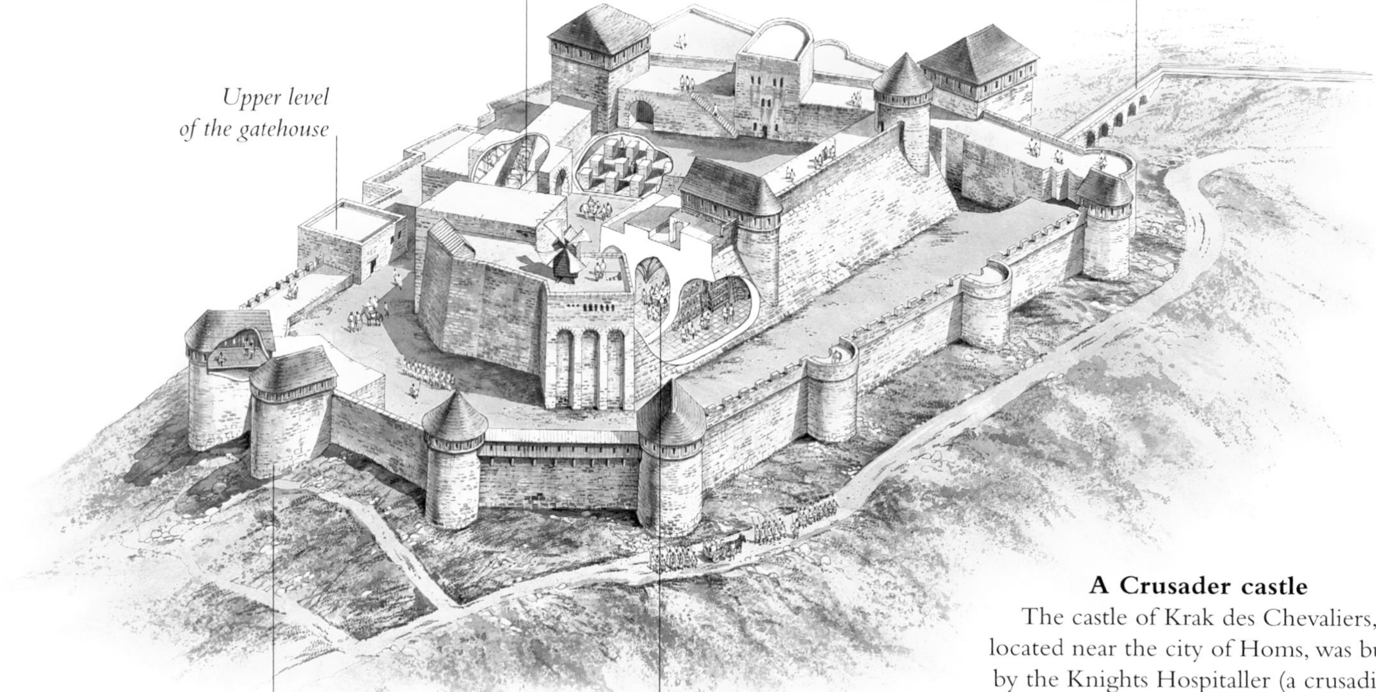
Entrance to the castle
Aqueduct supplying water to the castle
Upper level of the gatehouse
Thick walls and towers overlooking the approach
The Great Hall

A Crusader castle
The castle of Krak des Chevaliers, located near the city of Homs, was built by the Knights Hospitaller (a crusading military order) between 1142 and 1170. It was remodeled several times to repair damage sustained during sieges.

COUNTRYSIDE LIFE

In the Middle Ages, most people lived in rural village communities. Towns were rare. Country life followed a regular pattern every year. In spring the fields were plowed, the crops were sown, and the sheep were lambed and sheared. In summer the crops were tended and hay was made. In fall came the harvest. Each village was more or less self-sufficient, with its own blacksmith, craftsmen, mill, and church.

Harvest time
During the year each peasant family tended to their own strips of farmland, but in the fall the whole community banded together to help bring in the harvest.

Thatching
A thatcher was a craftsman who made watertight roofs from bundles of dried reeds.

Medieval plow
Plows turned the soil to make the fields ready for crops to be planted. Plows were pulled by teams of oxen.

Threshing
To separate the grain from the husk it had to be threshed, or beaten with a heavy flail.

Wealthy lords kept falcons for hunting

Each village had its own mill

People were placed in the stocks as a punishment

Village life
In forested regions with plenty of lumber, houses were built with wooden frames and thatched roofs. The walls were made from wattle and daub—woven strips of wood covered with a mixture of clay and straw.

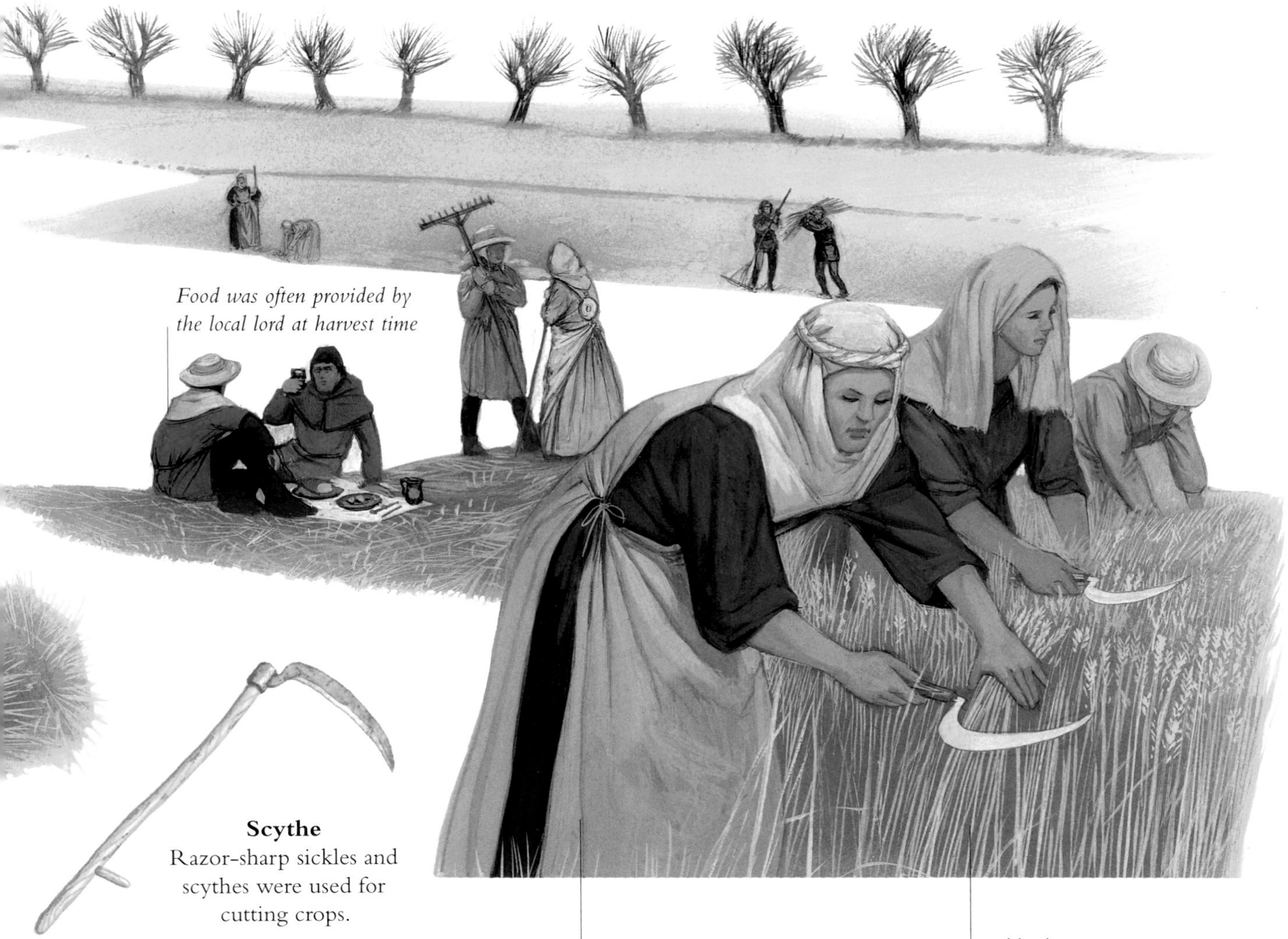

Food was often provided by the local lord at harvest time

Thick aprons for outdoor work

Sickles being used to cut corn

Scythe
Razor-sharp sickles and scythes were used for cutting crops.

Peasants' rebellions
This figure is John Ball, one of the leaders of the 1381 Peasants' Revolt in England.

Manor house
The lord of the manor (the local landowner) lived in a large house. His peasants provided food for his household.

LIFE IN TOWNS

Towns and cities grew larger in many parts of Europe in medieval times. Merchants and specialist craftsmen in these settlements joined together to form guilds. Life in these towns was no easier than life in the countryside. People started work when they were children, often leaving their family to be apprenticed, and people had only a few days off per year, usually for holy days.

Medieval towns

Medieval towns were noisy, crowded, and smelly. Houses loomed over the street to maximize the available space; sewage was often dumped in the street; and, in an age when literacy was rare, shopkeepers and craftsmen had to shout and holler to advertise their wares or services.

Overhanging upper rooms

A public market

Shop signs were often symbols of the owner's occupation—scissors for a tailor, for example

Some people had stalls outside their homes

Cutting cloth with a curved knife

Church windows

Guilds often paid for the windows in churches. This window, left, shows a member of the draper's guild.

Apprentices

Children were often sent away to learn a trade from a master craftsman.

Apprentices were usually given the worst jobs

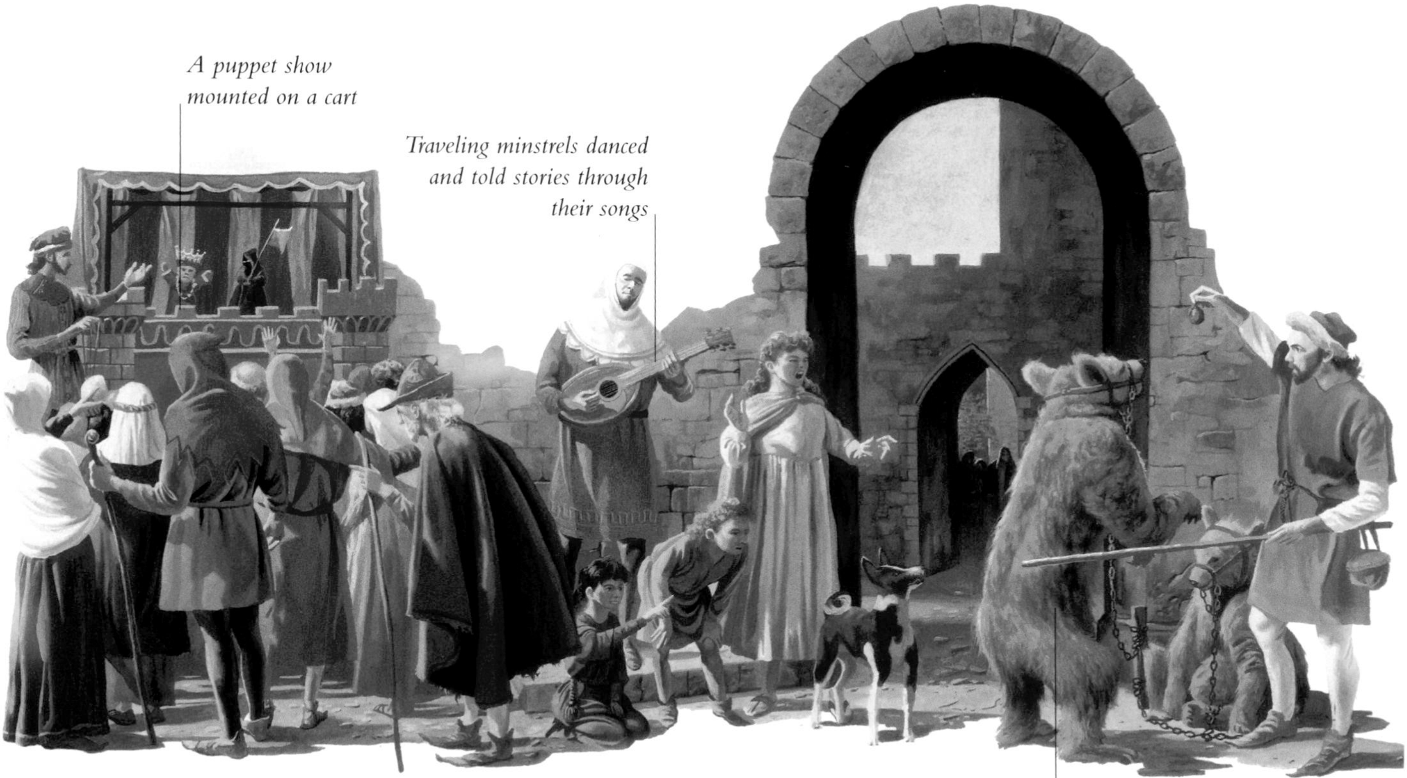

A puppet show mounted on a cart

Traveling minstrels danced and told stories through their songs

Captive animals, including dancing bears, were a common sight in medieval cities

Public entertainments
On holy days, when people were excused from work, they would often gather to watch public entertainments put on by traveling showmen and musicians.

Town seal
This wax seal shows the emblem of a European city, including two coats of arms and an image of the city walls.

Saint James of Compostela

A carved chess piece

Pilgrimage souvenir
People who could afford to went on pilgrimages to places associated with saints or notable miracles.

Chessmen
The game of chess was popular among the nobility. Lords often had highly ornate carved chess sets.

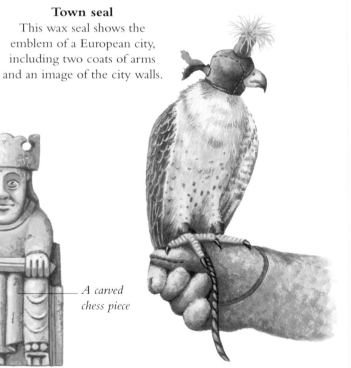

Falconry
Hunting with trained falcons and other birds of prey was a popular pastime for noblemen and women.

LIFE IN A CASTLE

Castles belonged to kings, noblemen, and knights—the most wealthy and powerful people in the land. A castle was a sign that the owner had money, power, and influence in high places (in most countries a nobleman needed his king's permission to build a castle). Small castles were homes and strongholds at the same time, while the larger ones often contained what were effectively small towns.

Wooden chest with lock
Chests were used for storing linen and other valuable goods. Kings often brought several with them when they traveled.

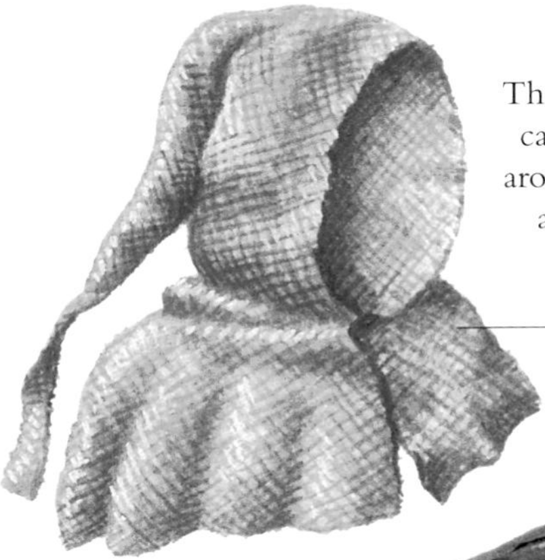
Coarse, cheap material

Capuchin
This style of headdress is called a capuchin. Part of it was pulled around the shoulders like a cape, and the rest formed a hood.

Handle used to lift off the cover

Beehive
Honey was almost the only source of sugar in medieval Europe. Straw beehives like this one were a common sight.

Infants were often cared for by nursemaids

Baby walker
Medieval carvings show that some children learned to walk using baby walkers just as they do today.

A castle kitchen
Castle kitchens were large spaces with enormous hearths and ovens. They sometimes provided food for the military garrison as well as the lord's household. Kitchens were often free-standing buildings to reduce the risk of fire spreading.

Fresh food
Castles had large vegetable gardens that provided fresh vegetables.

Aquamanile
Guests at the castle washed in scented water from decorative water jugs, or aquamaniles, such as this one.

Knives
Knives were valuable objects in the Middle Ages. Most men had their own personal knife. Table knives like these (left) would only have been found in the homes of the wealthy.

Fish
All kinds of fish ended up on the table, from eels to herrings. Whale meat was eaten as well. The church encouraged people to eat fish instead of meat on Fridays and holy days.

TRADE

In the Middle Ages few people traveled far from their homes. The world beyond Europe was a mystery, said to contain animals like the centicore—a cross between a horse and a lion with the voice of a man. But fact began to replace fantasy as merchants began to make longer voyages. Sailing ships became the most important form of transportation during this period. They could carry heavy loads over long distances at relatively great speed.

Merchant's mark
Merchants carried rings engraved with a personal mark. This could be pressed into wax seals on legal documents as a form of signature.

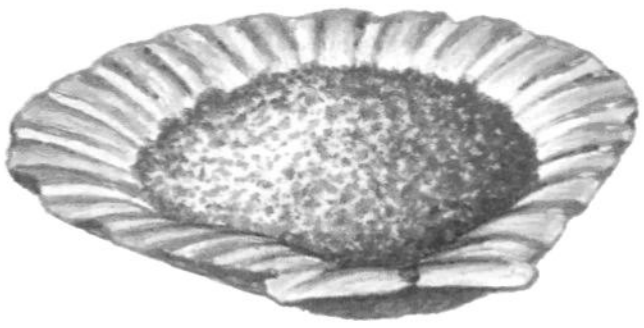

Lapis lazuli
The finest shade of blue for painters came from powdered lapis lazuli. This stone came from mines in Central Asia.

Astrolabe
Astrolabes were used to measure the angle of the stars above the horizon. This information was vital for navigation at sea.

Sheep trade
Sheep were sometimes driven long distances to market. Major fairs and markets could draw shepherds from all over the country.

Traveling merchants
During the Middle Ages many merchants became rich through trading in rare and exotic goods such as silks and precious stones.

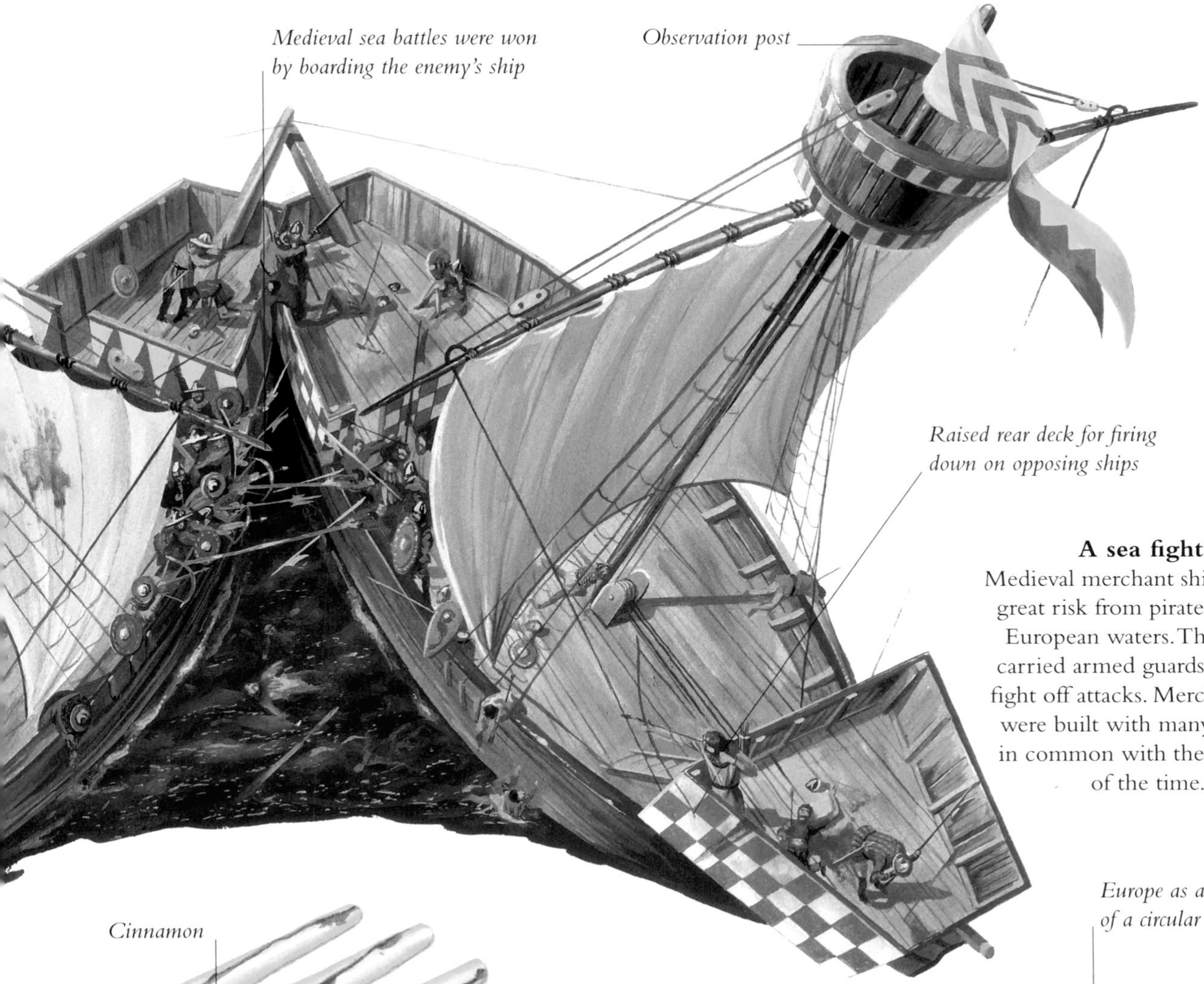

A sea fight!
Medieval merchant ships were at great risk from pirates, even in European waters. They often carried armed guards, ready to fight off attacks. Merchant ships were built with many features in common with the warships of the time.

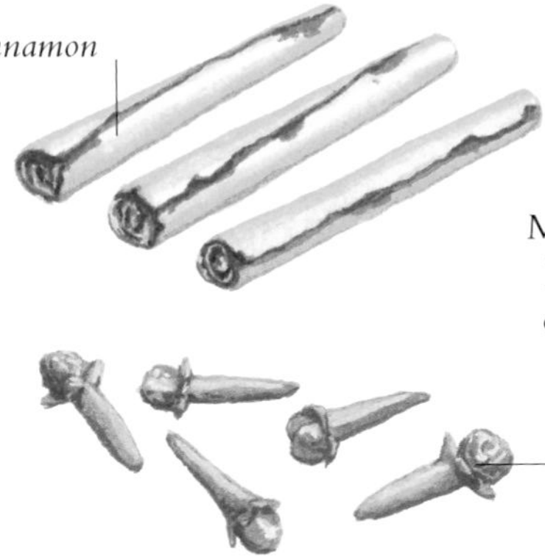

Spices
Medieval diets were much less varied than modern ones. Spices were valued as a way to add flavor.

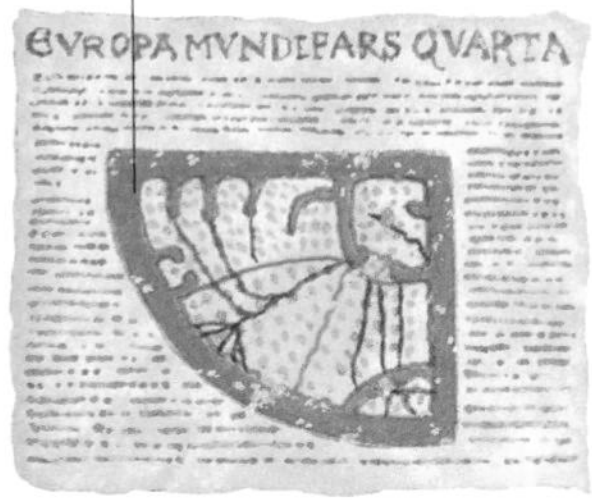

Medieval maps
Medieval mariners made detailed maps of coastlines, but they were unaware of what lay beyond the horizon.

Carts
Medieval carts were usually small, with only one axle.

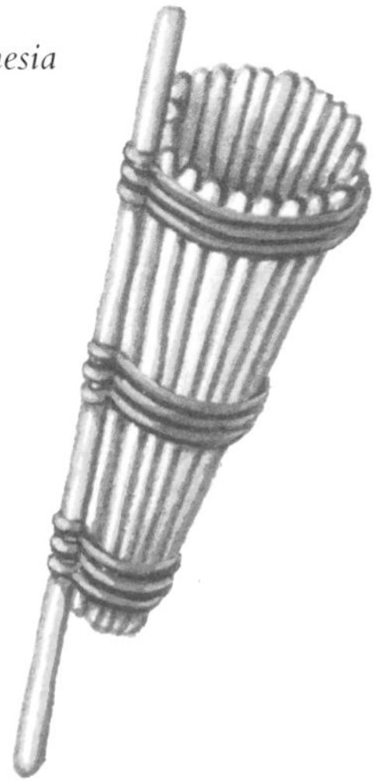

Creel
Creels were made from straw or wicker. They were carried on the back and used for heavy loads.

Coins
Coins were made from silver or gold. They were marked with the likeness of the king.

SIEGE WARFARE

During the Middle Ages, the science of designing and constructing fortifications advanced to the point where well-built castles could repel almost any attack. Unable to break down the walls or smash through the massive and cunningly designed gatehouses, attacking armies were left with only one other tactic: to surround the castle and starve the defenders into submission. This approach was known as siege warfare.

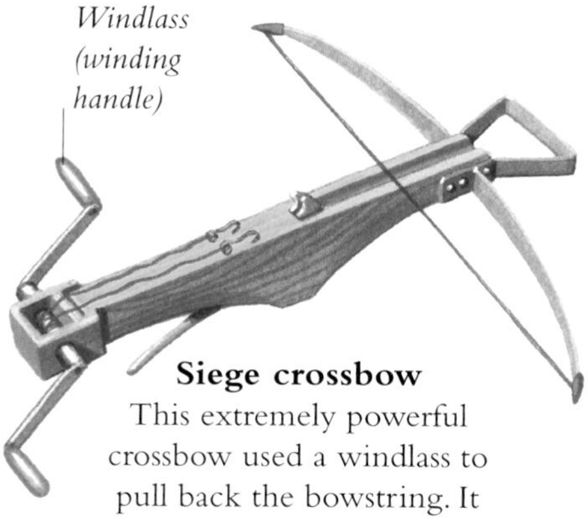

Siege crossbow
This extremely powerful crossbow used a windlass to pull back the bowstring. It was too heavy to use on the battlefield, but ideal for the defenders inside a castle.

Murder holes
If the attackers broke through a castle's outer gate, they would find themselves trapped in a chamber where the defenders could fire on them through holes in the ceiling called "murder holes."

A late medieval castle
Years of warfare led to many refinements in castle design. Round towers replaced square ones, as they were better able to deflect catapulted stones, and entranceways were protected by many layers of defenses.

Trebuchet
This type of siege weapon used a heavy counterweight and pivot to launch large projectiles into the walls of a castle.

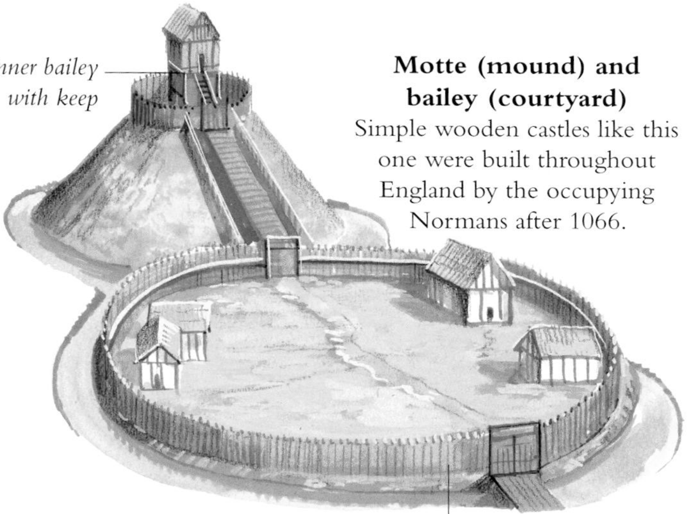

Motte (mound) and bailey (courtyard)
Simple wooden castles like this one were built throughout England by the occupying Normans after 1066.

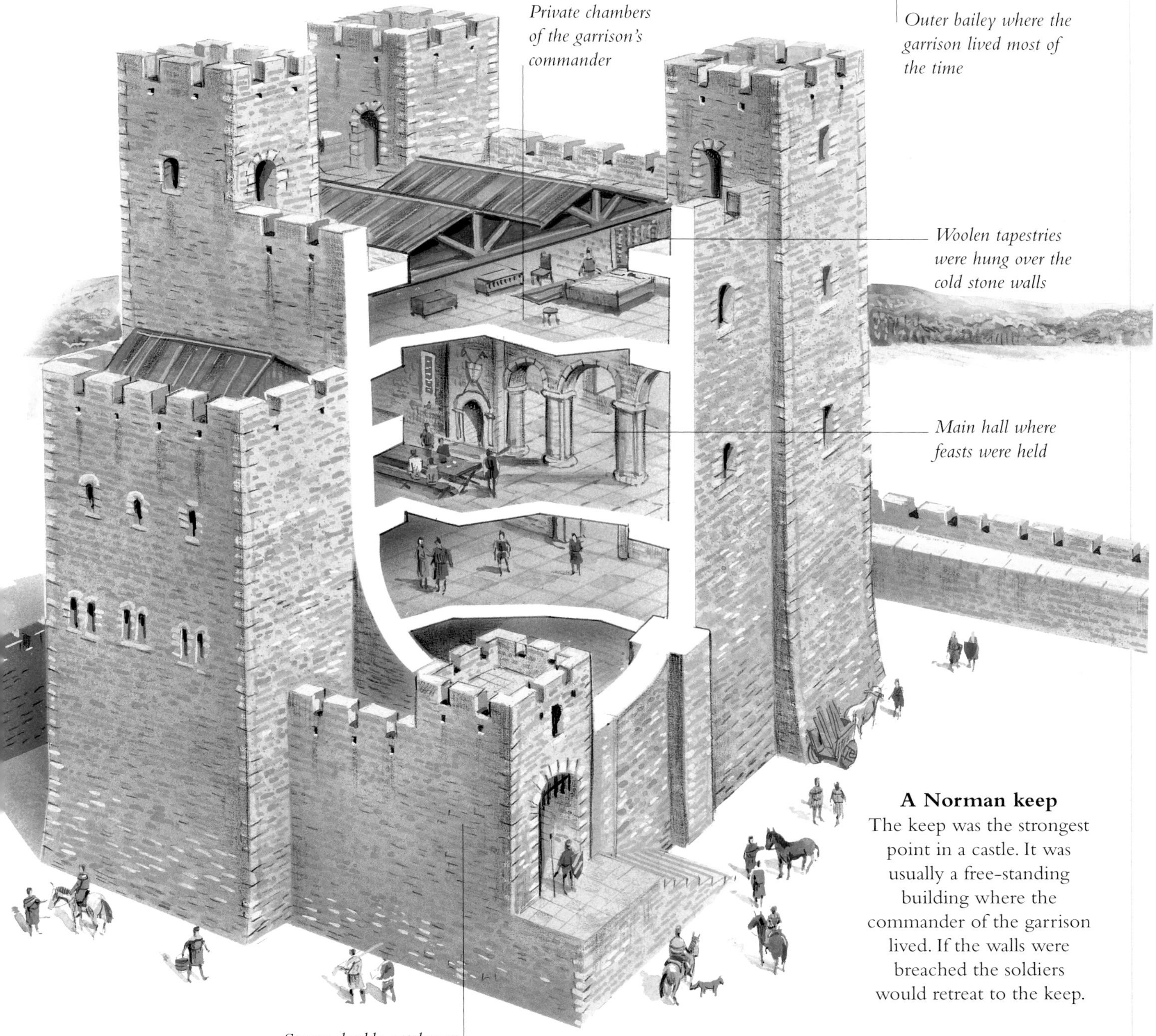

A Norman keep
The keep was the strongest point in a castle. It was usually a free-standing building where the commander of the garrison lived. If the walls were breached the soldiers would retreat to the keep.

LATE MEDIEVAL WARFARE

For the ruling elites of medieval Europe, warfare was the activity around which their lives were organized. The sons of noblemen were trained as soldiers from childhood, and their adult lives were dominated by military campaigns and jousting tournaments. The period also saw the rise of the professional soldier, with companies of highly skilled archers and pikemen fighting for whoever would pay them.

Lit taper for igniting the gunpowder
A hand cannon's short barrel made it inaccurate

Hand cannon
The earliest portable firearms were called hand cannons. They were powerful but dangerous to use, and often exploded.

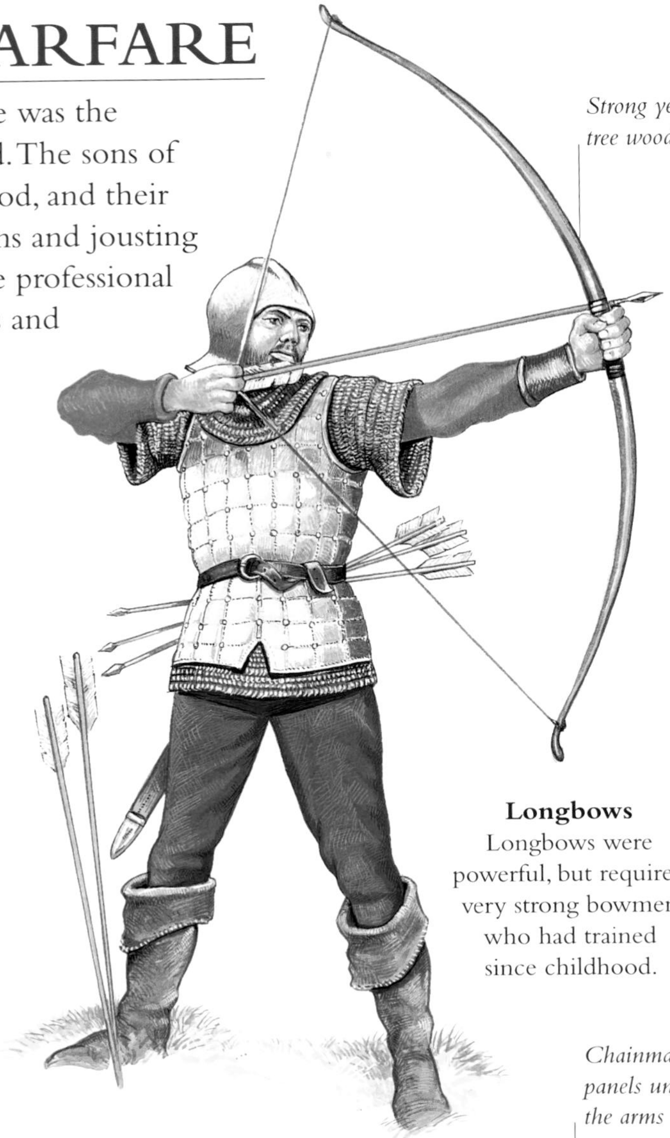
Strong yew tree wood

Longbows
Longbows were powerful, but required very strong bowmen who had trained since childhood.

Crossbowmen wore heavy armor as they had to stand very still while reloading

Arbalest
Heavy siege crossbows were called arbalests. They could fire a steel arrow, called a bolt, through thick planks of wood or even metal plate armor.

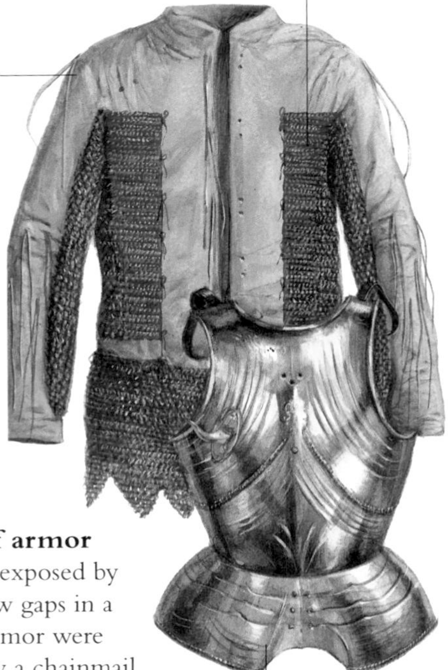
Chainmail panels under the arms
Padded leather
Curved steel breastplate

Suit of armor
The areas exposed by the narrow gaps in a suit of armor were protected by a chainmail and leather undershirt.

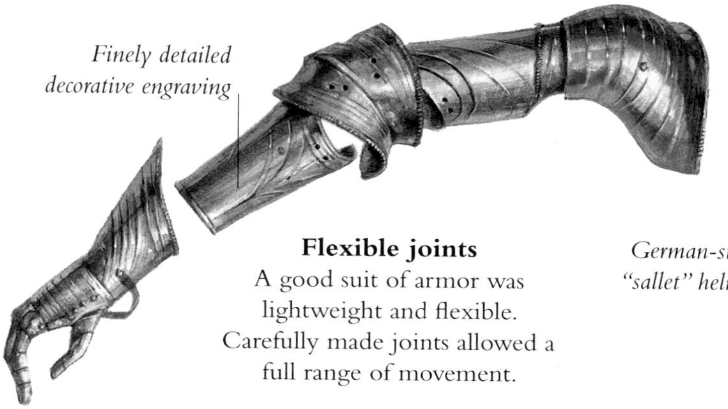
Finely detailed decorative engraving

Flexible joints
A good suit of armor was lightweight and flexible. Carefully made joints allowed a full range of movement.

German-style "sallet" helmet
Steel mace
A knight's personal attendant was called a squire
Reinforced overlapping plates at joints
Horse armor, or "barding"

Tournament armor
Knights taking part in jousting and combat at tournaments wore heavier and more elaborate armor than was worn on the battlefield.

END OF THE MIDDLE AGES

The Middle Ages did not end on a particular date, but after about 1400 things began to change. New ideas in religion and philosophy began to change the established social order. The spread of these ideas was made possible by the invention of the printing press. At the same time, the invention of gunpowder-based weapons challenged the dominance of the wealthy military elite, making it possible for ordinary people to rebel against their old masters.

Lifelike art
Assisted by the patronage of wealthy churchmen and nobles, artists were able to refine their techniques, creating ever more lifelike sculptures and paintings.

The printing press
Cast metal type made it possible to make books quickly and cheaply. Printed bibles revolutionized public attitudes to religion.

The age of exploration
Improved navigation techniques and better ships allowed explorers to travel farther than ever before, reaching the Americas in 1492.

GUNPOWDER

Gunpowder was first used in Europe in about 1250. It did not become a decisive factor in military engagements until the 14th century, however, when metalworking technology advanced to the point where powerful and reliable cannon could be made.

Urban rebellions

In the late Middle Ages, wealthy towns and cities began to turn against their aristocratic rulers. Tactical and technological innovations made it possible for their well-trained citizen armies to fight off mounted knights.

INDEX

Windmill Books Ltd
First Floor
9-17 St. Albans Place
London N1 0NX
www.windmillbooks.co.uk

ISBN: 978-1-78121-133-5

Designers: Mike Davis, Paul Drislane,
Design Manager: Keith Davis
Production: Richard Berry
Production Consultant: Alastair Gourlay
Editors: Tim Harris, Ben Hollingum
Editorial Director: Lindsey Lowe
Indexer: Ann Barrett

Printed in China